# THE BOOK OF DANIEL DREW

DANIEL DREW.  CORNELIUS VANDERBILT.

L.W. JEROME.  JACOB LITTLE.

CELEBRITIES OF WALL STREET.

# THE BOOK OF
# DANIEL DREW

A Glimpse of the Fisk-Gould-Tweed
Régime from the Inside

By
BOUCK WHITE

*with a new Introduction by*
Benton W. Davis

THE CITADEL PRESS     Secaucus, New Jersey

First paperbound printing, 1980
Copyright © 1910 by Doubleday & Co., Inc.
This edition published by arrangement with Doubleday & Co.
Published by Citadel Press
A division of Lyle Stuart Inc.
120 Enterprise Ave., Secaucus, N.J. 07094
In Canada: General Publishing Co. Limited
Don Mills, Ontario
Manufactured in the United States of America
ISBN 0-8065-0745-4

# INTRODUCTION

*"The Book of Daniel Drew"* is another favorite out of my old Wall Street Library. I am happy to see it chosen to take its place beside that great volume, *"Reminiscences of a Stock Operator"* in this new "Library of Stock Market Classics." Both books were prominent in my early reading on the subject and both were instrumental in creating a hobby interest in the stock market while I practiced law in Cleveland, and in later bringing me to work and live and write down here in the fascinating canyons of lower Manhattan.

In fact, as I write this, I can look directly across the Hudson River from my apartment over to Jersey City where, as you will read on page 239, Daniel Drew, just about 100 years ago, — "waited for Fisk and Gould. But they didn't come. I began to think they had decided to stay over in New York for the night. But shortly after dark, in they came. And they were a bedraggled pair of men. 'What in the world!' said I. 'You didn't have to swim over did you?' 'Pretty near', said Jimmy (Fisk); in fact, it looked for a spell as though we weren't going to get here at all. It's a beast of a day. We came over in a rowboat!"

You have undoubtedly heard of the early printing-

press operations in Erie stock and the sudden re-
moval of those operations across the river to escape
the wrath of Commodore Cornelius Vanderbilt.
Well, the story is all here. That Erie stock operation,
by the way, was the original "watered stock" in Wall
Street. But, for the origin of the phrase "watered
stock", go back to Chapter VI, page 44, — back to
Daniel's early days as a cattle drover: "That night,
when all the rest were asleep—the cattle boys used
to sleep in the barn on the hayloft—I went out to the
drove in the pasture alongside the tavern, and
emptied sacks of salt on the ground, scattering it so
every critter could get some. Then I saw that all the
bars were tight. I didn't want any of them to get
out and drink. I'll explain why when I get along a
little further. People have heard tell of the expression 'watered stock', that is used in Wall Street. This
is where that there Wall Street term came from. So
I want to write it down in proper order." Go on from
there into the fascinating story, though you may have
partly guessed the answer. You will also find the key
to the Drew psychology or, shall we call it, method,
in this story.

It is interesting to note that both *"Reminiscences"*
and *"Dan'l Drew"* are written in the first person and
in semi-fictionalized form. This form makes for en-
grossing reading when you know the writer is actually dealing with the real life story. The style in
each case is particularly appropriate to the subject.

Regarding *"Dan'l Drew"* — read carefully the
EDITOR's NOTE (following this Introduction) which
was written fifty-five years ago.

*"Dan'l Drew"*, as well as being intensely interesting per se, covers so very much ground, — the development of Hudson River navigation, early days
in Wall Street, the religious spirit of that age, and
the rationalizing of that religion with the buccaneer-
ing tactics of the Street. Dan'l Drew claimed to be
the first great Wall Street "speckilator." When you
have read this book I believe you will grant that he
was all of that.

Lest there be any doubt regarding the reality and
the power of Daniel Drew, another writer of those
bygone days wrote as follows: "In the present decade
among a host of lesser operators, Cornelius Vanderbilt and Daniel Drew are the central Titanic figures.
These men are the Nimrods, the mighty hunters of
the stock market; they are the large pike in a pond
peopled by a smaller scaly tribe. . . . Cornelius
Vanderbilt, and Daniel Drew—how great each in
his way, how similar, and yet how different they are!
Both commenced without a penny. . . . Vanderbilt's
intellect is the more comprehensive, Drew's the more
subtle. The genius of the former is constructive, in
building up values; that of the latter is destructive,
in depressing them, for Drew is a most robust archi-
tect of panics. . . . In personal appearance, how
totally dissimilar. Vanderbilt looks like an anax-

andron, a king of men. Seventy-six winters have not
bowed that stately form, or quenched the light of
that deep-set black eye. Three-score years and ten,
and more, have written upon the figure of his rival
(Drew) more of the physical signs of decay, but
through a wilderness of wrinkles, his steel-gray eyes,
twinkle with all the vitality of one and twenty."

Daniel Drew was born in 1797, in the village of
Carmel, Putnam County, New York. He had grown
up as a cattle drover, and his life of terrible priva-
tion in youth may have contributed to his "bearish"
view of life. In passing it might be stated that Vanderbilt, the great bull, who always operated on the
constructive side, died a wealthy man. Daniel Drew,
unfortunately for him, was "hoist by his own
petard." He was ruined by his own copybook maxim,
the one he lived by, the one he had always been fond
of reciting whenever he had trapped an unwary vic-
tim in the market. The maxim—

*"He who sells what isn't his'n*
*Must buy it back or go to pris'n"*

And so, our "sanctimonious and treacherous"
Daniel Drew, his millions gone, a ruined old man,
ostracized, near the end of his days was heard to
complain: "To speckilate in Wall Street when you
are no longer an insider is like buying cows by candle-
light."

*"The Book of Daniel Drew"*, then, is fascinating
and nostalgic reading, but, mainly, I regard it as a

Required Course for Wall Streeters, old and new. Read all about the game when there were no holds barred. It will greatly help you the better to understand the game today.

BENTON W. DAVIS

# EDITOR'S NOTE

A caution to the reader is necessary. From the fact that these papers are put in the first person throughout, one unwarned would get the impression that they were left by Mr. Drew in finished form, and that my task as editor had been merely to dig up from the rubbish of some attic a bundle of manuscript undiscovered these thirty years since his death, and hand it over to the printer.

This view would be the more natural, because of the following article (I quote it in part), which appeared in the New York *Tribune*, February 8, 1905:

> " A diary of Daniel Drew, containing pen pictures of former Wall Street celebrities and accounts of old-time financial transactions, has been discovered. It came to New York the other day in an old trunk which was shipped down from Putnam County to a grandniece of the financier from the Drew estate in Carmel. Yesterday, in going through her consignment, she came upon the diary. 'Jim' Fisk is mentioned often in its pages, and also Cornelius Vanderbilt. Events of 'Black Friday' are touched on."

The article goes on to state that the diary would be prepared for publication.

From this one might infer that the papers which follow were received from the pen of Mr. Drew in the connected form in which they here are given.   Which impression would be quite erroneous. As a matter of fact the material out of which this series of papers has been made, were in the most jumbled and helter-skelter form imaginable.   Even where I have had the clear words of Mr. Drew to guide me, I have had to "English" it for the easy comprehension of the reader.   For, as the pages themselves state, schools were not plentiful in our rural districts a hundred years ago; and an education of the book kind was not only hard to get, but was also little valued in comparison with practical skill—the ability to bring things to pass.   In altering his grammar and spelling, therefore, so as to make for easy reading, much of the tang and individuality which, to those who knew him, Daniel Drew possessed to an uncommon degree, has undoubtedly been sacrificed.   In order to whip the life story here recorded into something approaching coherence and clearness, I have had to shape the thing from the start.

In fact, my share in the preparation of this volume has had to be so large, even writing with my own hand parts which were needed in order to supply the connection—putting these also, as in the case of historical drama, in the first person—that I had doubts as to whether plain biography might not have been the better form, as being less liable to misconstruction.   But I decided to let it go forth in the first person throughout, provided it could be accompanied by a foreword of explanation. In historical drama, the poetic form is sufficient notice to the reader that the speeches are not stenographic reports, though the situations and spirit of the whole are true to history. In the present case I have sought to convey the same notification by means of this introduction. That errors have crept into a work pieced as this has been out of scraps and fragments, is to be expected. But I venture to state that these will be found to concern matters of unessential detail alone. In the drift and temper of the work as a whole, I pledged myself to absolute adherence to the originals.

The events narrated constitute a stirring and important era in our nation's history. The development of navigation on the Hudson River, brought recently to the front by the tri-centennial celebration; the Erie Railroad and its vicissitudes; early days in Wall Street; the religious spirit of a former age, a spirit which to-day in all of the churches is changing rapidly for the better; the Tweed Ring in New York City—these and other events touched on in the papers which here follow, are not without historical value. Some of the facts and viewpoints here given have not, to my knowledge, found their way elsewhere into print.

BOUCK WHITE.

Head Resident's Study,
    Trinity Neighborhood House
       New York City.

# CONTENTS

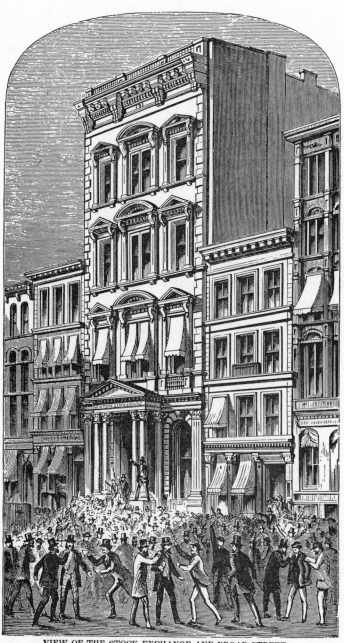

VIEW OF THE STOCK EXCHANGE AND BROAD STREET.

# THE BOOK OF DANIEL DREW

# The Book of Daniel Drew

## I

MEMORIES — that's what this thing is going to be. What I remember I'll put down. What I don't remember I won't put down. Or else I'll put it down cautious-like, so you'll know it isn't real gospel but only a sort of think-so. For after going on eighty years, a fellow gets a little mite rusty as to some of the goods packed away in his upper story. Whenever I talked with people I didn't jot it down word for word. Therefore it's only the gist of it that you get here in these papers.

Anyhow I never was much at writer-work. Jay was the boy for that. I mean Jason Gould. (He got to calling himself "Jay," and so the rest of us called him by that name, too.) In our doings — I mean, the doings of Jim Fisk, Jay Gould and me, for we were in a partnership together a long time — Jay would do most of the writer-work. "Jay, you're the ink slinger," Jimmy would say to him, and would pull him up to the table and slap a pen in his hand. He would do it so rough that Jay, who is a slip of a man, would wince. But Jimmy

3

had so hearty a way of slapping you on your shoulder with his big paws, that nobody could stay mad at him for very long together.

As I started to say, Jay had a high and noble way of stringing words together — a knack which I never could get. See that opening of his "History of Delaware County," which he wrote back in '55, before he came to New York to make money. It's worth reading over and over, if for nothing more than its moral teachings:

"History, with the more and more extensive meaning acquired by the advancement of civilization, by the diffusion of education, and by the elevation of the standard of human liberty, has expanded into a grand and beautiful science. It treats of man in all his social relations, whether civil, religious, or literary, in which he has intercourse with his fellows. The study of history, to a free government like the one in which we live, is an indispensable requisite to the improvement and elevation of the human race. It leads us back through the ages that have succeeded each other in time past; it exhibits the conditions of the human race at each respective period, and by following down its pages from the vast empires and mighty cities now ingulfed in oblivion but which the faithful historian presents in a living light before us, we are enabled profitably to compare and form a more correct appreciation of our own relative position.

"It is certain that the more enlightened and free a people become the more the government devolves upon themselves; and hence the necessity of a care-

ful study of history, which, by showing the height
to which man as an intellectual being is capable
of elevating himself in the scale of usefulness and
moral worth, teaches that the virtues of a good man
are held in sacred emulation by his countrymen for
ages succeeding, long after the scythe of time has
gathered the earthly remains of the actor to the
silent grave.    Such thoughts, or rather such reflec-
tions as these, inspire within the human bosom an
ardent desire to attain that which is good and shun
that which is evil, an honest and laudable ambition
to become both great and good; or, as another has
beautifully written: 'Great only as we are good.' "

You'll have to foot it many a mile to find writing
to equal that.  Fine, noble words seemed to come to
Jay natural-like.  If I could write in that fashion
I'd be stuck up.  But Jay wasn't; in fact, he didn't
use to like it when I would remind him of this
opening chapter of his "History of Delaware
County."

"Twaddle!" he'd say; "it's nothing but a lot of
gush, written when I was a youth out there back of
the Catskill Mountains."  Jay always was modest.
He didn't like to be pushed to the front.  Jimmy
was the boy — I mean Jim Fisk — to occupy the
front pew.  He never minded it a bit; in fact,
would rather sit there than anywhere else in meeting
— that is, so to speak; because Jimmy didn't go to
meeting really.

Well, as I started to say, I never was much on the

writer-business. So I don't want any one to suppose that I'm trying here to write history, like what
Jay wrote. I haven't got big enough words for
that. In these diary papers, I just set it down in
the first words that come to me. And I'm not
scared to put the whole story in, either. "What's
the use of digging up dead dogs?" some of the boys
might say. But I'm not scared. I have been busy
all my days, and now that I'm so old that they won't
let me speckilate in stocks as I used to, I've got to
keep busy. So I'm going to write out some things.
Goodness knows, nobody need be scared at it. Do
the best I can, these papers won't stay in order;
they're a mixed-up mess of stuff. The pages in the
forepart of a chapter get lost somewheres in the desk
before I get to the finish. So that, if I can't make
head nor tail to the thing three months after I've
written it, who else can? Then, too, people have
always said, "Nobody on earth can read Uncle Dan
Drew's quail tracks." So, what is there to be scared
of? Besides, even if the people should get the story,
what's the harm? The boys who would be mad
at me for ripping up old scores, as they'd call it, are
too thin-skinned. They are sensitive to the speech of
people. But I'm not sensitive. I don't care a hill of
beans for the speech of people. Never did. If people
want to know about some of the things that have
happened in my life-time, they are welcome. I shan't
make any bones of letting them know the whole story.

## II

JAY wrote his history about Delaware County in York State. My story — the first part — will have to be about Putnam County, on the other side of the Hudson. For I was born there — in 1797. It was in Carmel, on a farm above the Lake, on the "Pond Hill Road," alongside of Whangtown Brook. Follow up that brook until you come to a hill on the left as steep as a meeting-house roof. Climb to the top. And there, just at the fork of the road where it turns to go to Farmer's Mills, is where the house stood. There were locust trees in the front yard, and a well of cool water alongside the house, in the back yard. My father's name was Gilbert Drew. He was of English extraction. My mother was a Catherine Muckel-worth, of Scotch blood, as you could guess by the name. She was a master-hand in sickness, and kept in the house a store of roots and herbs. There was boneset and pennyroyal, smartweed, catnip, skunk cabbage, sarsaparilla, wild turnip, and such like. In those days it was a good thing to have a parent that knew something about medicine. Because the saddle-bag doctor was hard to locate just when you wanted him. He wasn't always very knowing either. "Old Bleed'em, Puke'em, and Purge'em," was what we used to call him — "Old Blisters" was another name.

I didn't get much schooling — somehow never took to it. In fact there wasn't much book-learning to take to in those days. Carmel then wasn't built up around where the village now stands. What there was of the village nestled around Old Gilead Meeting-house, at the other end of the Lake from us. Old Gilead was near Mt. Pisgah, and a good two miles from my home. It was a different kind of a place from Brimstone Hollow, a mile or two beyond. Old Gilead used to be known only as "Gregory's Parish," until he preached — Parson Nathan Gregory, I mean — that wonderful sermon of his from the text, "Is there no balm in Gilead?" whereby the entire meeting was so set on fire with godliness that they named the church "Gilead Meeting-house" from that day. Carmel was settled by people from Barnstable County, on Cape Cod, and had lots of religion even in its earliest days.

Well, as I started to say, in my day the preacher used to have both parishes, Gilead and another, called Red Mills, a few miles away. He would take turns, living for a spell at one place and then for a spell at the other. During his stays at Gilead he kept a school in his house. So that I got a little education. But it was only in snatches, so to speak. When you've got to walk three miles for it, the amount of book-learning you're going to bring back with you isn't going to be very hefty. Of course, there were the spelling-bees. But I had never got much beyond the "b-a, baker," in school; and so I always got spelled down the very first time round. But I never minded that very much. I never did care two pins what people thought of me. I'd take my place in any spell-down, no matter how many people were looking on.

Then, too, even when there was a parson-teacher at Gilead, there was no end to the things that used to pop up-and keep me from school. Whangtown Brook used to have some of the biggest trout you ever saw. And when a boy brings home a good string of fish for the table, his ma isn't going to scold him much for playing hookey from school. And I was needed a good deal around the farm. Not that we were poor. For those days we were comfortably well off — that is, compared to the rest of the people. We had a farm of nigh on to a hundred acres, and that was what lots of people didn't have. In those days nobody up in our part of the state had any great store of this world's goods. For this was, as everybody knows, just after the Revolutionary War. In the war, our part of York State was what was known as the Debated Country. The Red Coats were stationed down in New York City, the patriot troops up in the neighbourhood of Albany. This left Putnam and Westchester Counties between the two, like a grain of wheat between the upper and nether mill-stones, as Scripture says. The region was well nigh ground to pieces. First the Red Coats would overrun the county. Then the Patriots would take a turn at it. Until, by the time they both got through, the farms looked about as handsome as a skinned rabbit.

Sugar was very high. We used maple sugar a good deal. Father also would drive over to Fishkill on the Hudson, and get of the store-keeper a molasses barrel after the molasses had been drawn out. In the bottom of an empty molasses barrel is a whole lot of caked molasses that makes as fine sugar as a man ever put in his mouth. But even with these shifts, sugar and sweetening were scarce things. Sometimes, when we were to have company and sweetening was scarce, mother in making a pie would sweeten only one end of it. She would place it on the table in such a way that the company would get the sweet end; and we boys, Tom and I (Tom was my brother, a little older than me), would have to steer for the sour end. Molasses was good for medicine also. Because the itch was almost everywhere in those days. It was well nigh the most bothersome complaint we had. Lice are not so serious. After you get used to them they don't bother you much. But the itch is a pestersome thing.  Unless you keep it down with a powerful hand it will break out all over you.  And molasses-and-sulphur was a sovereign remedy.

Tom and I had to work hard, often during school term.  Father was old, mother being his second wife.  And our farm, besides, was almighty rough and hilly.  Some parts of it were as steep as the shingles on a house.  Then there were the stones and rocks to clear away.  How sick I got of prying those rocks out of the fields, with an old axle for a crowbar, and stone-boating them over to the boundaries to make fences of.

The woods were so plentiful that the farm was not of much use except for stock-raising.  And stock-raising means work pretty nigh all the time.  Because there were always poor spots in the fences.  And, trust me, there is no critter like a heifer or a bull calf for finding weak spots in a fence, particularly if it's a line fence.  And when your cattle get over into the other fellow's field, you have to get after them mighty quick.  Also our pasture lots were for the most part woods.  We had ear-marks in those days by which we could tell our cattle if they got mixed up with others.  For example, the left ear would be notched on the top with the right ear cropped off square and a hole in the middle.  So that if we found a critter with a notch in the right ear instead of the left, we knew he belonged to somebody else.  When you have to look through the woods for your milch cows, to bring them home at night for milking, with nothing to go by but the sound of the bell dingling from the cow's neck, and sometimes not even that, they would be so far off; why, it means that you've got work on your hands. When there was nothing out in the fields to do, the chores had to be looked after. And then, just like as not, mother would say, "Dan, I need a new broom." That would mean that I'd have to look up a straight birch sapling from the woods, and with a sharp jackknife cut one end of it into splints and bind them around, so as to make a new broom. We had to cart our farm truck, or young calves, eighteen miles across country to Peekskill-on-the-Hudson. From there a sloop ran to New York, for carrying passengers and freight. Later on, a line of market wagons went through Carmel to Peekskill twice a week, and gathered up the produce of the farms. But in the early days, each farmer had to do his own marketing.

So I reached the age of fifteen without much book-learning. Then came the War of 1812. And the school-teacher wasn't heard of any more. The farms, as I said, had been left so spoiled by the Revolutionary War as hardly to make grazing for a goose. And now, just when the farmers were getting on their feet again, along comes the War of 1812 and knocks things gally west once more. We knew in Putnam County that a war was on, even though there wasn't any fighting in our section. Because we used to get news regular, although it would be sometimes a little late in coming. There was the Red Bird line of stages from Albany to New York. They changed horses at Luddington's Tavern, in Carmel — these stages ran only in winter, because in summer travel from New York to Albany was by sloop. In the summer-time, also, when the boats were sailing on the river, there was another line of stages, running from Carmel to Peekskill, by the turnpike which went just south of the Fishkill Mountains across Peeks-kill hollow. We got our news from the stage-driver, as he drove up to Carmel in the great stage that was painted bright red, and with the bells jingling on the four horses. These stages would come once a day on their way through Somers, to Carmel, to Luddingtonville, and so on up north. (It took four days for the stage to make the trip from New York to Stockbridge, Mass., and Bennington, Vt., through Dingle Ridge.) There were also post-riders, who came into the town every Saturday afternoon on horseback with newspapers from Hartford and Poughkeepsie.

Then, too, we used to learn the news in a general way when the cobbler came to the house once a year to make up the year's supply of boots and shoes for the household. "Whipping the cat" used to be what we called his visit — I guess likely from his always driving the cat away from his work bench, for she seemed possessed to hang around and get his waxed ends jummixed up. This visit of the cobbler was quite an event each year. Father would prepare for it by swapping a pair of cattle or a load of potatoes down at Foster's tan-yard, a mile the other side of Luddington's Tavern, for a few sides of leather. Then the cobbler would come for a week or so and make the leather up into foot-wear. So when the news he brought was about a war, and about the goings-on in the great world outside, a boy of fifteen was going to listen with both ears. When the cobbler came it was the boy's work to whittle out the pegs for him. A boy would really get more news from the cobbler than any other member of the family, since he would be nearer to him.

In these ways, little by little, we learned about the victory of Commodore Perry on Lake Erie, and the big doings of our navy out on the high seas. But it seems that these victories on water hadn't done much good; because the military campaign along the entire northern frontier of our country was going against us. The English were pushing in on every side. It looked as though New York might be taken. The President had issued a draft for troops to defend the country. And men were paying as high as a hundred dollars for a substitute. That hundred dollars looked big to me. It seemed an easy way to earn a large lump of money. Times were getting harder and harder out on our hillside farm; for banks all over the country were stopping specie payment, and silver was getting as scarce as hens' teeth. So when, on top of it all, my father died, I decided that the time had come. I made up my mind to leave the farm in charge of my brother Tom (he being the oldest, he was by rights the one to stay home and take care of things), and go out and see the world, and make money as a substitute in the army. First along mother didn't exactly take to the idea. But I showed her I was sure to make big money. I was to get one hundred dollars out of hand; and as my board in the army wouldn't cost me anything, the money would be clear gain. It was a powerful argument, because she was thrifty. A hundred dollars all in a lump looked pretty nigh as big to her as it did to me. But just then she happened to think of another thing. For mother was old-fashioned.

"See here, Danny," said she; "you're under age, and to get into the service you'd have to tell a lie. And besides, you might get killed; and then where would the hundred dollars be?" I answered that I would agree to leave the hundred dollars with her to keep for me, before I started. As to my being under age, I told her not to bother herself about that point. I would take care of that. Women, anyhow, are apt to be squeamish about business transactions. Men are more sensible — they know that if a cat would eat fish she must be willing to wet her feet.   And I told mother that I would take care of the age limit. I calculated that, for a fellow as tall for his years as I was, I could fix my age all right.

And I did.   The Government was hard pressed for men.   So the recruiting sergeant didn't narrow me down very close when I told him I was of age.   I got my hundred dollars, handed it over to mother to keep for me, and in full regimentals of the State Militia, with knapsack on back and musket over my shoulder, I set out for Peekskill.   There I found a sloop going to New York, and got aboard. These sloops were big affairs.   They carried people, live stock and freight, all huddled together.   When the wind and tide were contrary, or when the wind died down altogether, they anchored, and you would be out all night just in making the trip to New York. In that case you'd have to sleep the best way you could.   But you could find a good berth on the hay or straw which usually formed a part of the boat's cargo.   As long as it didn't rain, you could pass a night very comfortable.

It was a great event in my life, this trip to New York.   When finally we came to where the Harlem River empties out into the North River, the man at the helm pointed it out to the passengers, and said, "there was the island, and the city was at the lower end of it."   Another hour of sailing brought us to where the city lay.   We landed at a wharf alongside where the Washington Market now stands. (The shore at that point has been filled in a good deal since that day. Back in those days, boats of light draft could sail right in and land pretty near to the market.) They marched me off along with the rest, and took me across the North River to Fort Gaines-vort, opposite New York City. It was near Paulus Hook (which is now Jersey City). There my company was stationed, I suppose to protect New York.

And now my good luck in enlisting showed itself. For my company didn't have to do a smitch of fighting. I just lived there in the camp, without it costing me a cent for food or lodging; and at the end of three months, on a February's day, a British sloop-of-war from Europe sailed into New York Harbour with the news that our Peace Commissioners at Ghent had succeeded in making a treaty. The war was over.

It was mighty good news for everybody. That winter had been one of the hardest New York City had ever seen. The weather was so severe, the North River froze over to Paulus Hook. Hickory wood sold in New York that winter for $20 a cord, and hogs fetched $11 a hundred. (That price for butcher's meat set me thinking, as will be seen a little later.) Milk was a shilling a quart. And the President, when the news came, had been just on the point of calling for 75,000 more militia. I was as glad as the rest. Perhaps a little more so.

I never was cut out to be a soldier. Not that I worried much about the hardships of life in camp. When a fellow has been reared on a hill-side farm, his cradle a sap-trough, and has been brought up to eat from wooden plates, he's used to pot-luck, and life in an army camp doesn't seem hard at all. Still I was glad when the news came of peace. In a battle there's always a danger from bullets and bayonets, and from cannon balls. I'm by nature a peaceable man. And I had cleaned up a hundred dollars in the space of three months. It was a good stroke of business.

I set out for home as soon as I was mustered out. And for a few days I was glad to be back. But I soon saw that I wasn't intended for a humdrum life. I had had a smack of big things, and now the everlasting chores on the farm didn't gee with my tastes. My brother Tom was there to take care of those things. (He said, with something pretty near to cuss words, when I spoke to him on the subject, that since I was such a gadabout, somebody had to buckle down and run the farm, in order to take care of mother.)

So I made my plans. Going to mother, I said, "Mother, I want my substitute money. I'm going into business."

"Goodness sakes!" she replied; "what is it this time? Some new fangle, I'll bet, to waste your money on."

"No new fangle at all," said I; "I'm going to be a drover. I'm going to buy up cattle for the city market. And I need the hundred dollars to start me off. I'm young. But that's the time to start in. Early sow, early mow."

"But are you sure, Danny," said she (for the idea began to take hold of her); "are you sure that you won't lose your money?" I told her I'd planned the thing all out; it was going to be a money-maker. She handed the hundred dollars over to me, and I became a drover.

Not exactly a drover, either, in the full sense of the word. I became a buyer of bob calves. The laws against bob-veal weren't very strict in those days — that is, they weren't enforced. If you could get anybody to buy the stuff, the law didn't poke its nose in and stop you. And so, I would go around among the farmers and buy a calf very soon after it had been dropped. I had my troubles. Bob-calves are shaky on their legs. Then, too, there's its mother to bother you. I found it easier to get around the law objection against bob-veal than the mother objection — so to speak — that pair of wicked horns, when you go to take the calf away from its dam! But the right kind of handling would do it. And then, by hurrying the calf to market, I would get the critter off my hands before it sickened and died. I dare say that the flesh now and then was pretty soft for real good eating. Peo-

ple used to say, "Veal bought from that young Dan
Drew can be sucked through a quill." But then,
folks who said these things were jealous of me,
because I worked hard and managed to get along.

Besides, with me it was a case of calves or nothing.
Because I didn't have the money to go into the
grown-up cattle business. You can buy calves on a
small capital — yes, sometimes without capital at
all. Because, a farmer who has a bull calf on his
hands and doesn't want to feed it, will often let you
have it on credit. Sometimes the farmer thinks
that a calf is so misshapen and puny that it is going
to die; and then he will be glad to get it off of his
hands on any terms. But when it comes to parting
with his grown-up critters, a farmer is almighty
particular about whom he trusts.

# III

THESE years of mine as a calf-drover were broken in upon a little later. I went into the circus business.

Some time after the War of 1812, the travelling circus came into fashion. The people in those days lived in little settlements. They were lonely. They didn't have much amusement. So, when times became settled once more and the farmers had recovered from the war, the Rolling Show came in and did lots of business. Only we didn't call it a show in those days, nor a circus — no siree! The people wouldn't have come near us. Because the preachers thundered against circuses and all such worldliness. To get the trade of the church people, we called it a "Menagerie" and "The Great Moral and Educational Exhibition."

Putnam and Westchester counties were headquarters for the circus business in early days, particularly Star's Ridge, in the town of South-east, and Purdy's Station, just below Croton Falls. I guess the reason for this was, because those two counties are just north of New York City. Being a beautiful farming region, with Bridgeport, Conn., and Danbury just across the State line, this region became naturally the winter quarters for the New York shows. The circuses would start out from our section each spring, and come back to us in the fall, for winter quarters. In this way all our part of the State got to talking circus. There was old Hakaliah Bailey, of Somers — Somerstown Plains it was, back in my day — five miles below Carmel. He brought over the first elephant ever seen in the county. "Old Bett," he called her. In front of the tavern there in Somers — the Old Elephant Hotel they called it — you can see even yet a pedestal with an elephant carved on top of it. And Seth Howe, down at Turk's Hill, near Brewsters', when he came to make his fine summer home there, had stone animals carved and stuck around the grounds here and there. Besides, there was Gerard Crane, of Somers — everybody has heard of "Howe and Crane's Great London Circus." Then there was Turner, of Bailey and Turner, of Danbury; and later on, Phineas Barnum, from Bridgeport. Isaac Van Amberg also started his menagerie from our section. The Weekses, also well-known in the circus business, came from Carmel. The town was full of circus, back in those early days.

So when Nate Howe, from down Brewsters' way — he was Seth Howe's brother — rounded me up one day as I was on one of my calf-buying trips, and said he was looking for a smart and handy young man like me, to be a driver and an all-round man with his show, I got the fever and started in. They put me at all sorts of work. In those days the circus was a one-horse affair compared to what it has grown to now, and one man would have to help out in a dozen different kinds of work. He would be a mule-driver, canvas-man, gate-keeper and feeder of the animals, sometimes all in one day. And most like as not, now and then he would have to turn in and help out with the clown's part. The clowns in those days had speaking parts. They cracked jokes on the politicians and local celebrities in the village where the show was exhibiting, sang the ballad, "Betsy Baker," and did flipflaps. Then, too, since there wasn't much advertising in those days, when we landed in a town and while the workmen were getting the canvas up, the one of us who was acting the clown for the day would go along the street, togged out in his tom-fooleries, and with a bugler parading in front. After he had got a crowd around him he would mount a barrelhead in front of the village tavern—about the time the stage arrived, if possible — and from that stump would announce the show, tell where it was to be found, and read off the list of the animals that would be shown. I used to like the part of clown. It was fun to crack jokes and set the boys and girls to laughing. I always did like a good joke, anyhow.

Inside the canvas we used to have the animals

arranged along one side, with the seats for the people along the other side. The performers' ring was in the middle, between the two. I was a good hand with the beasts, because I knew how to handle them. With the hay animals, such as deer, elk, zebu-cows and so forth, I was right at home, having been raised on a farm. Elephants were regarded in those days as dangersome; but my farmer training with horses and horned critters made me now a good man for handling risky beasts of all kinds. Then, when it came to the big cats, such as tigers and other blood-thirsty varmints, I knew how to get butchers' meat for them of the right kind and in the right way. Because I'd been, so to speak, in the butcher's line also. Upon landing in town, if it was the day for feeding them — we used to feed the cats only every other day, so as to keep them healthy; because in their native state they don't eat much oftener than that — I would look up some butcher and get him to give me a basket of bones and scraps for the cats. I would pay him by getting the clown to make mention of the butcher's name in some flattering manner, during the performance that afternoon. Sometimes a butcher would give me all the scrap meat I needed, on condition that he wasn't to be hit by any of the jokes — this would be after I'd hinted to him that the clown was going to get off some good jokes at those merchants in the town who didn't support the show. I knew how to handle men, as well as animals. And being smart and handy at all sorts of work, I was promoted higher and higher; finally I was offered a part ownership in the show. Like as not I would have taken it. But just then something happened: I got religion.

The churches were not very numerous in those days. So when a preacher wanted to get up a revival in a part of his circuit away from his meeting-house, he would use a grove, if it was summer time, or a schoolhouse, in the winter. It was good business policy for us circus people, on a Sunday, to be seen in church along with the godly; because it kind of gave respectability to our business — it helped out the "Great Moral Exhibition," on our show-bills. Never shall I forget that day, or that meeting, when I first got converted. First along during the meeting I was cold as an icicle — just a looker-on. But pretty soon the religious melodies began to get hold of me. Those were hymns with an edge to them, in those days. Seems as if hymns we sing nowadays aren't anywheres near so searching power-ful as those we used to hear:

> "Tremble, my soul, and kiss the sun;
> Sinner, obey thy Saviour's call;
> Else your damnation hastens on,
> And hell gapes wide to wait your fall."

I tell you, tunes like that don't let you forget them.

They keep ringing in your head, no matter how many years have passed since. In those days they didn't mince matters:

> "Far in the deep, where darkness dwells,
> A realm of horror and despair,
> Justice has built a dismal hell
> And laid her stores of vengeance there.

> "Eternal plagues and heavy chains,
> Tormenting racks and fiery coals,
> And darts to inflict immortal pains,
> Dyed in the blood of damnèd souls."

I got religion then and there. When the preacher called out, "Hasten, sinner, to be wise," I hastened. I didn't stop to ask what my old companions would think of it. (I never did care what people thought of me, anyhow.) All I thought of was to get to the mourners' bench. And so it wasn't long before I was up there, in front of the whole congregation. I told them I had a fervent desire to flee from the wrath to come.

It made considerable of a stir, this conversion of mine. For a circus man to come over onto the Lord's side, was a triumph for the army of Gideon. The brethren gathered around me with great joy. The preacher pressed me to tell the congregation how I felt. I rose and spoke. Words always did come sort of easy with me — that is, the plain,

every-day words. Besides, when a young fellow
has practised speaking from a barrel-head in front
of a village tavern, dressed in outlandish fashion,
and telling the people the way to the circus grounds,
he isn't going to be scared at a congregation of
people inside a church. So on the present occasion
I had wondrous liberty. In fact I gave in my testimony with such acceptance that the minister came
to me after the service and told me I ought to become
a preacher. This was a side of the matter I hadn't
looked at. In my testimony I had told the people
that "from this time forth I was going to serve the
Lord." But as to taking up preaching, that was a
different matter. There isn't much chance in
preaching to get rich. So, after turning it over in
my mind, I told him that I didn't feel any call.
And I went back to the drover's business.

I was glad that I had become converted.
Because the circus business didn't promise to bring
me in any such money as I felt I could make buying cattle, now that I'd saved up capital enough to
start in.

# IV

NOW began the real work of my life. For until this time I had been earning money hit or miss, as the chance offered. I was getting nowhere. But, starting now into the drover's business in good earnest, I found my main bent.

About this time a wave of prosperity was setting in throughout the country. The nation had recovered from the effects of the war. The banks were resuming specie payments. Trade revived. New York City was calling for butcher's meat. During the war she had had a long fast, so to speak. Now she began to eat. Her population was growing like sixty. City Hall Park had formerly been way up town. Now it was getting to be in the centre, with houses all around. To keep this big and growing city in butcher's meat was a work in itself. That was where we drovers got a living. Putnam County and the region round about is so hilly that it is fit for raising stock better than for anything else. A steer or a sheep can thrive on hillsides where a plough would tip over. Besides, it is on the same side of the Hudson River as New York, and only a few miles above it. Thus the Harlem Valley, leading down through Westchester County, soon became a channel through which drovers brought cattle to feed the thousands of hungry mouths in the city at the foot of Manhattan Island.

As a drover I had trouble first along, the same as when I went into the calf business, because the farmers didn't like to sell me their cattle on credit. But I managed to get around them in one way or another. I would ride up to a farmer's house — during this time of my life I was rarely out of the saddle except to eat or sleep, occasionally even driving cattle at night to save time, for hunger in the belly puts spurs to the heels — and, instead of starting in with talk about buying, I would say:

"Hello, Brother So-and-So" (the news of how I had got religion helped me with the farmers); "how are you off for fat stock?"

Upon his answering that he had a pair or so of fit cattle, I'd say:

"Well, now, I'm taking a drove into the city next week. If you say so, I'll take yours along, too, and sell them for you, for old acquaintance's sake. I know two or three butchers down there in the city, and calculate I can sell those critters for you at a top price." I had learnt good and early that if you haven't got honey in the crock, you must have it in the mouth.

The plan worked fine. That is, first along. I got several hundred head of cattle on these terms, and they seldom failed to bring a good price in the city. So that before long I had scraped together a nice little capital. To be sure, the farmers who let me have the stock on these terms would keep pestering me for the money. But I put them off with one excuse or another. Sometimes I would soften a man's anger by paying him part of what was coming to him, and tell him he'd have to wait for the balance until after my next trip. In cases where I couldn't quiet a creditor in this way, I had still another shift, for I always was a resourceful fellow. I would change my base of operations to another part of the county, so far away that the farmers I had traded with the last time couldn't reach me. Unfortunately, word would sometimes get around ahead of me, so that when I'd ride up to a farmhouse and try to get cattle without paying cash, I would be turned down. There was Len Clift, over near Brewsters', for one. I had agreed with him on the price of a calf. Then, as I was about to lead the critter off, I told him he would have to trust me a few days, as I was a little short of ready cash just at that moment.

"Trust you?" said he. "Wouldn't trust you no further than you can throw a hog by the tail."

I didn't get riled up. Getting riled up is poor business. A man isn't fit for a business career until he has learned never to get riled up; or leastwise, never to show it on the outside, even if he is all riled up inside. I sort of explained the thing to Len and coaxed; but he answered a plump "No" every time. "You'll get the calf when I get the money. Not a minute sooner."

"Len," said I, finally, when I saw that he wasn't to be moved; "you won't trust me for the price of one lousy little calf? All right. But, Len Clift, the time'll come when I'll have money enough to buy your whole farm. Remember what I'm a-telling you."

And the time did come, too. After I had made my fortune I bought his farm and made it into my country seat. I have got my family burying lot on that farm, now. "Drewsclift" I named the place. It's that beautiful farm just on the other side of the hill over from Brewsters' Village. The burying lot is out by the willow trees across the road from the house, down in the meadows. My parents had been buried in old Gilead Burying Ground at Carmel. I got the bodies dug up and carried over to this new burying lot, so I could establish a family cemetery. When a man makes a name for himself, he wants to make a family seat to go with the name.

But though I had a turn-down once in a while, such as this one from Len Clift, I found many a farmer obliging enough to sell me calves' and cows and steers and sheep on credit. A very good device, I found, was first to haggle with the farmer over the price, and beat him down to the lowest penny.  For, strange as it might sound, this inclines the farmer to trust you.  You see, his mind figures it out something like this:

"That there drover is anxious to get a bottom figure, because he's good pay, and means, when the time comes, to settle up promptly and penny for penny.  He wants to get a good contract because he is the kind of a fellow to live up to it word for word.  To be sure, he is a tight fellow to deal with, but at least he is a safe fellow, and so I guess I'll let him have this pair of cattle on credit."  In these ways, working now one plan and now another, I got together a nice little sum of money.

It was about this time that the field of business for drovers was widened to take in the great Mohawk valley.  The city on Manhattan Island was growing so fast that our little section up in the Harlem valley couldn't raise cattle fast enough to supply her butchers.  So a new region now was tapped, the country to the north, across the Hudson.  For some time back I had been on the look-out for a new place to move to.  Change of pasture makes fat steers; and it's sometimes good for a business man, too.  So I got to going on trips "out West," as we called it.  I would ride up north and cross over into the region around Cherry Valley (that is where the massacre in the Revolutionary War by those red savages took place).  There I would get a drove of cattle and start with them back towards New York City. We had regular routes which we followed with our droves. The taking of live stock overland to the New York market had got to be an established business by this time, with regular stopping places. There were tavern-keepers here and there along the route who catered to drovers. They would have a big pasture lot alongside the tavern, divided into two or three pastures to take care of several herds at once. When, hot and sore at the end of a day's drive, I reached one of these taverns, the inn-keeper would be there with his "Hello, Dan! I thought you'd be coming along about this time. Been expecting you these two weeks or more. Put your critters out in the orchard lot. The pasture there is as fine as a fiddle just now; and come in and rest your bones. Boy, take his horse."

From Cherry Valley we would strike across and into the old Schoharie Valley. This we would follow until we got to Middleburgh, an old Dutch settlement. We hired sloughters here to drive the cattle (in that locality they call a low, worthless fellow a "sloughter"). There we would put up for the night at a tavern called "The Bull's Head." I mention this tavern in particular, because of another "Bull's Head Inn" which I will tell you about later on. This "Bull's Head" at Middleburgh got its name from a big bull's head that was painted on a shed opposite the tavern, on the other

side of the road, to show that drovers were taken
care of there.   The tavern was a long, plain, two-
story house, just where the turnpike crosses a creek.
The creek flows down from the high hills back of
the inn, and had sweet and soft water at every
season of the year.   The cattle used to like the water
in that brook.   This whole valley is as level as a
barn floor, and flowing with pastures.

About nine miles further along from Middleburgh was an inn kept by young Brom Scutt, at a
place called Livingstonville.   He had a sign painted
and hung up, "Drovers' Holm."   (There used to
be a saying around, that that sign wasn't spelled
right;  but we drovers never set much store by spelling; we were a mighty sight more particular about
good feed and water in the pasture back of the tavern, than for good spelling on the sign-board in
front of the tavern.)   From there we'd go on to
Preston's Hollow and Cairo.   Then to Catskill on
the Hudson River.   Here we'd ferry across and
then would be on the New York City side of the
river.   (By thus skirting close around the Catskill
Mountains, we had saved miles and miles in the
journey from the Mohawk down and into the Harlem
valley.)   Then when we were safely on the east
side of the Hudson, we would veer in a south-easterly
direction into Dutchess County.   There were drovers'
taverns at Dover Wings, Hurd's Corners, Haviland's
Corners, Sodom, and Somers.   Then down into

and through the Harlem Valley, which I have mentioned before, and so across the Harlem River by the King's Bridge.  Once across the King's Bridge, it was but a day's travel down Manhattan Island to New York.

## V

I T WAS about this time in my life that I got
married — to an estimable young lady in
my home county. For, though my drover
trips were now taking me far afield, I didn't cut
loose from Putnam County altogether. Winter
time would find me back home. You can't drive
cattle in the winter time. The hard roads and
sharp ice would make them hoof-sore very quick.
For drovers, winter time is rest time. (For that
matter midsummer is also a bad time for the drover
business, because in very hot weather a drove of
cattle would sweat pounds of good fat off their
flanks before you'd get them across even one county.)
For drovers springtime and fall are the favourable
seasons. So every winter would find me back
in Carmel, doing what I could at odd jobs to earn
my board, until the roads thawed out again in the
spring.

Winter was the time for society affairs in Carmel.
I never was much of a hand for society, being more
fitted to size up a critter and buy him at a good figure
than I was to make much of a shine in social circles.
Still, I knew how to spark the girls. Of a winter's

night at Carmel we used to have high old times at sleigh rides and the mite societies. Then there were the paring-bees—we used to call them "apple-cuts" — and the singing school, nut-cracking parties, candy-pulls — what not? I was ratherish slow at getting started off to one of these shindigs. But once there and into the thick of it, I could carry my part with any of them. There was an apple-cut one night that I remember as well as I do my own name. We were playing the game "Wink and follow." After a while my turn came to be It. I caught one of the girls and said: "Laura, now I've got you." She looked me straight in the eyes and said: "Dan, you're not going to kiss me unless you're stronger than I be. And I know you be." I was. When it would come time for the refreshments, I used to step forward and help pass the fried cake, new cider, apples and hickory nuts, fine as anything.

Well, as I started to say, I got married. It was more or less this way. My brother Tom, two years before, had married one of the Mead girls, who lived over on Turk's Hill (just below where Seth Howe built his fine home with those imitation animals — I think I've wrote about it further back). Their father was a farm labourer. This Abigail Mead, my brother's wife, had a sister who was younger, just as I was younger than my brother Tom. Her name was Roxana — Roxana Mead.

(That's where the name "Mead Hall," at Drew Theological Seminary, comes from. That's my wife's picture in the Hall. But I'm getting ahead of my story.) What more natural, than that I and Roxana should get acquainted. When your brother has got a wife, and that wife has got a sister, there are going to be no end of chances for you and that sister to get to know each other. And, to make a long story short, we up and married. She was tall. So was I. Folks said we made a fine-looking pair as we stood side by side to be yoked together by the preacher.

I am sorry to say that I had lost my religion during these drover days. It's hard, anyhow, for a cattle dealer to keep religion. He is away from home too much. During these days I was always on the go — never was one of your lazy-bones; better to wear out shoes than sheets, was my motto. And when you're away from home you get sort of careless-like. You haven't got your own people around to kind of keep you straightened up. More than that, it is hard to keep religion when you haven't any one church to go to. In these days I was scurrying from pillar to post, sleeping outdoors or in barns, farmhouses, strange taverns — where not? And the upshot was, I by and by drifted from the means of grace. I backslided.

But I didn't slip back so far as to be unmindful

of my lost condition. Now and then I would feel some movings of the spirit when I would pass a burying lot, particularly if it was at night. The white stones would stand out so ghost-like, it would sometimes make me clutch the bridle to keep from shivering. And the old words I had heard so often in meeting, would ring in my ears:

> "Hark, from the tombs a doleful sound;
> Mine ears attend the cry.
> Ye living men, come, view the ground
> Where you must shortly lie.
>
> "And you, mine eyes, look down and view
> The hollow, gaping tomb.
> This gloomy prison waits for you
> Whene'er the summons comes."

At such times I accounted myself a mortal worm, fallen from grace, and open to all the bolts and fiery darts of heaven. From which it can be seen that, though I no longer had the joy which first I felt, but had lost the witness of my adoption, nevertheless the spirit was not entirely quenched within me. Accordingly, when a revival broke out in Carmel at about the time of which I am now writing, I went. The sermon that night was powerful searching, even to the dividing asunder of the joints and marrow. And before the meeting came to an end, I was wondrously saved.

> "Glory to God who treads the sky,
> And sends his blessings through;
> Who tells his saints of joys on high,
> And gives a taste below!"

I tell you, though I'm not much on singing myself, I swung in on the rest of that hymn:

> "Glory to God who stoops his throne,
> That dust and worms may see it;
> And brings a glimpse of glory down
> Around his sacred feet."

Besides, it was a help in business for me to be back among the church people; because, being married now, I wanted to kind of settle down at Carmel. But there were a number of farmers thereabouts who were cold-shouldering me, saying I owed them for calves and steers. And as they were for the most part church people, I was glad to get religion once more and be taken back into good company.

Now I began to be a person of consequence in the community. I was married. I was back in the church. And, what is more, I was a man of money. In fact, as to money, I was piling it up pretty fast these days. For New York seemed to be getting hungrier every day for fat steers. 'Most every one of my trips there helped now to line my jacket. Besides, at about this time I hit upon a scheme one day, as I was going to the city with a drove of cattle, which sluiced a lot more money into my pocket.

# VI

FORMERLY drovers into New York City had to take their droves to the old "Bull's Head," which was on the Bowery Lane, not far from where the Bowery Theatre stands. There the butchers from the stalls down on Fulton Street would meet the drovers coming into town and buy their stock.

But there was a butcher by the name of Astor — Henry Astor, his name was — who got into the habit, whenever a drover would be reported as coming into town, of leaving his brother butchers tippling at the Bowery "Bull's Head," skip out through the back door of the tavern, mount his horse, ride up the Bowery Road, and meet the drove before it got down to where the other butchers were waiting. Astor would stop the drove and pick out the prime beeves before any one else had a chance at them. By and by the other butchers got on to his trick and also began to ride up to the Bowery to meet the herds. In this way a new "Bull's Head" was established, way out on the Boston Road, where Twenty-sixth Street now is. (The "Boston Road" is now Third Avenue.) By my time this new "Bull's

Head" had got to be the cattle market, the drovers' headquarters for the city.

Henry Astor — I got to know him well — was one of the most thriving butchers in the city. He was a German. He had come over in the Revolutionary War as a sutler following the Hessian Troops. His brother, John Jacob Astor, came over a little later; and Henry started him in business as a peddler of knickknacks among the trading sloops that were tied up at the wharves. It was in this way, I guess, that John Jacob got in with the fur traders, and later made a peck of money; so that his son gave the Astor Library there, a little below where my "Bull's Head" tavern was located. But this is getting ahead of my story.

As I was driving my herd down through the Harlem valley one day, I got to thinking how anxious Henry Astor always was to get fat cattle. (I worked the scheme on any number of the New York butchers as time went on, so it will be understood that I'm now taking Astor merely as a type, because he is one of the best-known butchers of that time and because I got to know him perhaps better than I did the others.) As I was riding along, suddenly I hit upon the idea. And with me, to think of doing a thing means to begin to do it.

We came on along the Bronx River by old man Williams's bridge and across Gun Hill Road, which was deep and heavy — almost as heavy, I reckoned, as the time when the cannons sunk on that hill up to the hubs and General George Washington had to leave them to the British. Then crossing the Harlem on the King's Bridge, I brought the drove over to Harlem Village on the easterly side of the Island, about where Third Avenue now crosses 125th Street. There I put up for the night, since there was a good inn with several pasture lots alongside, in that village. I told my cattle boys to turn in early and get a good sleep, for we would be in New York City on the morrow.

That night, when all the rest were asleep — the cattle boys used to sleep in the barn on the hayloft — I went out to the drove in the pasture alongside the tavern, and emptied sacks of salt on the ground, scattering it so every critter could get some. Then I saw that all the bars were tight. I didn't want any of them to get out and drink. I'll explain why when I get along a little further. People have heard tell of the expression, "watered stock," that is used in Wall Street. This is where that there Wall Street term came from. So I want to write it down in proper order.

After the cattle had been well salted and the bars all safe and tight, I turned in and went asleep. Next morning I got up good and early. Didn't need any one to wake me. The cattle were lowing long before the sun was up, as though they wanted something or other almighty bad. By the time I got downstairs a couple of cattle boys were up and getting ready to let down the bars, to lead them out to water.

"Hey, there, what are you louts doing?" I called out. "Put up those bars right away and bring back that critter you've let out."

"But, boss," said one of them, "they're choked for water."

"What if they are?" said I. "Would you poison these critters by giving them water they aren't used to? These cattle are fresh from the country. This here is an island surrounded by the salt sea. The water here isn't what it is up country. We must get them used to this new region first. I guess I know my business. Not one of these critters gets a smitch of water until I give the word. D'ye hear? Go now; get a bite of feed, and we'll start for the city."

Thus I kept the drove from water; and as soon as breakfast was over, started them along the turnpike. At the same time I sent word ahead by a rider to Henry Astor, telling him that I was coming with some prime cattle and for him to meet me at the "Bull's Head" about noon. We trudged along, going slow; it was hot as mustard, and I didn't want to sweat any meat off my critters.

Below Yorkville—that's the village that used to be over on the Boston Road, about where Eighty-sixth Street now crosses it—was a little stream called the Saw-Kill, with a bridge crossing it. It was called "Kissing Bridge," because couples walking out that way used to kiss whenever they came to the bridge. It was a recognized custom. The bridge itself was below Yorkville, not far from where Seventy-seventh Street now cuts through. It was a low stone bridge, and hardly to be told from the road itself. But I guess young sparks and their sweet-hearts never failed to know when they were crossing it. Well, by the time the cattle got to that stream, on the drive down from Harlem Village, they were all-fired thirsty. The cattle boys, too, were glad to see the water. (We used to call these boys "ankle beaters," because they had orders when they were beating the cattle not to strike any higher than the ankle, for fear of bruising the flesh and making it unsound for market.) The boys had been feeling for the poor, suffering critters, and now were laying out to give them a good, long drink. But I had other fish to fry. I rode back to where they were. In taking a drove along the turnpike I used to ride ahead to pick out the road, leaving the boys to follow behind with the cattle. I said to them: "Boys, line up along the road there by the bridge, or those critters will get off away from you."

"Oh, they'll be all right," piped up one of the lads. "They smell the water already, and will make for it without any help from us."

"Make for nothing!" said I. I knew how to put command in my tone, when it was herd-boys I

was dealing with. "I don't want one of those critters to get to that there brook. Didn't you hear
me tell you this morning about the poison that's
in this salt air and this island water, to critters that
have been raised in fresh water-regions? Not a drop
do they get, and pelt them with dirt clods if you've
got to. Get them over the bridge dry-shod."

They minded me. They had to. They had
seen me plaster mud all over a steer when he didn't
go to suit me, and they knew I could do it to them,
too, if they didn't mind. I got the drove over the
bridge high and dry. Pretty soon we were at the
"Bull's Head." I told the boys to take the cattle
into the pasture pen that was back of the tavern,
where the well was. Then I went around in front
to the tap-room, as soon as I had put my horse
out, to look for Astor. He wasn't come yet, so I
went in to dinner. Then I waited for him on the
stoop in front of the tavern, alongside the Boston
Road. Pretty soon I saw him come up the turnpike, riding his horse. I got up and shook him
by the hand.

"Got my message, I see," said I, as he was getting
off his horse. "You know whom to come to when
you want prime stock."

"Well," said he. "I don't know as I'm buying
much to-day. Market's mighty poor. But thought
I would ride up for friendship's sake, and take a
look at your critters." (Being a German, he spoke

crooked English. It was curious to hear him. I
wish I could set it down here the way he spoke it.)

I was in hopes he'd go into the tap-room and take
something. Because when you're bargaining with
a man it's always easier if he's got something inside.
For then he takes a rosy view of things and doesn't
stop to haggle over pennies. Get ale inside of a
man, it makes him speak as he thinks. But Astor
wouldn't take anything. He only asked the landlord for a drink of water. Then I saw that I had
an uphill job on my hands. I was glad that he hadn't
come in a gig and brought his wife along, because
then I'd have had two of them against me; and Hen
Astor's wife, Dorothy, was a money-maker, just
like himself. She used to help him in the slaughter-
house, doing up butcher's small meats — that is,
the tongue, liver, kidneys and such like; she helped
make him the rich man that he got to be after a
while. I knew that with Hen Astor by himself I
was going to have my hands full. But I went to
it with a will. I asked him to wait for me a minute
while I stepped out to see if my horse was being fed.

With this as an excuse, I skipped around to
where my cattle boys were. I said: "My lads, I
guess those critters are used to the climate by this
time, and can now drink in safety. Buckle to and
give them all the water they can drink."

You should have seen them get to work. Cattle
boys get real fond of their critters. A drover likes

his critters because they mean money to him. "Ankle-beaters" often get to like them out of real affection. And you should have seen the cattle go at it, too. You'd have thought they'd not had a drink for an age. The salt had done its work. A quart of salt to every pair of cattle is a fair allowance; in the present case I had allowed them a little more than that. So that now they sucked the water in like sponges. Do the best they could, the boys couldn't keep the trough full. The steers fairly fought with each other for a drink. So I told off a couple of the boys to take part of the herd over to another pasture across the road, where there was a big pump, and start that going too. Then, when I saw that the thing was nicely under way, I went back to the tavern, where Astor was waiting for me.

"It beats all how these hostlers need looking after," said I. "If I hadn't gone out there to the barn they'd have starved that mare of mine. A thimbleful of oats no bigger than that, as true as you live, that's what they were giving my mare. And she as big as two ordinary horses. But how are you, anyhow?" And I seated myself beside him on the stoop. I took a fresh chew of tobacco, and offered him some. I thought it a good plan to sit and visit for a spell. It gets your customer into a neighbourly frame of mind; and then, too, in this present case it would give my boys time for the watering.

"I'm not so very chirpy," he grumbled. "How are you?"

"Fine as a fiddle," said I; "and what's ailing you?"

"All kinds of troubles," he went on. "The life of a cattle butcher, Dan, isn't what it used to be. There are so many in the business nowadays. And housewives come to my stall there in the Fulton Market and buy my best meats — top slices, no second cuts for them — and then, when I or Dorothy go to see them, they won't pay their bills. And the stall is getting so crowded, the hucksters and salad women have been signing a paper against me, because, they say, I've built my stall across the whole end of the market, and have crowded them out under the eaves, where they're exposed to the sun and weather. I'm a licensed victualler — I guess I've got some rights there. And then, too, the city fathers these days are getting so pernickety. You remember the market used to be on Maiden Lane — it was built over a running stream that was used as a city sewer. Very handy for us, because we could drop the swill and such like right through a hole in the floor. But the City Board didn't do anything else but talk everlastingly about 'nauseous and pestilential vapours,' and kept it up till we moved the market up onto Fulton Street. And now they're getting more pernickety still. Why, Dan, since the small-pox came they are getting so they won't allow our hogs to run in the streets any longer."

"Heinrich Astor!" said I (he liked to be called by his German name); "what won't they be ordering next? Pigs in the street are the best scavengers a city can have. You mark what I tell you, Hen; if they shut the pigs up, the gutters will get so full of slops and stuff, there won't be any living inside the city limits. Why, it would take a herd of swine to clean up what your slaughter-houses alone dump into the street."

"There you are again," he broke in. He was getting riled up. "That fussy old board of city fathers have gone and passed another ordinance, that butchers mustn't empty any more refuse in the street gutters. So now we have to cart the blood and guts way over to the river. I'd like to know how dogs, to say nothing of the hogs, are going to get a living inside the city limits, if this sort of thing keeps on. And without dogs, where would we be, at night? Why, just the other day a farm below me on the Bowery Road lost no end of chickens by the foxes."

"That loss of poultry will make more call for cow meat," said I; "and, Hen, between you and me, I've brought you some of the fittest beeves this trip that ever set foot on Manhattan Island. We'll step out and take a look, if you say so." I knew by this time that the boys would be through with the watering. So we went out.

Sure enough, when we got out into the pasture, you couldn't see a sign of a water-pail. And there, as plump and fat-looking as a man ever saw, stood the critters. I noticed out of the tail of my eye that Astor got interested all to once.

"There are two or three good-sized ones in the bunch," he remarked. "I suppose you want to sell the drove at a lump sum. I wasn't calculating on buying any stock to-day. But seeing it's you, I might be able to make an offer for the drove as a whole — say, at so much a critter."

"No," said I, "they go by the pound, this trip. Prime cattle such as these take a sight of time and fodder to fatten. I've had to get this herd together one at a time, the very best from a hundred farms. But it's worth the pains," I added, "when a fellow can bring to market a drove like this." He punched his thumb into two or three of the critters, and found them firm and solid.

"Tolerable good," said he, "tolerable good. But I'm afeared most of them will be tough. I suppose, though, I could use them up for soup meat. Tell you what I'll do. I'll give you two and a quarter a pound just as they stand, and for one or all."

I said that the figure I had set for this drove was four cents. He gave a snort and started towards the tavern as though disgusted. I didn't make any move to call him back; I knew that when a butcher finds what he thinks to be a drove of fat cattle, he isn't going to give up at the first crack. He likes the thought of a nice, fat carcass hanging from the hooks at his stall in the market. So, pretty soon, back he came.

"Donner and Himmel!" he exclaimed, and he was red in the face. "You drovers take us towns-people for suckers. I'll give you two and a half, and not a speck more. You can take it or leave it. Anyhow, I'm expecting another drover in from Long Island next week, and only came up to-day to just kind of look around."

I met him by coming down half a cent. I hadn't thought for a minute that I could get the four-cent price I had named. I had mentioned that figure in order to have something to back away from, when we got down to business. You must ask much to get a little.

He snorted off once more; but he didn't get so far this time. "Two and three quarters," said he, coming back. "And there isn't a cent in it for me at that figure, so help me Gott!"

I told him the very best I could do was three and a quarter, and only made it that figure because he was willing to take the whole drove. "It's the beneath-enest price I ever saw offered for choice stock such as these," said I. "It costs money, Hen, to pump corn into a heifer until her loins stand out like the hams on a hog."

He backed away. We dickered a spell longer. Finally we hit on a flat three-cent price. The cattle were driven on the scales. (They weighed up fine, as you can believe.) He paid over the money, and took them off down to his slaughter-pen, not far from the Bowery. I was happy, and he went off happy, too. Because a butcher likes to get heavy critters. To be sure they cost him more, but fat beef in a butcher's stall goes like hot cakes, where stringy joints wouldn't sell at all. So it was what I call a good bargain, seeing that both of us were pleased.

It can be seen now what a lucky thought it was for me — that salting device. The salt cost but a few pennies a bag, and by means of it nigh onto fifty pounds had been added to the selling weight of every critter in the drove — a full-grown critter will drink that weight of water if you get her good and thirsty. Thus I took in as my profits on this trip as fine a penny as a man could ask.

# VII

I FELT so rich from my stock-watering deal that I stayed at the "Bull's Head" tavern a spell. And, a day or two after the business with Astor, I started down to the city to see about getting a new saddle. My old one was so worn that the stuffing was coming out; for, although I had been making money for some years back, I hadn't felt like spending any more of it than I could help. My idea in those days was: Better a hen to-morrow than an egg to-day. Small savings, if you keep them up long enough, mean big savings by and by. If a fellow is going to be rich, he must get money working for him early in life. A swarm of bees in May is worth a load of hay; but a swarm in July isn't worth a fly.

Now, however, I felt rich enough to afford a new saddle. So I mounted my mare and started down to New York. I went by the Bowery Lane. I had to. That was the only road into the city in those days. I knew that it would take me past Hen Astor's house, and I had felt it would be best not to see him for a spell, if I could help it. But there wasn't any other way into the city. The Broad Way,

which is now the main thoroughfare right through
the middle of the island, hadn't been laid out then.
The place where that road now runs was swamp
and low land — "the Lispenard Meadows" we
called it.  A farmer who bought a tract of it was
joshed a good deal, his friends all saying it would
be a good farm for raising a fine crop of frogs.  So
I rode boldly down the Bowery Lane.

But just before I got to Henry's place, I thought
better of the matter and turned off to the right, across
lots.  I found a lane there that led into the meadows,
these being dry enough this time of the year for
safe walking for the horse.  The Broad Way by
this time had run up from the city a little beyond
and across the stream where Canal Street now is.
(Canal Street got its name when they dug out that
stream and made a good-sized canal there, in order
to drain the swamp and the Collect Pond just above
City Hall Park.)  I calculated on reaching this road
across lots, and then following it down into the city.
It took me some time to reach it, because I had to
wind in and out to dodge the water-holes.  But I got
out onto the Broad Way road at last.  Then I was
all right; for in dry weather it was from here on a
good thoroughfare into the city — almost as hard
and safe, in fact, as the Bowery Road.  It crossed
the Canal Street Brook on a low stone bridge.  Just
beyond was the Stone Bridge Tavern.  I knew the
locality, because around this tavern was a horse-

exchange, where old plugs and broken nags
were sold to the street hawkers and fish-men
of the city. Just above what is now White Street
I had to dismount; for there was a pair of bars at
this point to keep the cattle of the Lispenard Meadows from getting into the city. My mare wasn't
enough of a hunter to jump the bar; and I wasn't
anxious for it, either. Because a drover, if he is
going to lay up money, doesn't have any time to
break in hunters, or do much in the hunting business himself, either. So I led her through, backed
her once more, and was soon down to New York.

Reaching Wall Street, I hitched my mare to a lamp-
post and started out to the saddler's. There were
a number of good hotels down in New York at this
time, with horse sheds attached, such as the Franklin
House, over on the Broad Way, corner of Dey Street,
and the Park Place Hotel, corner of Park Place.
But the hostlers in those city hotels charged a fee
even for tying your horse under the shed. It has
always been my motto: Never feel rich, even though
you have money in every bank in town. There
are some young men so spendthrifty, they eat the
calf while yet inside the cow. But not I. In those
days a lamp-post was just as safe a place for a quiet
mare as a hotel shed; and was good enough for me.

I soon found that my dodging of Astor's place on
the Bowery had been in vain. Because, as I was
walking down towards "Dirty Lane" — that's the

name that used to be given to South William Street —
I happened to look back and spied him a-hurrying
after to catch up with me. He must have seen me
cut across lots to dodge going by his house; or
maybe he had come over from his stall at the Fulton
Market onto Wall Street, and had chanced to spy
me. At any rate, there he was, a-following after.
I didn't want to meet him just then and there; I
could see that he was in a temper. So I turned the
corner into William Street, and stepped into a tavern that was not far down the street. I guess I
wasn't quick enough; for a minute or two later
Astor came in the front door also.

"Hey, you," said he, busting in through the door
and puffing hard, "You tamned Dan Drew." (Hen
Astor's English was more crooked than ever when
he was excited.) "I vant to speak yust one word
mit you, you —"

But I didn't wait. It never pays to argue with a
man when he's excited, and Hen now was very
red in the face; I saw at a glance, that he was in no
state of mind to talk a matter over calmly. So I
hurried on through the tavern and out by the back
door. There I cut over onto the other street through
a lane before he could see which way I went, and
so lost him.

I decided, after thinking the matter over, that I
wouldn't stay in the city to get a saddle this trip,
after all. So I went back to my mare, unhitched

her, and was soon back to the "Bull's Head," safe
and sound. Then I rode away to Putnam County
for another drove of cattle.

The saying, "selling watered stock," has now got
to be well-known in the financial world. So I've
wrote down in this paper about the affair of salting
my critters. Some time later I became an operator
in the New York Stock Exchange; I hung out my
shingle on Broad Street. And the scheme was even
more profitable with railroad stocks. If a fellow
can make money selling a critter just after she has
drunk up fifty pounds of water, what can't he make
by issuing a lot of new shares of a railroad or steamboat company, and then selling this just as though
it was the original shares? But for this drover
time in my life, these smaller profits seemed mighty
big.

For I didn't let the salting scheme rest with only
the one trial. After I got back to Putnam County
I lost no time in getting another drove together
and hurrying it back to the city. Astor didn't care
to buy of me this second trip. Not that he kept
mad for any length of time. He was the kind of
a fellow to cool off after a few weeks. On this,
my next trip to the city, I found him as civil as I
could wish. But he wouldn't buy my cattle — made
a number of excuses. He showed his friendly spirit,
however, by introducing me to one of his fellow
butchers in the Fulton Market; so that on the present

trip I dealt with this other butcher. In fact, I found that the stock-watering plan, while a money-maker, had certain drawbacks. Because from now on it compelled me to deal with a different butcher 'most every trip. But that wasn't so bad as it might seem. For there were lots of butchers in the city; and in most cases I found that the butcher I'd dealt with the last time was willing to introduce me to one of his competitors, as a drover that handled choice stock. I took in profits with a big spoon.

# VIII

BY THIS and other devices, one way or another, I had by this time got to be tolerable well off. In fact I had become known as one of the richest drovers that brought cattle to the New York market. When, therefore, not long after, the "Bull's Head" tavern found itself without a proprietor, what more natural than that I should step in and take the position? I hadn't had any experience as an inn-keeper; but I'd had no end of dealings with inn-keepers. And I reckoned that a man who could make money taking care of droves, could also make money taking care of drovers. So I dickered with the people in charge, and got the place. I left Putnam County and moved down to the "Bull's Head."

By this time there was a little settlement growing up around the tavern, known as "Bull's Head Village." My tavern was the centre of this village. So that, although we were some miles out from the city, we were never lonely for a minute. It was the centre of the New York live-stock market. Drovers came to the "Bull's Head" from York State, Connecticut, Jersey, and Long Island, bringing their droves with them. Around my tavern there were cattle pens for the care of fifteen hundred head of cattle at once. There is nothing but the horse-market there now to show what the place used to be. New York's cattle yards have moved since then. They moved from the "Bull's Head," first up to Forty-second Street; then to Ninety-fourth Street; and now they are moving over to Jersey City. But in my time there wasn't a minute in the day when you couldn't hear there the moo of a heifer, the bleat of a lamb, or the neigh of a horse. Pretty soon a slaughter-house was built across the post-road and below the lane which is now 26th Street. Here and there, also, were little houses for the hired men to live in. There was a store for groceries and general merchandise. All in all, quite a village was growing up around the place. And I, as propri-etor of the "Bull's Head," was the king-pin of it all.

Not that I owned the tavern. That belonged to the Peter Lorillard family. They had had a farm where the "Bull's Head" stood, back in Revolutionary times. General George Washington stayed at the house once and took a meal of victuals there. When finally the "Bull's Head" tavern was built, the mahogany table from the Lorillard-house was put into the tavern as a part of the furniture. When I had any guests that I wanted to honour, I would set them at that table for dinner and tell them how General George Washington had eaten from it.

The tap-room of the tavern was on the corner. This was also the office and all-around room. The dining room was across the hall, and looked out onto the post-road, which is now Third Avenue. People eating in the dining room could peer out through the windows and see riders and vehicles passing well-nigh all the time, because this was the turnpike. It was the highroad to Boston. In that day all the through travel to New York City went by my tavern. Back in my time the tavern was seated on a hill, and you had to go down in order to reach the road. When the city streets were put through, this hill was cut down and a ground floor put in underneath.

Out in the hall, a wide staircase with a mahogany railing led to the second floor. Upstairs the hallways were narrow and crooked. A fellow could get lost in them. In fact these winding passageways, I'm sorry to say, were the cause of a good many fights. The "Bull's Head" was noted for its fine liquors, such as hot "Tom and-Jerry," toddy, and such like. A drover starting upstairs for bed, after spending half the night in the tap-room drinking or playing "crack-loo," would often get lost upstairs in trying to find his room, and sometimes would get so turned around that he couldn't even find his way back to the office. Then from somewheres in an upper hall he'd holler out loud enough to wake the dead. He'd get mad as a Durham bull. He

would call for some one to come and show him where
he was.  The sleepers near-by would turn out and
cuss him for making such a noise;  then the fat
would be in the fire.  Sometimes, instead of bellow-
ing for help, the man, when he found that he was
lost, would go into the first room he came to (since
we didn't have keys and locks in those days), swear
that it was his, and set to turn the other fellows out.
Which would also result in a hell-roaring fight.
In truth, the hallways were so crooked that I have
known of a perfectly sober man to come downstairs
of a morning, after a sight of muffled groans and
swear-words from somewhere upstairs, wipe the
sweat from his forehead, and out with a "Mighty
Lord, but it's good to get here;  I thought I never
would find that stairway."  Now and then of a night
I'd have a guest arrive at the inn late.  And then
I'd have to light a candle, take him upstairs, and
put him in with one of my boarders.  This would
sometimes make the boarder mad.  He'd cuss
around in high fashion because I hadn't let him know
beforehand who was going to be his bedfellow.  As
if I could help it that all of my rooms were full,
and another guest arrived.  Now and then I used
to have a fight on my hands from this cause, some
of my boarders were that unreasonable.

There was a big wheat-field behind the tavern,
and not far beyond that a grove of trees.  Being on
the post-road, picnic parties used to drive out from

the city and spend the day in the grove.  Cato's Tavern, further up by Yorkville, was more of a resort for society people of the city, in their drives into the country.  But for turtle feasts, turkey shoots and such like affairs, the "Bull's Head" was the leading resort.  In the fall of the year, around Thanksgiving time, we could put up a placard telling we were going to run a turkey shoot on such and such a date; and there would be going on to a hundred men there when the time came.  I would advertise it on the bill something like this:

Resting shot at 40 yds., . . . . . . . 10 cts.
Off-hand shot, at 40 " . . . . . . 5 "
Resting shot at 30    "    . . . . . . 15 "
Off-hand shot at 30 " . . . . . . 10 "
        Any shot drawing blood, takes the bird.

Perhaps these prices for shots may look to be ruinously low, seeing that it costs money to fatten up a turkey.  But in these turkey shoots the birds were not slaughtered as handily as you might think.  Because on these occasions I'd manage it so that the shooters got a glass or two of toddy, or of whiskey-punch sweetened with currant jelly, before the shooting began.  Something toothsome like that was usually a coaxer for another glass; and then the fellow couldn't shoot straight.  The liquor helped also in another way.  Because, when a fellow's got liquor aboard, he's pot-valiant. He thinks he can hit any mark at any distance; which leads him to pay for no end of shots, thus making more money for me without taking any more of my birds. So, even when, in order to get a fellow drinking, I had to give him the stuff first along without charge, in the end it more than paid. These turkey shoots were profitable in another way also. Because if the day was a good one, a lot of people would come to look on. So that, besides the fees for the shots, I made money from meals, shed room, horse feed, drinks, and such like.

These shoots and like affairs were held back of the tavern towards the "Winding Creek," as we called it — Crumassie Vly, in Dutch. (That's where Gramercy Park gets its name.) This creek flowed through the farm of Jim Duane, and widened out into a pond just where Madison Square now is. Alongside the pond was the Bloomingdale Road (that is now the continuation of the Broad Way). Around the "Bull's Head" village other settlements were beginning to spring up, so that we had neighbours on all sides. Not long before I came, there had been a yellow fever scourge in the City of New York, which had driven the people out to the suburbs for the summer. When the summer was over and the fever was finally checked, many of the people liked it so well in the open country that they stayed. Thus the suburbs were built up. There was a settlement below us on the Boston Road called "Bowery Village." Peter Cooper kept a grocery store there. The children used to spend their pennies with him, buying taffy, gingerbread, a bunch of raisins, or those round, sour candies that later on got the name, "Jackson Balls." Peter's house stood where the great Bible House now is. When he moved his home up to a spot back of my tavern on the Ruggles Place alongside the Gramercy Pond, he was that methodical, he took his house to pieces, marked each beam, and set it all up again on the new site. On another side from us was the farm of Jake Kip, alongside the East River. His house was a big double building, made of bricks brought from Holland. I was sorry when it burned down a little while later. Further over, just above us on the "Middle Road," as we called it, was Quaker Murray's summer house, set on a high hill. The hill is called after him to this day. (That's where Captain Vanderbilt dug his wonderful tunnel for the railroad, which maybe I will write of later on.) Sunfish Pond lay just at the foot of this hill, between my place and Murray's. Peter Cooper had his glue factory on the shores of this pond, and made no end of money there. The pond was a great place for eels, and was sure to have some visitors from my tavern, whenever a drover would stay over a day or two — that is, in seasons when the fish-

ing was good.   The pond used to dry up in summer.
That wasn't much inconvenience to me, because
in summer I was too busy, anyhow, to go fishing.
What fishing I did, I had to do in the cold season,
when the "Bull's Head" wasn't so full of drovers.

The whole region roundabout was filled with
gardens and apple orchards.   Peter Stuyvesant's pear
tree (the one he brought from across the ocean)
was still standing in my day, just below the "Bull's
Head" by the side of the Boston Road.   Along this
road all the way into the city, since it widened out
and was called the "Bowery," were the summer
homes of rich New Yorkers.   Over where Union
Square now is, the old powder house used to stand.
Above that, on the east side of the Bloomingdale
Road, was a neighbour of mine, the "Buck's Horn"
tavern.   It had a sign of a buck's head and horns
nailed onto a post by the side of the road, the house
being set some distance back.   There was a horse-
shed running out to the road.   It was a pretty
good place; but it didn't hurt me much.   I had
my drovers' trade all to myself.   The "Buck's
Horn" on that side of me, and Cato's on the other
side, were more for fashionable sports on their
drives out from the city.

There were several ferry lines running over to
Long Island.   One of them was an ingenious con-
traption.   It had paddle-wheels worked by six
horses, which walked around a kind of windlass in

the centre of the boat. The truck wagons and passengers would be placed on the deck along the two sides. Farmers and young work hands used to come into the city from Long Island by this ferry to market their crops. They all put up at the "Bull's Head." They were good customers of mine, these Long Island farm hands. Usually they were glad to get to the city, like a sailor to get to port. About all they thought of was to have a good time and see the sights, and would swap the farm produce they had fetched with them for board at my tavern. So I didn't have to buy much farm truck for my table. These Long Island farm hands were good-natured boys, and trustful; they left all the book-keeping to the host. Also, if they had any money, they gave it to me to take care of for them, while they were seeing the city.

In fact, besides my work as a tavern-keeper, I was also at this time a kind of banker. Because, with a village growing up around the tavern, there was no other place where money could be kept. So a big safe was built into the wall of the "Bull's Head," at the rear of the tap-room. It wasn't much like the bank safes to-day. This one was just a big iron box with double doors, and opened with an ordinary house-key. Here I would put the money that the people wanted me to take care of. Sometimes I had so much of it on hand that I was able to take it down to the banking houses in

the city and invest it there.  Seeing that I kept the
money for my guests, I didn't have the trouble
which some hotel-keepers have to-day, of people
jumping their tavern bill.  When a man would
hand me his money to keep, I would put it into an
unsealed envelope — a kind of open wallet — and
lock it away in the safe.  Since I was the only one
that had the key, I thus had the first call on that
money.  So, if a man got losing all the money he
had and more too, gambling — there was a back
room upstairs where "crack-loo" was played, and
sometimes drovers would keep at it all night and
late into the next day — I would see to it when I
handed him back his money on his leaving, that
his bill to the tavern was paid out first.  Also, if
there was any dispute over the size of his bill, I
was in position to carry my point.  But we didn't
have very many disputes of that sort.  Drovers
are a rough-and-ready, good-natured lot.  Whenever they would make a trip to the city they would
usually rake in a big walletful of profits, and so
were not close in counting the pennies, when it
came to settling their score at my tavern.

On such holidays as "Evacuation Day," when the
people celebrated the evacuation of the city by the
British troops in the War of the Revolution, my
house would be filled with young drovers and farm
hands from the country, come in to see the sights.
Sometimes I would have to put three in a bed, and

also stow away some of them in the barn to sleep on the hay-mow. These celebrations were something worth seeing. There would be a parade in the morning by mounted and foot soldiers, artillery, the fire companies, the Tammany Society, target companies, and such like. At these times City Hall Park, which had a great iron fence around it, would be surrounded by booths where they sold roast pig, cider, egg-nog, and spruce beer. The day would close with a display of fireworks. At other times the young farm hands, "with money to burn and boots to collop," as we say, could have good times at the Vauxhall Gardens, which were on the Bowery Road, just below Peter Cooper's grocery store. These gardens stretched clean over to what is now Broadway, on the site where Astor built his public library. They had a high wooden fence all around with a row of trees just inside. When you got in — the gate was on the Bowery — you found a beautiful garden with gravelled walks winding in and out between the flower beds. Around the sides, between the trees, were little booths for two or three people, with a table where ginger pop, cakes, baked pears swimming in molasses, and such-like delicacies were sold. In the centre of all was a pavilion for music and performances.

I didn't encourage my guests to go to such places, but to stay up at the "Bull's Head" and

spend their money there.  They could find enough
excitement at my place.  For my tavern was one
of the road-houses for the stage which went between
Park Row, New York, and Harlem Village every
day.  The stage would reach us a little before nine
in the morning, having left Harlem at seven o'clock.
Arriving at Park Row at ten, it would start back
in the afternoon at three, get to the "Bull's Head"
about four and arrive in Harlem at supper-time.
Also, there would be everlasting dickerings in horse-
flesh to furnish excitement and keep the blood
stirring.  For the "Bull's Head" was becoming
the horse-exchange as well as the cattle exchange
for New York City.  Those two lines of trade go
together, anyhow.  Farmers would bring in their
horses from the country to my tavern, and the city
people would come there to look them over.  In
this way, from being a master hand in judging
cattle, I pretty soon came to have great skill in
horse-flesh also.  It stood me in hand to be up in
it.  Sound animals find quick buyers.  Skill in
horse-flesh shows itself in selling an unsound animal.
After a time I got so that I could turn a good penny
in a horse deal.  It is a curious thing how a broken-
down plug can be doctored up and made into a
fairly good-looking beast, for purposes of a trade or
sale.  If he's got holes back of his eyes through
age, by working carefully you can prick a hole
through and blow under the skin, and so puff the

hollow up, smooth as the forehead of a two-year-old.  Another good dodge to make an old horse look young, is to take a file and bishop his teeth; for a buyer is sure to look in the mouth the first thing. Or you can sometimes burn into a horse's teeth the marks which go with coltishness.  With thick-winded animals a good dose of tar poured down the throat will often stop broken wind long enough to get the animal sold.  Roarers are harder to fix. They give you away 'most every time.  But even with this kind of beast there is a way, if you are on to it.  Well-greased shot poured down the roarer's throat will ease off the roarings and make him — for an hour or two — quite a sound-winded animal. Besides all these, a favourite device, when a young ninny would come along that didn't know a horse-colt from a mare, was to offer him the animal for sale with the harness on.  In such cases he usually thinks he is getting a bargain, because the harness seems thrown in.  Whereas the truth is, you have tucked that on to the price, and  meanwhile  the harness is covering up some galled spots on the animal that otherwise would stand out like a sore thumb.  In nine cases out of ten the young booby jumps at the bargain, like a hen at a goose-berry.

For amusement at night there was no end of things going on.  Of a summer's evening there were quoits, wrestling matches, and boxing bouts, out in the road in front of the tavern. While in the winter the guests would gather about the big fire-place in the tap-room, and smoke and chew while some one read the news out loud. Over in one corner was a table for checkers and backgammon. We didn't have spittoons in those days. We didn't need them; because I used to keep the floor of the tap-room good and clean by means of a layer of white sand from Rockaway. One newspaper would last a company for several evenings, because politics ran high in those days, and discussions would last sometimes far into a winter's night. When Andrew Jackson's bank measure went through, there was such high feeling, and the parties were that bitter, my guests sometimes had fist-fights before the discussion was over. Another topic of discussion one time was a book by a Mr. Fenimore Cooper, called "The Spy." It made no end of talk about the time of which I am now speaking. Because 'most every other man you met had his own idea as to who was the real original of "The Spy" in the story. I never read books of any kind, and novels are a sinful kind of book, anyhow. But I couldn't help hearing a lot about this book, because everybody was talking about it. And when finally it came out that the original of "The Spy" was no other than the same Enoch Crosby that is in the Gilead burying ground up in Carmel, I was mighty interested. I had a whole lot to tell about the man to the people who came to the tavern. It would be a mercy to put up a tombstone to mark Crosby's grave. I almost believe I would do it myself. Only just now I am giving orders for a tombstone in my own family burying lot at Drewsclift — a big cross, carved out of solid granite.

# IX

THESE talks of a winter's night around the fireplace in the "Bull's Head" tap-room, were great places for getting the news. Every man who had something new not only liked to tell it but was expected to. Because newspapers were not very numerous, and besides, there were lots of people who couldn't read it even when they had one. Accordingly news got around in great part by word of mouth. There was much excitement, I remember, over the news of the invention of brimstone matches — sticks of wood which would light themselves. For, one day, the news came to us that children had been seen down on the streets of New York City selling pine sticks about five inches long, with something on the end of each stick, so that by rubbing it the stick would break out into a blaze. It made a lot of stir when some of these pine shavings were actually shown in the tap-room one night, and it was seen that the back-log and flint-and-tinder were now out of date. But these loco-focos, as they were called, were rather expensive. So I didn't put them into the tavern right away. New-fangled things usually

cost more than they are worth; I was getting rich
by saving the pennies, here one and there one, like
a hen fills her crop, one grain at a time.  So the fire
tongs which hung by the fireplace for use by the
guests to light their pipes with cinders from the
fire, were not taken down.  I never was much of
a hand, anyhow, for new-fashioned things.

Another piece of news which was beginning to
be noised around, up in our tavern, was of a rich
country out West beyond the Alleghanies.  It was
not often that we got a traveller from so far away
as that.  So when we did, we made him tell all
he knew.  In this way I heard tell how there was
a rich valley out in Ohio, called the Scioto Valley,
where there was some of the finest beef cattle ever
known.  And these cattle could be bought out
there for a song.  A man by the name of Lewis
Sanders, across the Ohio River in Kentucky, had
imported three bulls and three heifers from England,
of the short-horn variety.  The Pattens (I think
it was), from the South Fork, in Virginia, had also
taken with them into that Western country some
blooded stock, and had brought out the bull Pluto.
A blooded short-horn cow, Venus, bulled by Pluto,
had helped to people all the pastures throughout
the Scioto region.  This importing of foundation
stocks from England was also helped along by
General Van Rensselaer, up at Albany, who had
just been bringing over from Europe the bull Wash-

ington, and two short-horn heifers. The short-horns make one of the best beef breeds I have ever seen. Our American cattle were mostly of the Devon, the Hereford, the Sussex and the Norfolk, of England; the Ayrshire and the Galloway, of Scotland; the Kerrys, of Ireland; the Alderney, Guernsey and Jersey breeds of the Channel Islands; with the Holsteins and Holstein-Friesians from Holland. All of these imported breeds, out in the rich Ohio and Kentucky reservations, had bred into an even finer beef cattle than on their native soil. Perhaps this was because of the rich grass and good quality of water. The short-horns were particularly sought out by us drovers, because they were beef breeds. In that day beeves were more important than dairy cattle. Beef is easier to transport than butter or cheese, because it will drive overland of itself. In that day we didn't have hardly any other means of transporting food-stuff long distances, except to drive it on its own legs. Not that the short-horns are not good ·milkers, too; but they are especially good for butcher purposes.

When I heard these stories about the Western lands, I became mighty interested, because the city of New York was growing so all-fired fast, it was hard to find enough beeves in the regions roundabout; so that the price of fit cattle was going higher and higher. I pondered the matter. I made up my mind. Calling Chamberlain to me one day —

he had been my bartender at the "Bull's Head," and had married my daughter — I said to him:

"Roswell," said I, "you've got to take care of the place here for two or three months. I'm going out to Ohio to get a drove of cattle." He looked at me with eyes as big as saucers.

"What's that?" said he.

"Just what I say," I answered. "I'm going to bring some of those there critters from the West, right here into the New York market."

"How in the world are you going to get them over the mountains?" said he. "It's a wild-goose chase; they'll die if you drive them that far."

"Leave that to me, son," said I, "leave that to me. I calculate to manage it fine as a fiddle."

So I began to make my plans. First I went to Henry Astor, the butcher. He had been pretty well riled up against me once, because of some deals we had had together. I think I've wrote about it, somewhere in these papers. But he got over being mad after a time, and he and I had become good friends once more. He had made a peck of money as a butcher in the Fulton Market. So much, in fact, that he had retired and now was a kind of private banker. I went to him and got a loan of money to make the Western trip. I saw that it wouldn't pay to drive just a herd of ordinary size that distance. I had to do it on a big scale

or not at all.   So I got the money from him — he
made me give all-fired heavy security — and started
out.   I took a Mr. Robinson with me.   He later
went in with me in the banking business, when I
became a Wall Street operator.   He was an A
No. 1 drover; I wanted that kind of a partner.
I also took along our cow-dogs.   A good cow-dog
is not to be picked up everywheres.   A drover
learns, when he once gets a good animal of that
type, to keep him.   They are marvellous intelligent.
I've had cow-dogs that knew almost as much as I
did about driving cattle or sheep.   And they are
faithful, too.   They aren't spiggot-suckers, like
some of your hired help.   They will work for you
night and day, and for pay only ask a few bones
and a pan of milk at night.

We started out in the stage coach, going by day's
journeys through Jersey and Pennsylvania — Robinson, the dogs, and myself.   The dogs were lots
of company on the journey out.   Much of the way
through Pennsylvania the woods were thick;   the
dogs, following behind, would do some hunting
on the side, and often brought in a rabbit, partridge,
or such like game.   It took over a week to get to Ohio.
Out there I found that what I had heard tell about
the richness of that Western country was gospel.
The Scioto Valley was full of fat beef cattle which
could be bought — for cash — at a price that would
have made a farmer out East turn up his nose at the

offer.  I had no trouble in getting together a drove
of fine cattle and other stock — over two thousand
head in all.  Then we started towards home.  I
didn't know how long it was going to take to get
back.  Because this was pioneer work.  No drove
of cattle had ever been taken across the Alleghany
Mountains before.  So I was anxious to get started.
Besides, I wanted to get them into the New York
market before the heat of summer came on.

We got along prosperous.  The spring of the
year is a good time for drover's work.  In the first
place, it is the right time to buy the cattle from the
farmers.  Then again, at this season the roads are
soft, so as not to lame the animals.  And besides,
there is lots of water for drinking purposes, and
plenty of pasture at night.  In taking a big drove,
the order of march is for the drover to ride ahead,
sometimes several miles in advance, in order to pick
out the road and to make arrangements for shelter-
ing the animals at nightfall.  In the present case
that work fell to me.  Another duty of mine was to
find fit places for fording the rivers — either a natural ford, or else some places where the animals
could get down into the water safely, swim over,
and get up again onto the bank opposite.  Because
those were early days in the Western country.  The
roads didn't have bridges at all places.  And although there were ferries for the stage-coach, there
wasn't any ferry big enough to take care of two

thousand head of live stock.  So we had to swim or ford the rivers.

In driving a herd, the cattle are placed first.  The dogs are trained to follow along just behind and alongside the cattle; because the sheep will come along behind of themselves, being timid.  They don't need much tending.  After the first day or two they get to know the cattle, and crowd in close behind them without any urging.  It's curious, anyhow, to see how a drove of live stock will form itself into a herd after one or two days of marching. They seem to get acquainted with each other, they become a kind of a big family — the cows, the sheep, the dogs, the horses and the boys.  They get introduced, so to speak, and hang together after that as though they had growed up on one farm.

This flocking spirit was a great help on the journey. Because pretty soon after leaving Ohio and getting over into Pennsylvania, the country became so wild that, unless the animals had learned to herd together, they could easily have strayed and many would have been lost.  In fact, the country became so much of a wilderness after a while that I wasn't always able to find cattle boys when I wanted them.  On a long drive like this, you don't have cattle boys for the entire journey.  Boys such as you hire for this kind of business are youngsters, and aren't allowed to go far from home.  Therefore, we used to pick up a set of boys in the settlements we passed through, take them with us for a day's drive, and let them go back the next day, taking a new set in their place.  But when we came to the mountains, the settlements were so scattered that sometimes we had to use the same set of boys for several days' journeys.  The farmers along the road were very obliging.  They seemed to know that this was the first of what would probably become a frequent custom, and so helped me along.  Fodder and living were cheap out there, anyhow.  At night-fall, when I would put up at a farmhouse and ask for accommodations for the drove, they would let me have it at a most reasonable figure.  Sometimes I paid these bills by leaving with the farmer the lambs or calves that had been dropped during that day's march.  They were very trustful farmers out there.  All I would need to do, sometimes, would be to say:

"Neighbour, a couple of miles back, down by that ledge of rock, you'll find a ewe.  She dropped a lamb yesterday, and we left her behind.  Pretty good pair  Send your boy down and you can have them.  We can't stop to take them with us.  These new-born youngsters would delay our march."

Two or three of that kind would sometimes pay our entire bill for the night's lodging.  Besides, there were the cattle that got sick.  A critter is often too sick to drive; when, if he can only have a little spell to rest up under a cattle-shed, he'll

get well again and thrive. I helped pay my
lodging bills by means of these sick critters which
I left behind. Besides, the farmers were glad to
have a drover come to take their own fatlings. Often
I could make a swap, leaving some new-dropped
calves or lambs, and take instead good healthy
stock.

There were places where we had to camp out
at night. When we got up into the Alleghany
Mountains and started crossing that wilderness,
there were sometimes no farm clearings for mile
after mile. When nightfall would overtake us here,
we would have to shift the best way we could. But
you get used to sleeping out, after a while. Cut
browse for the horses, let the critters pick a meal from
the grass and leaves, wherever they can find it; and,
with a blanket over some hemlock boughs, make
a bed for yourself; in the morning you eat as though
there was a wolf in your belly.

Real wolves sometimes used to scare us. Wolves
are very fond of veal, and at that time they had not
yet been cleared out of the Western mountains.
The states were trying their best to get rid of the
pestersome varmints and used to offer a bounty
for wolves' scalps. In fact, in some places the killing of wolves was quite a business. A trapper
could take a wolf's scalp to the justice of the peace
and get a scalp certificate payable by the tax-gatherer
when the next tax was gathered. But he didn't

have to wait for the tax-gatherer, because these scalp certificates were good at 'most any store for merchandise. The country out there was so uncleared that there were still plenty of wolves in the mountains. In fact, some trappers were so abandoned, and the bounty on scalps so high — for a full-grown wolf, $40, and for whelps, half that price — that they would keep a she-wolf and her litter of whelps out in some secluded place in the mountains, in order to sell the scalps when they were full-grown. We met with this danger. But here again the herding spirit of my critters was a help. At night, when they would hear a pack of fifteen or twenty wolves a-yelping in the darkness, the cattle and sheep would crowd in together, shivering with fear. They wouldn't need any dogs or boys to round them up. In fact they would hug in so tight that they would well-nigh smother to death a weakling that might be in the middle of the herd.

With all my care I lost a sight of critters before I got the drove through. There were those devoured by the wolves; and the stray-aways, because we couldn't stop to hunt up a lost steer, if he got too far from the drove. Also, some died of mud-fever on the legs and belly, due to sloppy roads. Then there were the accidents that happen on a journey through a wild country and across deep and sometimes swift rivers. Out of a drove of two thousand, we lost four or five hundred at least. And, do the best we could, we made slow time. Delays were all the time happening. A horse would get a wind-gall on the fetlock, or my mare would get a swollen hock and would need to be coddled. Finally, after delays and losses, we got the drove into the New York market.

And now I found that the trip was worth all the time and pains which it had cost. I had picked up the cattle dirt cheap in Ohio, and the price of young, fat critters in the New York market was so high that I cleared up over $30 on every head of cattle in the drove.

# X

I HAD done so well on the Ohio trip that I followed it up with several more. These times I went into Kentucky and even as far west as Illinois. Because now I knew that it could be done, and also more or less how to do it. There were accidents and delays. But New York was growing so fast and the price of butcher's meat was climbing at such a rate, that I found each time a fine profit when I had cleaned up the deal. I gave Astor back the money he had loaned me, and had enough besides to pay me for my trouble.

Of course, these Western trips didn't take up all my time during these years. I paid attention, off and on, to running the "Bull's Head." I was also making short trips out around New York to pick up a herd of cattle here and there. There were some fine grazing bottoms out through Orange County. I got to know some of those southern counties of York State, as well as the near-by regions of Jersey and Pennsylvania.

One day something happened to me whilst on a cattle trip I was taking up near the Harlem River, which had a great effect upon my life. It was my remarkable escape from death by lightning, and my return to religion. For I had by this time — I grieve to state it — backslided once more. The life at the "Bull's Head" tavern was not very favourable to growth in grace. Besides, I was trotting about here and there. Churches were not very numerous, and my religious life got like the dead ashes in the fireplace, here and there perhaps a live spark, but the fire, for the most part, died out. I say, there were still some live sparks; because all during this time of my backslidden state I had periods when I was under conviction; which means that the spirit was still striving with my soul. But I was not yielding to these strivings of the spirit. I seemed to have become hardened. Now something was to happen which was to bring me back once more within the fold, never again to wander.

I had driven up to Manhattanville, in the upper part of Manhattan Island, some miles from the Bull's Head village. I was in a gig, for I had a man with me. My visit was for the purpose of looking over some cattle which were on a farm up near that town. We reached the place, tied the gig at the gate, and went out into the field where the cattle were. Whilst I was looking them over I noticed a hard thunder-shower brewing, and hurried through the work. This I could do easily, because I had by this time become one of the best judges of critters to be met with anywheres. I could take in the parts of a steer with one sweep of my eye. As soon as the job was done we got back to the gig and started to drive to shelter before the storm should break. But it was providentially to be otherwise. We had hardly got the horse unhitched and started on our way, when the storm broke all around us. We tried to press on. Suddenly we were blinded by a blaze of light brighter than a hundred suns at noonday. I guess it was followed by a terrific thunder-clap. But of this I am not sure, because, after that blaze of light, I don't remember anything.

How long I lay unconscious I don't know, but it must have been some time. Because, when I came to, the rain had ceased and the storm had cleared away. I found that my companion had also been stunned and now was likewise coming out of the fit. When we got back some of our senses we looked around. There before us the horse lay, dead in the harness. It was by a miracle that my life had been spared. Then and there I gave myself once more to the Lord. As can be seen, it took a great deal of the grace of God to reach me. He had to try so many times before he finally got me landed safe and sound on his side. I promised that I would never backslide again.

Not that I was ever very bad. Even in my backslideful states I had never been a profane, bad man, and I had always held infidels in great horror. Over in Greenwich village, across Bloomingdale Road from the "Bull's Head," was the house where a man by the name of Tom Paine had lived. He had written a bad book called "The Age of Reason." To reach his village from my side of the island, I had to go through the potter's field, where public hangings used to be held. The gallows stood right in the middle of what is now Washington Square. On top of that gallows many a poor fellow used to stand, never to walk again — "jerked to Jesus" is what we called it back in those days. I don't see how any one, if he had any spark of grace about him, could go by that gallows and across that potter's field to the road where Paine's house was, without feeling a horror for bad men and infidels.

I was glad, after I had fully recovered from the fit into which that stroke of lightning threw me, that I had gone through the experience, and had become at last soundly converted. Because, as it later turned out, the drover business was not to be my work all through life. Just as I was beginning middle life, I left it, said good-bye to my life at the "Bull's Head" tavern, and got into the steamboat business. An owner of steamboats ought to be religious and respectable-like. It may not be so bad for a drover to stay away from church, because his business is a rough-and-ready business, anyhow. People don't expect much of him. But a steamboat proprietor is in a higher seat. A man of prominence is called upon to be godly in his walk and conversation; he should hold his head up — like a hen drinking water. There was Peter Cooper. He was godly. He was superintendent of the Sunday-school, there below the "Bull's Head," from which the Bowery Village Church started. He was a man that feared God and went to meeting on Sundays. I was glad that I, too, was now on the Lord's side. And though I have suffered many losses since then, I am thankful to say that from that day to this I have never lost my religion.

# XI

MY START into the steamboat business came about more or less haphazard. There was a little boat run between Peekskill and New York, by Jake Vanderbilt, a brother of Cornelius Vanderbilt. It was in connection with a boat designed to compete with this one of Vanderbilt's, that I made the start.

This was back in the early days, when steamboating on the Hudson River was just getting under way. The old sailing sloops were still in use, but were rapidly becoming back numbers. A sloop would sometimes take nine days in going from New York to Albany. When the *Chancellor Livingston* made the trip once in nineteen hours and a half, people thought it a miracle, and gave her the name, *Skimmer of the River*. But even the sloops were an improvement over the old stage-coach, because the fare by stage-coach from New York to Albany was $8, and it never took less than two days and one night. Besides being slow, the sloops were also inconvenient; yes, even danger-some, because the winds on the Hudson are fluky, squalls rushing out, often without any warning, from

behind the headlands which line both sides of the
river. The boom of one of the old packet sloops
was sometimes ninety feet long, and when it jibed
unlooked-for, would sweep everything before it.
There was Dunham, a merchant of New York City
and of a considerable name. He was making the
trip one day on a sloop down from Albany, when
the sail jibed; the boom knocked him overboard
like a nine-pin, and he was drowned. So when
Fulton, with his partner, Livingston, showed that
steam-engines could be put into a boat and would
propel it even against wind and tide, it made a great
change.

For some years, however, the effect of the new
invention was not noticeable. Because Fulton had
got a grant from the Legislature giving to him and
Livingston exclusive right to steamboat navigation
on the tide waters of York State. This kept rival
boats off. At last, some time before I started in,
this monopoly had been done away. It came about
through that famous suit of "Gibbons against
Ogden." Thomas Gibbons was the owner of a
steamboat, *Bellona*, which plied between New
York and Elizabethtown, New Jersey. (He was
the one who built that beautiful estate down at
Bottle Hill, New Jersey, which I bought from his
son, William Gibbons, and turned into the Drew
Theological Seminary, years after.) Ogden had got
from Fulton and Livingston a grant to carry on

their monopoly. So, when Gibbons started in, Ogden had him arrested. Then Dan Webster, Gibbons's counsel, made that famous speech of his before the Supreme Court, which broke up the monopoly and opened the tide waters of all the states to free navigation. When Gibbons found himself free to run boats, he went ahead with lots of push. He got a young man by the name of Cornelius Vanderbilt, who had been running a sailing sloop between New York and Staten Island, to be captain of his boat, the *Bellona*. This ran from New York to Elizabethtown, where it shipped its passengers to the stage-coach, which carried them on to Philadelphia and the South.

Vanderbilt did so well there that he became superintendent of the line, and used to go up to Bottle Hill to report to the owner concerning the boat. Gibbons by and by sold the boat to the Stevens Brothers, of Hoboken. Then young Cornelius Vanderbilt took up navigation on the Hudson. He started a small boat called the *General Jackson*, to run between New York and Peekskill, and put his brother Jake on as captain.

Those early steamboats were funny things, compared with the great boats which are seen to-day, such as the *Drew*, and the *Dean Richmond*. Back in the early days they didn't have any pilot-house. The steersman was nothing more than the old sloop steersman; only, instead of working a tiller at the stern, he was placed up on top of the cabin, with a tiller wheel connecting to the rudder by a rope, and was exposed to the wind and weather. His station was directly over the engine. He signalled to the engineer by tapping with a cane on the roof. One tap meant, "Go ahead"; two taps, "Back up."

Well, as I started to say, the *General Jackson* one day blew up. That line between Peekskill and New York had interested me more or less, anyhow, because it had become the great way of getting back and forth between the city and my old home in Putnam County. But I hadn't thought of going into the business myself. I counted on buying and selling cattle all my life. But one day, soon after Jake Vanderbilt's boat, the *General Jackson*, blew up, a friend of mine came and told me about a new steamboat, the *Water Witch*, which he was planning to run as a competitor with the Vanderbilt Brothers on the Peekskill route.

He talked me into investing a thousand dollars in the boat. I had some money lying around loose. My cattle trips, together with what money I made from running the "Bull's Head," had been bringing me in good profits. I was glad to make a small investment in the steamboat business, even though it looked somewhat risky.

And it was risky. The thing turned out a loss the very first season. As soon as we put our boat on, Captain Cornelius Vanderbilt, who was a spunky fellow, built another boat for the Peekskill route, which he called the *Cinderella*. We ran each other hard. The result was that my boat lost that season $10,000.

Cornelius met me one day on the wharf, just at the time when our boat was running behind like old Sambo. He was in high spirits. "You'll meddle with my business, will you?" said he, in a joking way. "See here, you drover, let me tell you something. You don't know anything about running boats. You know a good deal about judging cattle. That's your line. Boats is my line. Water transportation is a trade all by itself. You don't understand it. Stick to your steers, Drew, stick to your steers."

That got my dander up. I got in with a man named Jim Smith. We two went up into Putnam and Westchester Counties and stirred things up good and lively. We told the people up there that they had been charged too much by Vanderbilt. We asked them to come in and put money into our line, because we were an independent company trying to take the side of the people against the monopoly which had been oppressing them. They flocked into our pen, because this Peekskill route was their main means of communication with New York City. It stood them in hand to build up a competing line. Now we were in shape for business. We had money — working capital. We began to slash the rates. We showed the *Cinderella* what business enterprise was. We kept at it until the fare was a shilling — twelve and a half cents a head — from Peekskill to the city. More than that, we showed the other boat that we were able to keep that game up just as long as they wanted it.

When I met Captain Cornelius the next time, I served him with his own sauce. I said: "Hello, Captain; do you think now that I know anything about the steamboat business?"

"Drew," said he — Cornelius was a frank man to own up when he had made a mistake or had misjudged anybody, "I don't think anything about it. I know you do." Cornelius was very nice to me after that, even sociable-like. He used to come around and call on me. We got to be good friends.

In fact, we got so friendly that Smith and I sold out our boat to Vanderbilt and let him have control of the Peekskill route once more. We did this without letting the other fellows in our company know. We were afraid they might put some obstacle in the way if they knew it beforehand. As a matter of fact, when they heard of it they were as mad as a wet hen.

"Because, Drew," said they, "we went in with you and Smith to break up the monopoly and in order to get decent transportation for our region. And now, after putting our hard cash into the thing and providing capital enough to bring the other

side to their knees, you skunks up and sell us out —
you make terms with the enemy behind our backs,
and we lose what we put in."

But I had other irons on the anvil. I didn't feel
called upon to keep myself back, just in order to
provide better transportation for Putnam County
farmers. I had my own fortune to make — my own
career to carve out. Any fellow, except he's a
natural-born fool, will look out for number one first.
There were bigger prizes to be got in the Hudson
River steamboat business than the Peekskill route.
It was these that I was after. The Hudson River
Association was running a line of boats from New
York to Albany. Captain Vanderbilt had had a
falling out with one of the directors of that association, and had put two rival boats on that route
so successfully that he had compelled them to buy
him out; he agreeing to withdraw from the boat
business on that route for ten years. This left the
coast clear. If Vanderbilt, by running competition boats, could scare them into buying him out at
a good figure, I didn't see why I couldn't do the
same. So I bought two boats, put them on the
line to Albany, and ran them in competition with
the River Association. This lasted for a year. At
the end of that time it turned out as I had expected.
The Association took me in with them on a pooling
arrangement, my boats sharing the total earnings
of the partnership.

This lasted a little while, and I was feeling big to be in with the company that was running so big a line of water transportation. By and by I wanted to make still more money. So I hit upon a scheme. While I was still in the Hudson River Association, I put another boat on the route as a competitor. Only, I ran it under the name of another fellow, giving out that he was the owner, so as to keep my own part in the matter hid. Then I cut prices on that independent boat in such a way as to hurt the Association like sixty. Whenever we would hold a directors' meeting of the Association, if they were not already talking about it, I would steer the conversation around to the subject of this rival boat, and ask if something couldn't be done about it. Because, as I showed them, if we allowed that boat to run against us so freely, other fellows would be encouraged also to put boats on, and we would soon be nowheres. Finally I got the directors to pass a resolution to buy up this troublesome rival. And I got them to appoint me the agent to go and see her owner with our proposition.

"I think I can find him right away," said I. "His office is only a spit and a stride from here, so to speak." They said they would hold the meeting until I got back. So I left the room, went out, walked around the block, and came back with my report.

"A penny more buys the whistle," said I. "I've

seen the owner and he is willing to sell. Only our figure isn't quite high enough. He says he is making money hand over fist. Pretty soon he thinks he will be able to put another boat on. But he doesn't want to be mean. He is willing to sell if we do what he thinks reasonable. If we tack $8,000 more onto the offer, he'll close with us."

The directors debated. The boat was hurting us. Anybody could see that. I put a word in now and then, hinting how this pestersome competitor was probably in a position to hurt us still more, unless we got him out of the way right off. Finally we voted to give the $8,000 more which the man had asked. I left them there in the meeting, went out, walked around the block again, came back and said the man had accepted; and if they would make out the papers then and there I would take them over to him and get the deed of sale.

I saw from this incident that I could match my wits against most anybody's. Besides, this $8,000 which I had turned into my pocket out of the company's funds was not only so much clear gain to me, but was so much clear loss to them. So now I became bold as a lion. I saw that this Hudson River route to Albany was making no end of money, and I wanted to own it, hook, line and sinker. So I picked a quarrel with one of my fellow-directors, and started out on a rival line of my own. My *Westchester* was a good starter in this fight. Still they had the best of me, because their boat was the handsomer. So I bought the *Bright Emerald* for $26,000, and ran her as a night boat to Albany. More than that, a little later that same year I bought the *Rochester* — paid $50,000 for her. The Hudson River Association hit back by buying the *Swallow;* and now the fight was on. We raced each other up and down the river, trying to beat the other fellow in rates, and boasting that each had the swiftest boat. Finally, it came to a race between the two. Both boats started at four o'clock one afternoon, from the dock near to the ferry which ran to Jersey City. This was in 1836. Up the river they ran, nip and tuck. The *Swallow* was so anxious to win that she speeded her engine beyond what it was built for. She got a little in the lead, but couldn't hold out. Just below Hudson her engine broke down. She had to stop a few minutes for repairs. This gave the *Rochester* the lead. By the time the *Swallow* got under headway once more, my boat was so far in front that she couldn't overtake us. At Van Wies Point, a hundred and forty miles from New York, the race ended. My *Rochester* had won. This finished the fight. I had got the fare down so low that the Hudson River Association, weakened as they were by that loss of $8,000 (which was just so much additional ammunition in my own magazine), gave in. I bought them out. And whereas the fare had been so low until then that I

myself couldn't have stood it very much longer,
now that I was in control, I put the rate to Albany
back to $3, and made enough money to pay me for
all I had lost in the fight.

Those were the days before the railroad. Since
the Hudson is so wide and deep and slow a river,
while both banks are rocky and high so as to make
railroad engineering difficult, steamboat navigation
between New York and Albany came many years
before the railroad. Thus the traffic by water was
large. Competition boats were springing up all
the time, and we were everlastingly running each
other. Steamboat rivalry was very high in those
days. In making speed on our trips, we got so we
didn't make full stops at the landings to let passengers
off. When we would come near to a landing, we
would put the passengers who were to stop off in
a rowboat and towed it behind the steamboat. Then
the steamboat would veer in towards the dock and
slacken her speed a little. This would permit the
steersman in the rowboat to sheer his boat alongside the dock, and as she went past the passengers
had to scramble out and onto the dock. Sometimes they landed on the dock, and sometimes in
the water. One day, while trying to make this
kind of a landing at Poughkeepsie, several passengers
were drowned. The Legislature then passed a law
putting a stop to these landings "on the fly." This
craze for speed was bad, also, because it put the

boilers under such pressure of steam that it wasn't always safe. In a close race engineers would tie down the safety valve, plug up the mercury pipe in the pressure gauge so the stuff wouldn't blow out, and then crowd on steam until the boiler plates would bulge out into bumps as big as a saucepan; and the boiler would be weaker for the remainder of its life. Besides that, the pilots would take a hand, and in racing with a rival boat would sometimes in a narrow place in the river crowd the other boat onto the shoals or against a barge.

Rate-cutting was so sharp that I had to try all kinds of schemes and dodges to keep my end up. A good scheme, I found, was to make different rates for alternate nights — fifty cents for one night, and $1.50 for the next night. This worked well. For people, hearing tell of the lower rates, would forget on which night the lower rate was given, and when they got to the wharf all packed up and ready to travel, were usually willing to pay the extra rate rather than go back and wait over another day. Sometimes we carried people from New York to Albany for two shillings. And one time, when a rival boat, the *Wave*, started up, our boats carried passengers free. The *Wave* wasn't very heavily financed. She lasted just three days. Sometimes we would even pay passengers a shilling to take our boat rather than the boat of the opposition line. But this wasn't so wasteful as it might seem, because after you've got a passenger aboard your boat and out in the middle of the river, he's at your mercy. For the first hour or two he thinks he's getting off fine. But by and by he gets hungry; besides, night is coming on, and he wants a place to sleep. Then we would stick on enough extra for meals and sleeping privilege, not only to make up what we had paid him for taking our boat, but also to pay us a profit besides.

Since I was now the chief owner of the big line of steamboats on the river, I was powerful, and new competitors didn't have much chance. I felt that competition had to be put down with a strong hand. There was a man by the name of Hancox. He put on a small boat in opposition to our regular line. He called it the *Napoleon*. It was a poor boat. It didn't have much show, anyhow. But it wouldn't do to take any chances. His New York pier was further down than ours. So one morning in June our boat, the *DeWitt Clinton*, was waiting at her dock working her engines full stroke. When the *Napoleon* was a short distance from the lower side of the dock, the hawsers of the *DeWitt Clinton* were cut with a sharp axe. She sprung out under a full head of steam and hit the *Napoleon* just forward of the wheel. You'd have thought it would have put that miserable little boat out of commission altogether. It didn't succeed as completely as that. But it careened her over until her guard was under water, and gave her passengers a scare that they didn't forget for a long time.

But there were still other ways of getting around a competitor; and we left no stone unturned. Hancox, who wasn't man enough to continue the fight on a business plane, began to squeal. He put out an advertisement like this:

## "TO THE PUBLIC:

"It is the first time in my life that I have been forced to appeal directly to the public; but after having been persecuted as I have been for the last three days by one of the greatest monopolies of this country, my duty towards my family, as I owe them a support, makes it necessary that I should inform the public of my situation.

"I purchased the steamboat *Napoleon* last winter, and associated with myself E. C. Corwin, and James Cochrane, who became equal partners with me in the boat, and the Articles of Co-partnership were drawn in such a manner that the boat was to run to Albany and nowhere else. Recently, the monopoly, after ascertaining that I was determined not to remove the boat from this route has made extravagant offers, made in such a way that I was to be left alone; and consequently, as my means are small, I must, without doubt, be ruined and my family beggared. I now simply appeal to my friends to assist me in supporting the *Napoleon;* for as long as she does not lose, no money that can be provided will prevent me from running.

But if she does, an injunction will be immediately served on the boat. I can also state that E. C. Corwin has spurned their offers, even at a sacrifice of $6,000.

"J. W. HANCOX."

When a powerful company like mine is threatened with competitors on all sides, it does not pay to fool with a man, even though he is just a small toad in the puddle. One of the ways we used to work it in order to get passengers and hurt an opposing line, was by employing runners to go to the other's dock and discourage passengers from going by that line. These runners used to be very enterprising fellows. One of their favourite dodges was to scare the passengers by saying that the boat they were about to take was unsafe, in fact was liable to blow up any minute. This dodge was particularly useful if any of the passengers were women. So this man Hancox, a few days later, squealed again, in another advertisement:

"MONOPOLIES AND PERSECUTIONS

"Are the people aware of the disgraceful manner in which the Hudson River monopoly persecutes the steamboat *Napoleon* and her owners, especially by hiring the most abandoned and profligate wretches to run against her for passengers and making use of the most disgraceful language to prevent passengers from going on board of her? They are guilty of the foulest lies and assertions. We had been, we thought, on the free waters of the United States, but if this is the manner in which the people are to be driven from their lawful and honourable pursuits, away then with our boasted freedom!

"Are the people aware of the manner in which we have been driven from pillar to post for the last few days? When they found they could not terrorize the owners of this boat, they said, 'Let's crush them. They are poor and cannot stand against such monopolies as we are but a few days longer.' Will the people suffer this, or will they patronize the *Napoleon* and keep the fare at One Dollar, and thus sustain the poor in fair rates and honourable pursuits?

"NAPOLEON."

# XII

IT WAS a caution, the shameful practices that some of the steamboat owners back in those days, in their ambition to get started and make headway against our company, adopted. An empty leech always sucks the hardest, and a new competitor is usually a fiercer one than a competitor of long standing. They used to make use of the public print in these steamboat rivalries. If companies are going to fight for traffic, let them fight it out in their own field, say I. There was the *Alida*, which was some time later put on the river to run against us of the established line. The way she boasted of her accomplishments and ran down all other boats, was a shame to see. She put out a card like this:

### "STEAMER ALIDA

"The splendid day boat *Alida* is now the only day boat for passengers to depend upon. She makes all landings and arrives in Albany and Troy two hours ahead of the old boat, the *Drew*. The *Drew* is twelve years old, and her machinery is now so worn as to be nearly broken down. On

Wednesday her passengers did not arrive in Albany until ten o'clock at night, too late for the cars, and this morning she was seen with but one engine at work. Those travelling should patronize the only opposition on the river, and more especially as she is far the fastest boat. Fare, .50."

She put on such airs as a speedy boat that we couldn't stand it. So finally, when the *Daniel Drew* was built and had finished her first season, this advertisement was given as wide circulation as printer's type could give it:

"The steamboat *Daniel Drew*, having discontinued her trips on the day-route for the season, will for the purpose of gratifying the curiosity of certain individuals, hold herself in readiness until the 27th of the present month, to make a trial trip from New York to Albany with any other steamboat now built, for $1,000 or upwards, on one week's notice from this date, the boats to start from the foot of Thirtieth Street, North River, at eight a. m., to run with their usual tackle as used in their ordinary business. Any person or persons having a steamer that they think can beat her have an opportunity to make a profitable trip by calling on the subscriber."

They didn't accept the offer. So we didn't have to run the race; but we were ready for them.

After getting control of the Hudson River Association, I got in with Isaac Newton. Up to then I had been in with a couple of men, Kelley and Richards. But I wanted to be in big company.

Isaac Newton was a leading steamboat man of
New York City. The kind of a proposition I made
to him was this: We would start a line of steamboats, and call it the "People's Line." He would
be the president and I the treasurer; and we would
show the country what steamboating ought to be.
He fell in with the idea and we formed the line.
He owned the *North American.* That was the
first steamboat to use blowers for an artificial blast
in the furnace of the boilers run by an independent
engine. He also owned the *South American.*
These were good boats. But when we formed
the "People's Line" we built a great new boat
and called it the *Isaac Newton.* It was the first
of the floating palaces that were soon to make the
Hudson River famous throughout the world. It
was three hundred feet long, and had berths for 500
passengers. When she started off on her first trip
the people crowded the wharf black to see her sail
away. She was so big they thought she was too
bulky to be pushed against the tide, and that she
would either tip over, break down, or something
else. But she sailed away fine as anything. And
the people clapped their hands. Then we added
the *Knickerbocker.* She was built for us by
Smith & Dimon. She was a fine boat and had
as many as twelve staterooms in the ladies' saloon.
We took the engine for her out of the old *DeWitt
Clinton.*

Pretty soon we bought the "*Oregon*" of George Law — "Live Oak George" was the name he was known by in steamboat circles, he was that brisk and fearless.   He was the one who offered to run his boat with only one wheel against the old *Hendrick Hudson*, for $1,000, and wasn't taken up on it.   The *Oregon* was a boat we wanted for our line; because Law had made her well-known. I in particular was anxious to get her, because she was a thorn in the side of Captain Vanderbilt.   Vanderbilt and I never got along very well together. From the first we were more or less running each other.   This *Oregon* had beat his boat, the *Commodore Vanderbilt* (he got to be known as "The Commodore" after a while, because he owned so many boats;   but when I first met him, he was just plain "Captain") in that famous race from New York to Croton Point and return.   It was a distance of 75 miles.   Vanderbilt was all-fired set on winning that race.   He made big preparations.   Got his boat in the best of trim.   The people saw that he was going to win or bust.   So everybody came out to see.   It was almost as exciting as the bulletin boards in the city when they announced Scott's victory at Churubusco (because this was the time of the Mexican war, and there were a lot of New York boys in Scott's army).   Well, they ran the race, and the *Oregon* won.   They said the race might have turned out different, only

Vanderbilt got worked up with excitement, and mixed in at the wrong moment. When his boat was about to turn the point up at the far end of the course, be grabbed the control of the thing away from the pilot. Wrong signals were given to the engineer. Instead of slowing up to make a turn, the boat went around at full speed. This lost her so much distance that the *Oregon* got the lead, kept it, and won the race. It was an awful blow to the Commodore's pride. In fact, it was because he felt so sore over it, that I wanted to own the boat that had beat him. So we took the *Oregon*, and run it on our line.

I have always suspicioned that this defeat was one of the things that disgusted the Commodore with the steamboat business, and made him leave it for other things. Because pretty soon he was giving all of his time to railroading, and didn't bother with steamboats much more. When railroads were first coming in, he had stuck up his nose at them. In talking with me about them, he would refer to them with a sneer, as "them things that go on land." He was a lover of water craft, and didn't like to see anything come along that promised to hurt sail and steam boats. But when he lost that race to the *Oregon* it hurt his pride something terrible. It wasn't long after that before he changed his mind about railroads, and was after their shares lickety split.

# XIII

I WAS now as busy as a dog licking a dish. For I was soon to be interested in those same railroad contraptions that Vanderbilt had gone into. I had lots of faith in him and his judgment, since he seemed to turn into money everything he put his hand to. And seeing I had done so well by following his lead into the steamboat business, I felt I couldn't make much mistake by following his lead once again, into the railroad business.

The spread of railroads was now almost as rapid as the spread of steamboats had been a few years before. When once it was found that locomotives could pull a train up a grade, it was a discovery. Because now railroads could be built even through hilly country. When iron rails came in and took the place of the old straps laid on beams of wood, which were everlastingly curling up into snake-heads and derailing the train, that was another big invention. By now it was seen that the railroad was not just a curious toy, but was a practical way of getting across the country; and every city and town wanted one.

I didn't have to go out of my way to learn about

this new invention. It crowded itself in on me. Along the entire length of my steamboat route from New York to Albany, one of these new-fangled things was a-building — a railroad was being cut through the steep rocks on the east shore of the river. By and by when it had got up from New York as far as Poughkeepsie, we ran a line of steamboats from Albany to Poughkeepsie, connecting with the train from New York. When the road was finished clean up to Albany, the railroad crowd were so boastful, they thought they were going to run steamboats off the face of the earth. And they made no bones in saying so. President Boorman of this Hudson River road came to me just as soon as the last rail to Albany had been spiked down.

"Drew," said he, "you might just as well hang up your fiddle. We've got you whipped. Own up. Your steamboats can't hold out against these things that go along the rails 30 miles an hour like a streak of lightning. Give up the boat business. Boats can't live on the Hudson River any longer. It won't pay you to fight."

But I wasn't going to knuckle under. I told him, modest-like, that he did have a big thing there in those steam buggies of his. But I was going to stick to steamboating for a spell yet. And as to driving me off the river, I guessed I could take care of that.

And I did, too. Even after the railroad got into full running, my boats carried just as many

passengers, yes, even more than before. The railroad got people used to travelling, and that helped
all kinds of transportation. Besides, the great
West was beginning to open up. There was Kansas,
and the rush of people to get out there and save it
from being a slave state. For John Brown and
his Kansas doings got into the papers and helped
to make the prairies known to the people. Lots
of families, whether they cared about the darkey
question or not, got the fever to go West. And
what pleasanter way could there be than to sail up
the Hudson to Albany, change there to an Erie
Canal boat, out through the Mohawk valley to
Buffalo, and then by water through the Great Lakes?
It was a sight cheaper to cart household goods
that way than to pay railroad freight charges.

But I haven't any cause to poke ridicule at railroads. They have proved mighty good friends to
me and my fortunes. For it wasn't very long after
this that I got into the business myself. It came
about something like this: Transportation was
stretching out from New York City not only in
a northerly direction — but Boston and New York
also wanted to be tied to each other by a fast route.
Boston and New York were almost as closely knit
together as Albany and New York. People and
goods were going back and forth between them all
the time. I knew this, because my "Bull's Head"
tavern had been on the highway which led from

New York City down east to Boston. But the
stage-coach couldn't take care of the traffic now.
So a line of steamboats started up from New York
out through Long Island Sound. I and George
Law — "Live Oak George" — established it. That
bridged over a good part of the distance between
the two cities. Then from Stonington a railroad
was built the rest of the way to Boston. The traffic
that went over this part-water-and-part-rail line,
soon showed that it was to be a money-maker; that
this was what the two cities had long been waiting
for. As soon as I saw that, I wanted to have control
of the railroad end of the route, as well as of the
steamboat end. So Vanderbilt and I went in and
bought enough shares of the "Boston and Stonington Railroad" to control it. In fact, his family
and I were pretty closely tied up together in those
days. Because at this time, besides the partnership
between him and me in this railroad, his brother
Jake was with me in the Stonington Line of steamboats. But my life hasn't had so much to do with
Jake. He was never the pusher that his brother was.

I was getting busy now in still another direction.
Some time before this, since the best fishing is in
deep waters, I had become a broker in Wall Street.
By this time that section of New York City had
gone through a wondrous change from what it had
been in my first visits to the city. Wall Street wasn't
any longer the market place of a big village. It

was becoming a money centre. Banking houses were going up there, and an Exchange Room for trading in railroad and steamboat shares. Railroads now were spreading over the country like measles in a boarding school. There was need of some place where their shares could be bought and sold. Wall Street got to be that place. The big commercial men of the nation were in New York. They lived in the aristocratic section, on Pearl, Broad, Water, Beaver and Whitehall Streets. So it was natural that they should locate the Stock Exchange right in the centre of their part of the town, at the corner of Broad and Wall Streets.

My banking enterprise up at the "Bull's Head" had got me more or less familiar with handling money. I had learned to find my way around in Wall Street's doings. So now I started in on my own account. The firm was "Drew, Robinson & Co." Robinson was a Nelson Robinson whom I had known up at Carmel. He had also been in the menagerie business — used to ride in the ring, all bespangled with shiny gold and silver lace. As soon as the fiddler was through (because in our old circus days they didn't have the big brass bands that circuses have now), the clowns would come leaping into the ring with a "Here we are again," and then Robinson and the rest of the circus performers would parade in and go through their monkey-shines. The "Co." in our firm name stood for Robert Weeks Kelly (the Weekses were also big people in the circus business up in Carmel). This Kelly, though, had made most of his money in the drover business. He was a shrewd, thrifty drover, and after Chamberlain died he became my son-in-law. So since we three knew each other well, we started together in the banking and broker business.

With so many fish-poles going at once, I was kept tied close to business. Never was much of a fellow to take vacations, anyhow, and during these days I wouldn't have had a chance even if I'd wanted to. There were some business men who kept drawing off their thoughts to politics and affairs of state. And if a fellow had been so minded, he could have taken up a deal of his time in talking about such things, because there was lots of excitement those days. There was the Mexican war. And then the Slave question down South got people all stirred up. But I was too busy to bother with such things. When a fellow is making money he gets busier every year. Because the more money he makes, the more investments he has to search out, in order to keep his money working. And the more investments he has, the more money he's going to make. Which means still more time in finding safe employment for it. And so on. Such far-off things as wars in Mexico, Missouri Compromises, and Slave Wars in Kansas, could not be allowed to come in and take my thoughts away from business.

But I did now and then take time off to see the sights. For instance, there was the big celebration when Henry Clay visited the city. He came up to be present when the body of President John Quincy Adams was brought on to New York from Washington. I had always regarded Clay as a great man. He had been the one to import Devons, Herefords and a lot of fine short-horns from England, and was helping to introduce these breeds into the Kentucky and Ohio lands. New England's favourite was the Devon. There was also the long-horn Texas cattle, which was being boasted about by the Westerners. But I never took much to those long-horns. They are but one remove above the buffalo, and are ungainly critters. The polled Durham of Ohio is far better for ordinary purposes, being quiet at the feeding rack and troughs. I kind of took to Henry Clay because he was so hot to get the farmers out in his section of the country to take up with high-grade breeds of cattle. On his farm in Kentucky they used to say that he had as fine a fat stock array as a man could ask to see. Those Western soils, anyhow, helped a whole lot in improving the breeds of live stock. There was the red hog of New Jersey, which formed the foundation for the large and heavy animals exported to the West Indies; when sent West it took on plumpness and became that fine-grained meat which corn-growing countries always give to a healthy breed. The same thing happened with the white hog of Pennsylvania. Before he was sent to Northern Ohio, he was a tough and lanky animal; but out there he became fine and plump. Out West also they got to crossing the Berkshire and China breeds upon the common hog, and made something finer than had ever been seen before. Those Western States were great in improving the quality of butcher's meat. Henry Clay would, to my thinking, have made an A No. 1 President if he had ever been elected.

But after a while we didn't have so much time over at our banking house of "Drew, Robinson & Co." for discussing breeds of cattle. We had our hands full in handling the business that began to come in. When you are loaning money, buying and selling railroad and steamboat shares, and such like, it keeps you going. If you don't look out, one slip will make an almighty loss. In fact our house made a slip at the start. One of our customers was a fellow we had known for some time. He owed us $30,000. My partners were for extending the loan. I was against it. They begged — talked about old friendship's sake, and such like. They got me to consent. Result — we lost the money. That taught me a lesson. Sentiment is all right up in the part of the city where your home is. But downtown, No. Down there the dog that

snaps the quickest gets the bone.   Friendship is very
nice for a Sunday afternoon when you're sitting
around the dinner table with your relations, talking
about the sermon that morning.   But nine o'clock
Monday morning, notions should be brushed away like
cobwebs from a machine.   I never took any stock in a
man who mixed up business with anything else.   He
can go into other things outside of business hours.
But when he's in his office, he ought not to have a relation in the world — and least of all a poor relation.

I also saw from this incident that I was not a
good hand for working along with other people,
being better fitted to go it alone, so to speak.   I
saw, or perhaps kind of felt, that there was going
to be lots of money in the stock-market business.
So I began to turn my efforts more and more in that
direction.   And if my partners wouldn't go with
me into speckilation, I could go without them.   When
you are doing just a banking business and nothing
else, your returns may be safe, but they're almighty
slow.   The same with running a steamboat, or a
railroad.   But if you can buy up the shares of a
company and sell them again inside of a year or
two, you can often turn more money into your purse
in a twelve-month than you can make by slow
business profits in twelve years.   For instance, there
was the Lake Champlain Line of steamboats, which
we controlled.   We might have just settled down,
and in a poky way run those boats and made our

profits, slow and sure. But I was in for bigger things. So we sold that line to the Saratoga and Whitehall railroad, and I put the money in the form of cash for speckilating. My experiences had told me that I had skill in getting deals worked through, and that these would bring quicker gains than the slow-poke method of regular business. So I went into operations in the stock market.

People have coupled my name along with Fisk and Gould. But it will be seen from what is here being set down that I was in advance of both of them. Here I was, an operator in Wall Street, when the Stock Exchange was new. I was a middle-aged man on the Street when Jim Fisk was a baby in the cradle, and before Jay Gould had seen the light of day. I might almost say I was their Wall Street parent. Many of their schemes and methods they learned from me. I was the pioneer. The way to manipulate stocks and work Wall Street dickers was well-nigh unknown when I first went into the business. I thought up many of the schemes out of my own brain. Those who came after had nothing to do but copy my ideas. Gould and Fisk — they were pupils of mine, both of them. I helped to make them. They were a pair of colts; I broke them in. It is easy now to lay out a campaign for working the market. But back in my early days, it wasn't so easy by a long shot. I had to invent ways of doing it. I had no guides to steer by.

# XIV

I WAS getting now to be a power in the financial market. Accordingly I wanted to live right in the city, and no longer out in the suburbs. I got a house on Bleecker Street, just where Mulberry Street runs into it — No. 52 Bleecker, it was — the upper corner towards the Bowery. That section had formerly been the blackberry region for Manhattan Island. When I was at the "Bull's Head," Bleecker Street was a lane lined with blackberry bushes, and in the berry season was a great place for picnics from far and near. It was also a good region for snipe shooting, and also for hunting rabbits. But by now you would hardly have recognized the place. For the city had grown up into it. The digging out of the stream just below into a canal (where Canal Street now runs) had helped to drain the frog-meadows up in the Bleecker Street section of the island. The Broad Way was pushed up to Union Square (as it was by and by called), and tacked onto the Bloomingdale Road which continued it up to the middle of the island kitty-corner. Where Grace Church now stands, there used to be an old high-peaked barn; but that farm was now being cut up into building lots, and criss-crossed by city streets.

The church I attended was on Mulberry Street, not far below my house. And now I set in to go to meeting every Sunday; I was also present on prayer- and class-meeting nights. I never lost my religion after this. You won't read in these papers of any more backslidings by Dan Drew. It took a good deal of the grace of God to reach me. But when finally he got me landed safe and sound within the fold, he held on to me. I have never slid back from that time to this. Of course, I have had my cold seasons. Every person has those. You can't live on a mountain all the time. Now and then I have found myself in the valley. But I have never failed to get back to the mountain-top experiences.

We used to have glorious times in that old Mulberry Street Church. From the Bowery village by Peter Cooper's grocery store, where he was superintendent of the Sunday-school, the church moved first down to the north side of Seventh Street. But the revivals there were so powerful, the neighbours began to object. Some good saint would get the power and would be well-nigh out of his senses. Suddenly he would come to, and with mighty "hallelujahs" would tell of the things he had seen. I don't see why people should object to shouting Christians. I'm not a shouter myself.

But in a love feast I can get good and happy along with the rest. And I like it. If the saints on earth haven't any right to be happy, I should like to know who have. Come, let our joys be known, say I. We are travelling through Immanuel's ground, to fairer worlds on high. Let those refuse to sing who never knew our Lord. The soul that knows its sins forgiven by the atoning Blood applied, and has had vouchsafed unto it the sprinkled conscience and the inward witness, let that man raise his Ebenezer, say I, and shout his joys abroad.

Well, as I started to say, some of the neighbours didn't just take to the revivals that used to be held in the old Seventh Street Church; and in those days the preacher would get up a revival every winter. I must confess that some of the meetings did last pretty late into the night. But so much the better. When a sinner has sung: "Show pity, Lord, oh, Lord, forgive; let a repenting rebel live!" and sung it over and over until his knees are well-nigh cramped beneath him, and then when he is ready to despair, for seeing himself slipping down the hill into the Devil's lap, if the burden all to once rolls off from him and he gets through and comes out onto the Hallelujah side, that man isn't going to let that meeting come to an end very soon. He is going to relate his experiences. He is going to tell what the Lord has done for him, and keep on telling. And he is going to wrestle with other sinners at the mercy seat until he gets them through also. And if it's twelve o'clock midnight before the meeting is over, he isn't going to care.

But the neighbours did. They said the church was a bad thing for property values. So they raised some money and bought two lots near Third Avenue. These they gave to the trustees of the church on condition that they move the meeting-house over there. The trustees consented and the building was put up. One day Zekiel Moore, a merchant and member of the Seventh Street Church, saw a vacant plot on Mulberry Street near Bleecker, and got the idea of building a church there. So Jake Bunting called a meeting at his house on Crosby Street, and the thing was started. There were great doings when our new meeting-house was finally dedicated. Dr. Bangs preached the sermon that afternoon. How some things stand out in a person's memory! It was from Luke I, 79. The sermon was meant mostly for us who were saved. This was as it should be. A dedication sermon is to the saints rather than to the sinners.

The preacher described the darkness out of which we had been delivered. I could almost feel the heat of the flames as he pictured the thing, and showed how we had been snatched as a brand from the burning. Although I had been in the back-sliding class often and long, I was no longer in that state of alienation nor appointed unto wrath. My delight was now in witnessing and testimonies. I could with joy gaze into the lower depths, which once used to send shivers and goose-flesh all over me.

> "Waken and mourn, ye heirs of hell,
> Let stubborn sinners fear;
> You must be driven from earth, to dwell
> A long forever there.
>
> See how the pit gapes wide for you,
> And flashes in your face.
> And thou, my soul, look downwards too,
> And sing recovering grace!"

There was a time when that sort of thing would have made me hang onto the seat in front to keep from slipping down into the pit. But now my feet had been placed upon the rock. I was no longer building on the sands, but on solid foundations. Hay and wheat and stubble — the fire will consume these. But the rock stands, when the nearer waters roll.

These thoughts may seem poky and dull to some. That is because they have never experienced religion. It was in this Mulberry Street Church and in the big marble church on Fourth Avenue, which a little later I was instrumental in building, that I spent a good share of my time out of business hours. When a man goes to prayer meeting and class meeting two nights of the week, and to church twice on Sunday, and on week-days works at his office from morning till night, his life is made up of about two things — work and worship.

In order to know what a man really is, you've got to see him now and then away from his office. Business isn't the whole of life. Business shows one side of a man. His church and home life show the other side. That is where a good many of the revilings against me have come from. They have come from people who have seen me only at business. Everybody knows that business is one thing, and a man's church and home life another thing. I have had to sharpen my wits — count the pennies close — in order to make money. But there has been something to Dan Drew besides just getting rich, and I want people to know what this other something is. Unless a business man is also a converted man, with the witness of the spirit within him, he is like a hog under an apple tree — so busy crunching the fruit that he doesn't have time to look up to where the fruit comes from. It isn't fair to judge a man by his down-town life alone. Business, anyhow, slobbers a fellow up. It's like teaching a calf to drink out of a pail — you're sure to get splashed and dirty. Business is a scramble for the cash. Nobody looks for manners around the meal tub.

## XV

RAILROADS were now all the rage. And at about this time the greatest railroad in the world, for its day, was finished, "The New York & Lake Erie." It was called, for short, the "Erie." I was soon to make a bag of money out of this Erie Road. So I came to know a good deal about it. The road had been a long time a-building. Young Pierson, of Ramapo, well-nigh lost his fortune in the job. If it hadn't been for English investors coming forward and buying the stock at a time when Americans had got sick of the thing, it would have fallen flat as a pancake and there wouldn't have been any Erie Road at all. Pierson had worked like everything to get the Legislature to give a subsidy. In this he was backed by the southern tier of counties in York State. Those counties for a long time had felt sore that the Erie Canal had not been built through their section rather than through the Mohawk section. And they put up such a howl that the Legislature had either to give them a canal of their own, or else build a railroad. Pierson — he was the son of old Judge Pierson of Ramapo — pushed the thing and got a grant of money from the Legislature. But this hadn't carried the road to completion. It hung fire. It was built only half-way to Lake Erie — was like a bridge thrown half-way across, about as much use as no bridge at all. The Legislature wouldn't grant any more money. Also American capital got cold feet. The thing looked bad. It was at this time that English investors came to the rescue. They put up their good money, bought the road's paper, helped the thing out. So that by and by a pair of rails was laid clean through to Dunkirk.

Then there was a great jubilee. All the people in that part of the state joined in the "Hurrah." They had been jealous of the Erie Canal section of York State. Now they could hold their heads up with any. Because, what is a canal with its poky old boats, compared to a railroad 500 miles long, with trains scooting over the rails like a streak of lightning! Thirty miles an hour now wasn't considered remarkable; soon the trains could keep up that speed the whole distance. To celebrate the completion of the road two trains of cars ran over the route. There were many invited guests — the President, Dan Webster, and lots of the other big wigs. It was in the spring of the year. When finally they got to Dunkirk at Lake Erie, they had a big barbecue. Under a tent were victuals for well-nigh a thousand people. Whole roast pigs

and oxen were served on the tables.  There was a
great sign hung up, with poetry on it:

> "'Tis done, 'tis done, the mighty chain,
> That binds Lake Erie to the main."

The road first along ran to Piermont on the Hudson.  They hadn't been able to get through the
Bergen Hill, which lay just back of Jersey City.
So had to go up to Piermont as the next best place
of reaching the Hudson.  Washington Irving's
country seat was on the river on the opposite bank.
He could look over and see the trains come down
to the shore; for there was a pier a mile long that
ran out into the water from Piermont.  It had to
be that long, because the Hudson is shallow at that
point.  (Right where Washington Irving had his
estate was where the three patriot soldiers got
Major André when he was trying to escape from
West Point, during the treason of Benedict Arnold.)
That place, Piermont, had formerly been a fishing
village called Tappan Slote.  The place had supported three fishing sloops.  But now three steamboats took the place of the sloops.  Great shops
and engine-houses were built, and a switch-yard.
Piermont — a long pier running right into the
mountain back on the shore; I suppose that's where
the village got its new name — became a boom town.
This plan of having the eastern terminal of the

road at Piermont had its drawbacks. It was twenty-four miles up the river from New York City. Steamboats could take care of the travel all right in summer. But in winter it was a different matter. In that day there wasn't so much traffic in New York Bay and on the North River as there is now. So that in a cold winter the floating ice, not having anything to break it up, used to jam, and freeze solid from shore to shore. The Erie Railroad boats to Piermont in winter had to have a channel cut for them through the ice. Sometimes they had hard work keeping even this open. The channel would sometimes get so narrow that the boat could just skimp through. Skaters on the ice would come alongside and jump onto the guard-rail of the steamboat, or onto the false prow.

However, in spite of this difficulty the railroad did well almost from the start. For one thing, the people living alongside were so proud of the thing that they pitched in and helped it in every way they could. They looked upon the Erie Road as a patriotic achievement. Because people as far away as Europe were talking about this wonderful engineering feat that America had put through. More than that, the road ran through a prosperous region. From Rockland to Chautauqua, there were rich farm lands on both sides. It tapped the Delaware and Hudson Canal at Port Jervis. Branch lines quickly spread out on both sides and served as feeders. The grazing lands of Sullivan, Delaware and Broome Counties now had a way of getting their stuff to market. The road paid good dividends.

I had kept my eye on the road while it was a-building. Because I knew something of the country it went through. My Western cattle trips had made me acquainted with Ohio and the great region west, which this road was now to lead into. And my shorter drover trips out from New York had made me more or less at home in those counties that the Erie Road passed through. I knew that that southern York State country was a rich one. It had been peopled for a long time back. During the Revolution those southern counties had been an important section of the state. The Tuxedo Gap through the Ramapo Mountains was, in General George Washington's day, the only road between New York and the western counties. (I knew a whole lot about that Ramapo section. When a man travels through a country on horseback, with a drove of three or four hundred critters a-plodding along behind him, and pitching camp at nightfall wherever he happens to be, he picks up a sight more information about a locality than you can get out of books.) That is why General George Washington fortified the Tuxedo Gap when he was looking for the red-coats to advance from New York City and New Jersey. He knew that that was the only pass by which they could get through, and he wanted to keep them away from his army which was up in the Highlands. Back in my drover days these fortifications were still standing. They ran out from the south side of the mountain, a mile and a half up from Major Suffern's mansion. (That mansion is where General George Washington made his headquarters when his army was camped there.) In this gap, and on top of the high "torn" — that's a Dutch word for steeple — before the railroad came with its smoke and dust, you could look wellnigh into New York Harbour. They used to tell the story that General George Washington used to climb to the top of that hill and watch for the British through a spy-glass. Just a little beyond this, a mile or so to the west, is where our droves of cattle, and in fact all the traffic which went through the gap, used to cross the Ramapo River. The railroad when it came built its bridge right alongside the old turnpike bridge. Back in my drover days, Judge Pierson had his iron works there for rolling and splitting iron, and making cut nails. The river here in this gap furnished fine water power. And the mountains round about are so full of iron ore that in a lightning storm you could hardly get away from the fiery bolts, no matter which way you ran. To be there in a lightning storm would make a sinful man wish he had listened to what the preacher said and had made himself thunder-proof against the wrath of God.

Why, to show you the richness of that country, long before the railroad was even thought of, out beyond Pierson's Iron Works Major Jake Sloat had put up a big cotton mill. It was in a Dutch settlement. Sloat was very anxious to keep a good tone in his settlement. He had a grocery and general store, and wouldn't allow a smitch of rum or intoxicating drink to be sold anywhere in the place. The mill was in a beautiful grove. Dutch girls worked in the mill. Their homes were back in the woods all around, here one and there one, very cosy little cottages. It was a God-fearing people. Judge Pierson also kept liquor out of his village. So that all the way through that section it was a poor place for drovers to stop off in. Because, since they weren't allowed to sell liquor, no one would put up a tavern. They figured that without a tap-room, a tavern wouldn't pay expenses. So we drovers would plan to go through that section in the daytime, and reach some tavern further on. Because, if we landed there at night, it was a case of sleeping out under the open sky.

Not far from the Tuxedo Gap, up in the mountains, was a woodchopper's settlement called Johnson-town. They made a living by burning charcoal, which they carried down to the Ramapo River for use in the iron furnaces. They also whittled out wooden spoons and chopping bowls, which they sold. They were a good people. But they didn't know very much about the goings on in the great world outside. When the railroad trains began to come through this Tuxedo Gap, those woodsmen heard the screech of the engine as it went through the woods — it was pretty nigh all woods in those days, so that a squirrel could almost go through four counties from tree-top to tree-top, without touching ground — they thought it was the scream of some new kind of wild animal; for the woods then were infested with panther and other varmints. So one night they gathered with axes and pitchforks in that part of the woods where the screeching had been heard night after night, to make an ambuscade for the beast. When the engine finally came rushing through the woods and the darkness, with a long tail of light streaming behind, those mountaineers rushed away scared. This new kind of varmint was too much.

The Monroe Iron Furnace, about three miles beyond Sloat's Burg, was where Parrott made his guns, which became famous in the Civil War. There was an iron mine six miles up from there in the mountain, whose ore was said to be the sovereignest in all the country for the making of cannon. (That's why the Parrott gun became so noted.) It was great iron, also, for making nails; and some distance from there, at the South Fields, back in my drover days, was a flourishing nail works. Only smart and handy chaps were employed in those works, because a nailer had to work like sixty. A nail is so small that, to compete with the maker of wooden pins, a nailer had to get a certain number of nails made out of every heating of the rod. Even as it was, and work as hard as they could, they couldn't force wooden nails from the market altogether. Many of the pin-makers had got to be so skilled in making wooden nails that they held their own even when iron nails came in. But wooden pins were not all of uniform size; they used to cause much profanity on the part of house and barn builders. So it was a good thing, I have always thought, when iron nails finally took the place of wooden pins altogether.

This particular section was not good for drovers. There was good fishing in the ponds. Ramapo, they used to say, was an Indian name, meaning "place of round ponds." And these bits of water were scattered all through the mountains on both sides of the Tuxedo Gap. So that, if a fellow could only have stopped over for a spell, he could have had good sport with a fish-pole. But the region sent only a few cattle to market, and these were for the most part stringy things, mere bags of bones. The woods were too thick and the mountains too wild for grazing. But when you got out a little further west, beyond Tuxedo Gap, you came out by Centreville. (This was changed to "Turner's" when the railroad came, because old man Turner kept a tavern at that place right close to the tracks, with a flourishing grist mill back of it. He used to feed the travellers; Turner's Restaurant got to be famous the whole length of the Erie Railroad because of its fine victuals.) Here you came into a region flowing with milk and butter. Some of the finest short-horn beeves that ever came to the New York market were picked up in this valley. The pasturing was of good quality in summer, and in winter the fodder was plentiful. From here all the way along the route of the Erie, it was a great breeding section. It made big money by selling critters to us drovers, long before the railroad came.

# XVI

YES, I knew something of the richness of that country through which the Erie railroad was being built. So, when it was at last finished, I hankered to get it into my hands. I felt that I could make money out of it. When you own the hen, you own the eggs also. And when you control a railroad — that's the same as owning it — you own what the road makes.

I went about it like this. There was by this time a chain of railroads through the Mohawk Valley and the central part of York State. They coupled together, a little later, to form the "New York Central." This chain of railroads out of Albany could be made, in connection with my steamboats on the Hudson, a bad competitor of the Erie for the through western traffic. With my Hudson River boats I was in a position to favour this Central Line with rates on the through traffic and so make myself an enemy of the Erie whom it would stand them in hand to make terms with. To make doubly sure, I set my trap at the other end also. Out on Lake Erie was a line of boats connecting with the Erie Railroad and forming its route to the far West. Softly I bought a controlling interest in this steamboat line. This gave me power over the Erie in that direction. I took still a third step. Out in western New York there was a line of railroad connecting both the Central Line and the Erie. It was known as the "Buffalo and State Line Railroad." Without letting anybody know what I was doing, I got enough stock in this dinkey little road to control it.

Now my trap was set. I let it be known that I was planning to give the railroad which ran through central New York a better through rate, both on the Hudson River steamboats and on the "Buffalo and State Line" connection with the West, than the Erie could meet. I also hinted to the Erie Company that it would very soon have to give me a bigger slice of the through rate, for the use of my Lake Erie line of steamers.

The Erie people got interested in me then almighty quick. For I had their line bottled up, corked at both ends good and tight. "What do you mean," they asked, "by giving that New York Central crowd better rates than you do us?"

I answered, sort of cool-like, that I hadn't thought the Erie would care very much. They had never seemed to give much thought to Dan Drew one way or the other. I said I was kind of surprised that they even knew I was living.

"What do you mean by that?" they asked.

"Is it that you want to be a director of the Erie?"

I hemmed and hawed, chewed my tobacco for a spell, and then said I'd think their offer over. Some time before the Erie's annual meeting I let it be known that, inasmuch as they had asked me to take a position as director, I might see my way clear to accept if I was elected. I put it kind of mild, like that. But I was just itching to get in on the inside. Like a dog around hot porridge, there was something good there, if I could only get to it. I could hardly wait. Finally the election took place, and they sent me word that I had been elected a member of the Board of Directors. I was at last on the inside.

But even this wasn't enough. To be a director is something. It gives you Wall Street tips ahead of the people who are on the outside. But I wanted something more (I always was ambitious, never contented, but always pushing on to something better). So I now took steps to get the road completely under my thumb. In order to do this, I saw I'd have to get her to borrow money of me. That's the sure way. When a man is in your debt, he's your slave. You own him body and breeches. You are the cat, he is the mouse. You let him have a little space to run about in, and he thinks he's going to get away. But you are only playing with him. You can stick out your paw and claw him across the back any time you wish. So I set about to make them borrow money, and to borrow it of me.

This was not so easy to do as one might think. Because the Company was prosperous. It didn't need any more money. The road was so wonderful an achievement that it was almost a mark of patriotism for the people in that region to patronize it and help it along. It was not only a York State thing, it was an American institution — the first great trunk-line railroad the world had ever seen. So money flowed in from all sides. Conductors, engineers, brakemen, track-walkers, proud to be working for such a fine and great enterprise, were honest and faithful. No wonder the road paid dividends. This was during the panic of '57 that I set about to get control of the road. Money everywhere else was tight — so much suffering, in fact, that the New York Common Council put labourers to work grading the new Central Park, in order to relieve the distress. And yet, with stocks everywhere else slumping, banks failing, great commercial houses toppling on every side, that very year the young and thrifty Erie Railroad paid no less than eight per cent. dividends. If a road could do that so soon after it was built and while it was getting onto its legs, so to speak, what wouldn't it do when it had settled down to real business? Yes, it did look like a hopeless task, to make a road that was as flourishing as this borrow money of me.

But I was like a steer that smells the clover; he will either find a hole through the line fence, or make one.

This Erie enterprise in my life, let me say right here, got a lot of people to disliking me. "Because," they said, "before Dan Drew got hold of it, the Erie was one of the best and most thriving properties in the country — America's pride — longest and finest railroad in the world — the bringer of blessings to all the southern tier of counties in the Empire State. Whereas, when he got through with it," so these enemies of mine said, "its treasury had been squeezed dry, the road brought to bankruptcy, its rolling stock run down, and the road-bed become a death trap and a taker of human life. And the evil didn't stop with him," so they went on; "for when this Dan Drew finally let go his clutch on the finances of the road, he had set at work a chain of influences which were to make the road a by-word, and set back the development of a third part of York State for the space of fifty years."

Oh, they ripped it onto me good and hard. I suppose I have put up with such abuse during my life as have few other men that ever lived. But, being of a peaceable disposition, I have forgiven these enemies of mine all the hard things they said. I always turn the other cheek, as it were. A quiet cow can get along with short horns; and if, when enemies revile you and say all manner of evil against you, you don't answer back, but just go on your own peaceable way, it sort of takes all the spunk out of them; by and by they get over being mad, and stop their mud-throwing. Anyhow, I never did care pea-shucks what people were saying about me. So many have taken a kick at me that if I were tender I suppose I'd be so sore by this time that I couldn't sit down; but my saddle leather, so to speak, has become tough, so that I don't mind their kicks any more.

The truth is, I was hard pushed for funds when I started in on this Erie business. My fortune had stopped growing. And no matter how much a man has, when he comes to a point where he stops getting richer, he is scared. The panic of '57 had cut off a number of my dividends. I was doing nothing more than holding my own. I wasn't making any progress. Each night didn't see me any further along towards becoming a rich man than the morning. I wasn't getting ahead. Every man of spirit wants to be getting ahead.

Besides, with this panic year of which I'm now writing, a new state of affairs came about in financial circles. The panic was known as the "Western Blizzard." It put old fogyism out of date forevermore. The men who conducted business in the old-fashioned, slow-poke method — the think-of-the-other-fellow method — were swept away by this panic, or at least were so crippled up that they didn't figure much in the world of affairs afterwards.

A new generation of men came in — a more pushful set. I was one of them. We were men now who went ahead. We did things. We didn't split hairs about trifles.    Anyhow, men of thin skin, with a conscience all the time full of prickles, are out of place in business dickerings.    A prickly conscience would be like a white silk apron for a blacksmith. Sometimes you've got to get your hands dirty, but that doesn't mean that the money you make is also dirty.    Black hens can lay white eggs.    Take that blacksmith.    During the day he gets all grimed up.    Then at night he washes, and now is as clean as anything.    And his money is clean, too.    What better kind of man is there than a blacksmith?    It isn't how you get your money but what you do with it, that counts.

Well, as I started to say, I wanted to get the Erie Railroad in my debt.    I went about it in this fashion: The road, as I guess I've wrote, went to Piermont, twenty-four miles up the Hudson.    They would like to have come straight down to Jersey City.    It would have saved that twenty-four mile trip by water, which was so bothersome in winter.    But there, square across the path, was Bergen Hill.    The trouble with this hill was, it wasn't a gradual rise that a railroad grade could work up to and over by slow degrees.    The Hackensack meadows came smack up to it on one side, and the Hudson shore smack up on the other, with this hill between, stiff as a line fence. But the Erie was so prosperous, holding its own even in this panic year of '57, that the directors now decided to go ahead and try the well-nigh impossible task of getting into Jersey City.

Some time before this, passengers to New York had got into the habit of leaving the Erie at Suffern Station, and getting on to another road which brought them into New York by the way of Paterson, New Jersey. A short-cut road over this route had been built by private capital. Or rather, this short cut was a chain made up of three roads; the "Union Railroad," the "Ramapo & Paterson" and the "Paterson & Jersey City." All of them were short. The "Union" in fact was only half a mile long, but was needed in making the final connection with the Erie. These were all narrow-gauge roads — that is, narrow-gauge for that time. They would be called standard-gauge to-day, for they were built on the English standard, five feet eight and a half inches wide, which has since been adopted by all the railroads of America. But the Erie was a six-foot road. Right here was one difficulty. The Erie rolling stock couldn't run on this narrow gauge, nor could the narrow-gauge cars and engines run on the broad track of the Erie.

This short cut through Paterson, when it got to within two miles of the Hudson River, followed the track of "The New Jersey Railroad & Transportation Co.," through a hole in Bergen Hill into Jersey City. That was then the only way through that hill. It had been cut at the lower end, where the mountain was nowheres near so broad and so hard to tunnel as it was further up. But this cut through the hill was already taken. It was the only thoroughfare from New York to Philadelphia, Washington and the South. So it had all it could do to handle its own traffic. And for the Erie Road, with its great trunk-line traffic, to try to use that same passage-way would have blocked it tight. So an independent hole through the mountain was needed, and further up, too, where the tunnelling was hard.

But the directors took the bit in their teeth, so to speak. They voted to buy this Paterson short cut consisting of the three roads running out to Suffern, and, leaving the narrow gauge as it was, to lay a third rail so as to accommodate the Erie's six-foot rolling stock. They also voted to dig a tunnel under Bergen Hill, and to build a long dock and terminal in Jersey City.

I was happy. Here was the chance I'd been waiting for. I set about softly to increase the difficulties the road was meeting in this job, so as to get her to a point where she would have to cut her dividends, find her balance by and by on the other side of the account sheet, and finally have to raise a loan. I didn't let the other directors know what I was doing. In order to keep my place on the Erie Board I made believe I was working for her interests. So, all unbeknownst to them, I began to put obstacles in the way of these improvements which the road was undertaking. Not big enough obstacles, of course, to stop the improvements altogether. All I wanted was to get the road into hot water, so it would become a borrower.

I had two or three ways of thus stirring up trouble. One was by means of the Rockland County representatives in the Legislature at Albany. Piermont and the other sections of Rockland County hated to see the terminal of the road moved to Jersey City, like a cat hates mustard. Because to be a great railroad terminal was booming Piermont and the surrounding towns. Her population was growing. She promised to become a city in no time. They didn't take at all to the idea of losing this, and of having the terminal moved to a city in another state. York State had given some grants of money to see the railroad built. So now the Rockland County people got up all kinds of objections in the Legislature against changing the charter of the road so as to permit it to go down into Jersey City. These difficulties at Albany gave me a chance to depress the securities of the road, by hinting around through Wall Street that the road was losing its favour with the powers at Albany, and that it apparently was no longer to be York State's pet institution, but an outlaw from now on. The bill was at last put through.  But not until I had made it help my end.

In the tunnel which the road was trying to dig, I had a still better handle against them.  Thousands of travellers go through that hole to-day, and most like as not hardly give a minute's thought to the trouble that was had in digging it.  But there was trouble.  The boring of tunnels in those days wasn't the easy thing it is getting to be to-day.  Vanderbilt had done it, under Murray Hill in New York City.  But that was a short and easy thing to do.  Murray Hill wasn't very high — he could put a lot of air shafts down through from the top.  The road to Philadelphia had also done it; but, as I said, this was at the lower end of Bergen Hill, where the thing was easy.  Up where the Erie was trying to do it, the thing was all-fired difficult. Bergen Hill is made of trap rock, about as hard a thing as is known — so hard, in fact, that they use the rock for paving stones.  Over in Hoboken the people in winter cut paving stones out of the ledge in their back yards.  Besides, engineers didn't have anything but gun-powder; and the only way they could drill the blasting-holes was by one man holding and turning the drill, while two others hammered it in.  More than that, in the state of engineering science of that day, there was no guarantee that with so long a tunnel they could keep it straight and true, so as to know where they were coming out.  Best of all —

for my purpose — the popular mind was in a scary condition in reference to so big and risky a job. People were open to all kinds of rumours.

Accordingly, while the work was going on, I softly started reports through Wall Street to the effect that the tunnel wasn't getting along as prosperous as had been hoped for — difficulties were being met with — it was all right to try to dig narrow tunnels through small hills; but to dig a tunnel for a six-foot railroad, through a mountain as big and hard as Bergen Hill, was being found a different matter. And there were dangers, too, I hinted, which hadn't been calculated on. The workmen were getting scared to be so far in the bowels of a mountain, where they didn't know what might turn up any minute in the shape of unknown caverns of water, cave-ins, foul gases and such like.

Investors are skittish folk. It's the business of Wall Street to catch the slightest hints and act upon them; which makes it the easiest place in the world to get rumours going. Accordingly, when these hints were dropped by one like myself, who was known to be on the inside of the Company's councils, investors took them at once for valuable points as to the state of Erie's affairs. A rumour, particularly if it comes from some source on the inside, only needs to be started. It spreads then of itself and keeps getting bigger. Capital got scared. As soon as it was learned that the Erie Railroad in this

Bergen Hill tunnel had bitten off more than it could chew, in fact seemed to be getting sick of the job and might give up in disgust, investors became suddenly uncertain concerning the stock. Erie slumped from sixty-three down to thirty-three. So that the road now couldn't raise money like she had used to.

This set-back came at the time when she needed the money most, because just then her pay-roll was enormous. There were new supplies to pay for; workmen in the tunnel to pay off every month; the costly right of way through Jersey City; freight-yards in that city; a big new station to build; and a long dock out into the water; and the job of getting a charter through the Legislature at Trenton and through the Jersey City Council. The Company just had to have money. There hardly had been a time when she needed capital more than she did just now. But capital now wasn't friendly. The directors met in a sad-faced session and asked what could be done.

When they were most in the dumps, I stepped forward. I announced that I would be the road's helper. Since the other men of money were getting cold feet and seemed to be losing faith in the enterprise, I would let them have a loan of my money, all that I could raise. If they wanted a million and a half, I'd see, in some way or other, that they got it.

They took me up. I paid over the money, and took as security a chattel mortgage on the rolling stock. I had the sow by the ear at last. From now on, for almost ten years, I had the Erie Railroad in my breeches pocket, so to speak. It is always an advantage in Wall Street operations to be on the inside of a railroad or a big industrial concern. You know, then, the monthly earnings before they are given out to the public. You get earliest notice of any favourable or unfavourable happening. You have access to the transfer books and know where all the circulating stock is. Any dangers that have arisen to the road's property, or any new connection favourable to the road's earning capacity, is known to you long before the outside investors have got the tip. So that you can go onto the Stock Exchange and speckilate in those shares with your eyes open, whilst the rest of the speckilators are going it blind. An insider's position is as good as money in the chest.

Besides, I had now another advantage as well. Not only could I predict well-nigh every turn in Erie shares. I could do even better. I could make it turn in either direction I chose. I had the horse by the halter, so to speak, and could lead him where I wanted. If my operations on the Stock Exchange made it needful for the stock to go up, I could give out that the road was prosperous — and her stock would go up. Or if I was in a Bearish temper and wanted her shares to slump, I could make the road unprosperous for a time, and then stocks would go down to the point where I wanted them. I worked it something like this: Erie shares would be selling, say at ninety. I would give orders to my broker to sell Erie heavily short. By selling short a Wall Street operator puts out contracts to deliver the stock, say sixty days from that date, at present prices. If within those sixty days the price goes down, he can buy at the lower price and collect at the higher price named in the contract. Well, after I had got my short contracts placed, the other fellows, of course, taking my offers, because they figured that the shares were likely to go up rather than down, I would give out a statement to the effect that I, as owner of the chattel mortgages on on the road, was about to foreclose. Or I would have one of my under-fellows get out an injunction forbidding the road to pay any more dividends; or I would start a rumour that the road was going to rack and ruin. Immediately there would be a panic in Erie quotations. Her shares would slump; and before the sixty days were up, that former price of ninety would have shrunk to, say, sixty-five. So that now I would buy my shares at sixty-five, sell them for that contract figure, ninety, and thus pocket $25 clean profit on every share dealt in. If this particular deal had amounted to fifteen or twenty thousand shares, and I cleaned up $25 on every share, any one can see what a fine little sum it would amount to.

Thereupon I would turn round and work it the other way. I was now short of the stock — that is, was sold out. I would therefore buy large blocks of it at the low figure of $65 a share. Now it stands me in hand to have the stock go up in value. So I give out a statement to the effect that my little difficulty with the road, which had been noised abroad some weeks before, has been settled; I have decided not to foreclose my chattel mortgage after all — the road has found a way to fix up the matter with me, is very prosperous, in fact is likely to declare a big dividend shortly. Immediately, with these refreshing rumours spreading abroad, Erie stock begins to go up. By and by she touches again the top-notch figure, say, ninety. Now I sell, and in this way clean up $25 more on every share of stock I had dealt in.

This is the advantage of operating from the inside. You win both going and coming. When stock is going down you are a Bear, and make money by its fall. When the stock is going up, you are a Bull, and make money by the rise. In fact, I worked this so prosperous, that after a while they made it into a kind of a proverb. It got to be a saying around the street: "Daniel says 'up' — Erie goes up. Daniel says 'down' — Erie goes down. Daniel says 'wiggle-waggle' — it bobs both ways!"

# XVII

I HAD by this time got too rich to live down in Bleecker Street. I was becoming one of the big bugs in the financial world. There weren't so many back in those early days — Jake Little, Vanderbilt and a few others. If these fellows could have big, fine houses to live in, I thought I ought to have one too.

So I went way up to Seventeenth Street. I decided if I was going to move at all I might as well make a big move while I was about it. I bought a lot there on the corner, facing Union Square. That square had been the parade ground for Company Drill and General Training, back in my "Bull's Head" days. Now it had been turned into a public park. Some fine houses were being built around it. So I wanted to live there, too, and be in the company of the money kings.

I built a big house, a four-story mansion of brown stone, on the lower corner of the street. For I had money now. A man with a big jar of butter can spread his bread thick. My site extended back some distance along Seventeenth Street, and I put up a barn, with a cow-shed and horse-stable joined to the house. I have always had a hankering for cattle. Though I was now a city dweller, I was bent on keeping at least a milch cow. The smell of cattle now and then, particularly when he is cooped up in a city, sort of does a fellow good. It makes him feel young again. Sometimes when I have been worried well-nigh to death in some tight place in my speckilations, I have got up of a morning and walked out through the back yard and into the cow-stable — for I had built my home in such a way that by walking out through the conservatory on the first floor I went down into a little back yard, just beyond which was the stable and cowshed. Once there, the smell of the cow and horses would take me back to old days, and make me forget my worries. I could go back to the breakfast table a new man, ready to face anything. Family prayer after breakfast would also help to put spirit in me. We didn't have much form or ceremony in these daily devotions. Getting my family around me, I would read a portion from the Scriptures. Perhaps then we would sing a verse or two of a hymn, particularly if we had a preacher staying with us — I gave preachers the run of the house — then we would kneel and I would offer prayer. Then from the family altar I would step out through the back yard, and if my hired man wasn't around, would harness the horse myself — I had a black horse for many years — to take me down to the Street. I had a doctor's gig to ride in, and would drive down the Bowery Road to Wall Street. There I would send a boy with the rig to a livery stable not far away; and he would also bring the rig back for me at the close of business that day. To have the reins in my hands and to feel the tug of the bit, would carry me back to old days when I was driving along the "Mud Road" or the "Horse Pound Road" up at Carmel looking for calves and heifers.

I was glad that I had made the move up into the big house on Union Square. Because it gave me standing among the boys on the Street. This was the time when Wall Street was beginning to get important. The early cow gets the dew, and those who were on the Stock Exchange back in those days made money. For the Civil War was coming on. We didn't know it then. Still, we knew that something big was on the anvil. There was a stir in the air. Nobody knew what was going to happen next. And we made big bets, so to speak, as to what would come off on the morrow. Even the most unlikely speckilation would sometimes win, affairs were that unsettled. The very existence of the nation was uncertain. Nobody knew just where we stood. At such seasons, speckilators have good times. When excitement is high and one thing as likely to happen as another, it gets people worked up to venture big sums.

When the Civil War finally broke out, I wasn't sure for a spell whether I wanted to see York State go into it or not. Because, if the nation went to smash, and our state was mixed up in it, we would be in the smash-up, too. Whilst, if we stayed out of the muss, and the smash-up came, we could save our bacon. Because our state, and particularly New York City, was in position to get along even if there wasn't any nation. In fact, there might be advantages in being independent of the rest of the country — a sovereignty all by ourselves. Fernando Wood, who was Mayor of New York when the War broke out, suggested this in a message to the Common Council. He wanted them to consider whether it might not be to our advantage to become a free and independent city. Said he:

"Why should not New York City, instead of supporting, by her contributions in revenues, two-thirds of the expenses of the United States, become also equally independent? As a free city with but a nominal duty on imports, her local government would be supported without taxes upon her people. Thus we could live free from taxes, and have cheap goods nearly duty-free."

It was a puzzle, and I for one couldn't just make up my mind. We in New York were a commercial set. We didn't have New England's hot-headedness to get excited over Negro cotton-pickers down South.

And if the general smash-up was to come, it was true that New York as a free and sovereign city, having such a fine harbour location, could get goods from Europe free of duty and keep all of that tariff money to herself. But then, on the other hand, it was to the advantage of us money kings to have a big country to operate in; because railroads cross the country without regard to state boundaries. We wanted a big landscape so we could do a big business. It was a hard thing to decide, whether to go in for the War and stand by the Union, or stay out and make ourselves free and independent. But Abe Lincoln came to New York and made a speech in Cooper Union. That turned the people towards the preservation of the Union. It wasn't much of a stump speech. Lincoln's voice, I always thought, was too husky to make him a popular talker. But people who came away from Cooper Union that night got the notion that this question of standing by the Union was really of considerable importance. The speech made a lot of talk over the city, and even roused some of the boys on the Street, who commonly were calm-headed like myself. Then when, on top of that speech, the shots were fired on Fort Sumter, it made such an almighty stir among the people generally that we Wall Street men had to get in step. A fellow would have been very unpopular then, if he had stood out against the War. It was now a case of fight it out, no matter what the cost.

What won't make butter must go into cheese. If the War must come, I decided to make it help my fortunes. And I must say that I soon began to wonder how I had been of two minds as to the advantage or disadvantage of a war. For I saw very quickly that the War of the Rebellion was going to be a money-maker for me. Along with ordinary happenings, we fellows in Wall Street now had in addition the fortunes of war to speckilate about and that always makes great doings on a stock exchange. It's good fishing in troubled waters. As I look back now, I see that I never made more money, or had four years that were all in all more genuinely prosperous, than those four years of the War. Commonly, the things that belong to guns and battles and soldiers don't appeal to me. I made some money once — I guess I've mentioned it in these papers, somewheres — by wearing a knapsack for the Government, in the War of 1812. But I saw even as a boy that this thing they call patriotism is a mighty slow way in which to roll up a fortune. I have noticed since, that the fellows who are all the time hurrahing for their country don't get fat bank accounts. For instance, there was all of that talk about the Missouri Compromise. When I was getting started in Wall Street there were people who talked of nothing else but Missouri — discussing sometimes way into the night. And they are for the most part poor men to-day. Whilst all of that time I was giving myself to business, and piling up money.

But now I saw that I could turn this very thing of war into a helpful friend. Because, with McClellan's Peninsular Campaign, a tall business began in Wall Street. I found myself getting really interested in the movements of armies and such-like things. For now it stood me in hand to keep track of the doings at the front. In fact, we financial men organized a way for getting early news from the seat of war. A silver key will open any kind of a lock. We had on our pay-roll sutlers, reporters, private soldiers and officers even up to generals. Also, there were politicians in Washington, even a Congressman or two, whom we used to pay. We found that it was a good plan also to have an understanding with telegraph operators, because when they were sending important messages to the Government from the seat of war, they could favour us by sending the news also to us—sometimes before they sent it to Washington. Big officials who wouldn't accept money could usually be reached by giving them some shares in the stock we were manipulating. (We didn't dare make offers of this kind to Abe himself. Lincoln was an unpractical man, so far as making money went. All he thought about was to save the Union. He used to get very peevish at some of us money kings.) During these days of the War we who were on the inside could call the turn of a stock long before the general public.

This made very profitable business. In fact, I got to taking a great interest in the Boys in Blue. I came to look upon them as heroes. Their pay, to be sure, would have to come out of the taxes. We rich men would have to foot most of the bill. Still, I didn't let that thought bother me. I felt that the Boys in Blue, sometimes tramping all night through fever swamps and across mountains, or lying in the camp hospitals sick and wounded and dying, earned all the monthly pay they got. Because they were beating the waters, so to speak, and we in Wall Street were getting the fish. There was the Antietam Campaign, for instance. It was worth a good deal to a Wall Street speckilator, that one campaign. Because, whilst the people all through the North were still wondering what was the fate of that expedition, we, by our underground telegraph lines, so to speak, knew the outcome of the campaign, and turned it to such good use in the stock market that we made almost enough from that one deal to pay the wages of every Boy in Blue in that army. When Richmond was finally taken, I for one was sorry to have the War come to an end, so great had been my change of view towards the whole affair.

# XVIII

ONE day, big Bill Tweed dropped in on me at my house on Union Square. He had got interested in Erie speckilations some time before, and as I was the head and front of Erie, he used to come to see me in regard to turns in the stock. His old Bowery boys, anyhow, had been in large part butchers' apprentices. I had known the New York butchers since earliest days. So I had been in close touch with Tweed's rank and file for a long time back, even when he was foreman of the "Big Six" Engine Company, and had got into trouble with that other engine company for blocking their way to a fire so his company could get there first. (It had been those butcher boys then which had stood by him and had helped him out of that trouble.) So, when he went into politics, I was glad to get in with him personally, because he was becoming a person of importance in the affairs of the city. It's always an advantage to a big operator in the Street to be on personal terms with political leaders.

Tweed had in turn seen that it stood him in hand to be on intimate terms with me. After he had got out of the chair business, which his father had built up before him down on Pearl Street, he had got into Erie speckilations good and deep. Erie shares had got to be the leading speckilation on the market. For, as head of that road, I had found ways of using its shares in Wall Street whereby I could sometimes make a turn of ten points in Erie inside of a month. A stock that bobs back and forth as suddenly as that, is going to be followed by a great crowd of speckilators. Tweed was one of these. He thought he could make more money speckilating in Erie than he could by making chairs. So he gave up that business, and put all of his money into Wall Street — mostly into Erie.

On the day that I am speaking of, I saw that he was grumpy over these Erie ventures of his. He was as cross as two sticks. I used to take my visitors up into the sitting room on the first floor, facing the Square. (Why, in the plush rocking-chair in that room, Jimmy Fisk sat and talked with me the very morning of the day he was shot.) Well, as soon as Tweed came in and was seated, I saw at once that he was all het up about something or other. He started right in. He said I and my Erie crowd were no better than a crew of blood-suckers; and he swore profanely. He had been brought pretty near to busting up, so he said. And he told of the pile of money he had lost, how it had crippled him up, and such-like.

I let him go on.  It's a good thing to let a loser talk.  I could well believe that what he was saying about his losses in Erie was true.  Because he had been one of the outsiders in that stock.  What's the use of being on the inside if you don't have the advantage over speckilators who are on the outside?  And he had been one of these.  Green wood makes the hottest fire — it's so full of sap.  But I didn't say these things to Tweed.  I was afraid it would only make him madder.  Soft words quench more than a bucket of water.  He was already mad enough, goodness knows.  He pawed around like a horse with the colic — said that the points I had given him on Erie hadn't been worth a hill of beans.  He even said I had fooled him on purpose!

"And a pretty go you've brought me to, Dan Drew," said he.  He sputtered like a tea-kettle when it's boiling over.  Tweed was a big, thick-mouthed fellow; when he got excited he would spit out his words so you could hardly understand him.  "You have gone and drained me dry!  Busted me!  Busted my father, too!  The old man's all broke up over it!  He says I've taken the bread out of his mouth to pour into Wall Street.  I can't go home any more without he curses me up hill and down.  He says he'll throw it in my teeth at Judgment Day for taking the bread out of an old man's mouth. — And the business is gone! — That dad of

mine worked a lifetime to build up that chair
business! And now it's been swept away! And
where's the money gone? I'll tell you where it's
gone! It's gone to build such fine brown-stone
mansions as the one you're living in right at this
minute! And if you don't begin to do something
for me, Drew," said he, "I'm going to get back at
you! Sweet Jesus! Do you think I'm going to
be a sucker and let you hook me like this all the
time? I took the points you've been giving me,
thinking you were on the square. And you've
done me dirt! When you've let me win once, you've
turned around and sucked it all back the very next
day!... And it don't go any longer, Dan. You
fellows in Erie have got to take me in with you.
That's all there is to it. Or I'll make it so hot for
you, you'll wish you'd never been born!"

I let him go on. Big barkers are small biters.
I knew that if be blustered around like that beforehand, he wouldn't do much. It's the still fellows
that I've always been scared of. There's Vanderbilt. One of his mottoes used to be: "Never
tell anybody what you're going to do until you've
done it." When he was going to rip a fellow, he'd
never let that fellow know beforehand. Beware
of quiet dogs and still waters. So I let Tweed have
it out in talk. Anyhow, he wasn't so poor as he
tried to make out. He had a diamond in his shirt-
bosom which looked as big as an engine's head-

light. And he went around town with a coach and a team of horses. I suppose it cost him more to support his kept women, than it would an ordinary householder to take care of a home.

By and by he got over his fury. Then I began to talk. I called him "Bill"! Tweed was a man that had a lot of good in his heart, spite of all that his enemies say against him. I always found I could do more with him by kindness than in any other way. You need smooth wedges to get into a knotty piece of timber.

"Bill," said I, "why don't you get into Congress again? You've got gifts."

"Congress!" said he. "Congress is the pokiest old hole under heaven! Any young squirt can go down to Washington and, if he's got the gift of gab, can cut a figure. But as to money-making, there's nothing down there for a man of talent. I suppose I know more Parliamentary Law than anybody in Congress. But that doesn't make any money for you. I can make more in six months as Street Commissioner of New York, than I could in Congress in a hundred years. All they talk about down there is Fugitive Slave Laws. I'd like to know what in thunder I care about Fugitive Slave Laws! I never was interested in niggers, anyhow. They're no good. I've got a lot of them now, over there in that ward by the river. But they don't stay fixed like my Sixth Warders do. They're all the time flopping to the other side, particularly now that the War has set in. I've got to have money. My expenses are heavy. I can't live like one of your goody-goods. And if you big wigs don't take me in with you, you'll wish you had."

I turned on him sort of cool-like. "Bill," said I, "how would you like to go in with a street railway deal? You are a Commissioner of Streets for the city. I guess you have a lot to do also with the Common Council, don't you?"

"I should say I had," said he. "I've got a ring in the nose of every mother's son of them."

"Well," said I, "have you been following that application of some New York parties up at Albany to get a franchise to lay a pair of steel rails down Broadway?"

"Yes," he replied; "a little."

"Has it occurred to you that those fellows in the Legislature — the Assemblymen and Senators — would turn a pretty penny, if they were allowed to dispose of the Broadway franchise?"

"Of course, they would," said Tweed. "I'd like to know what earthly right they have to meddle with New York City affairs. This is our hunting ground. They had better keep off."

"Just what I was thinking of," said I. "And they tell me that Vanderbilt is starting in to head that Albany proposition off on his own account; because, in the charter of his Harlem Railroad, there is a clause permitting him to extend his tracks down Broadway, whenever the Mayor and Aldermen of New York City give their consent."

Tweed began to prick up his ears. He was a quick fellow to arrive at your meaning. He had a shrewd headpiece. It's true that women could lead him around by the nose. (The same with Richard Connolley — "Slippery Dick," we used to call him. That woman of his whom he picked up from the Turkish Bath where she had been an attendant, used to play him all kinds of tricks, and he wasn't any the wiser. If it had been a man, Dick would have seen through him at once.) But in other ways Tweed was very knowing. He now listened close.

I then went on to show how we could work the Common Council in such a way as to squeeze Vanderbilt in his Harlem-Broadway enterprise, and make a neat little sum out of it.

We became friends again, whereas it had looked pretty· squally half an hour before. Tweed was a gunpowder fellow. He got mad quick and got over it quick. Now that I had promised to help him get back by this Harlem-Railroad deal some of the money he had lost, he was willing to be on good terms again with me.

## XIX

THE Harlem Railroad was the offspring of the stage-coach that used to run by my "Bull's Head" tavern. That stage line was from Park Row, New York City, up to Harlem Village, above where 110th Street now is. As the people moved out from New York and settled up in that section, Harlem grew to be a good-sized town. When railroads were at last seen to be practicable things, a line of rails was laid from that village down to New York, and was called the Harlem Railroad — because it went to Harlem Village. The rails were not laid along the Old Boston Road. It would have scared the horses. Anyhow, the stage-coach people didn't like the new-fangled steam buggies any too much, and never would have allowed their post-roads to be encroached upon in that fashion. So the rails were laid a little to the west of the Boston Road, where Fourth Avenue now runs.

The Harlem railroad first along wasn't much thought of. Its stock just before the War sold as low as eight dollars a share. But, instead of allowing it to stop with Harlem Village, they now began to run it up through the Harlem Valley, where I used to drive my critters down from Putnam County to the city. By and by it got clean up to Brewsters'. Vanderbilt about this time had a lot of loose money, and began to invest in the stock of this railroad. His friends laughed at him. They thought the shares were hardly worth the paper they were printed on — said the road would go up the spout soon or late. But he kept at it, and by and by owned a big block of stock. I got in, too, and soon owned considerable of it.

The depot was down on Fourth Avenue at Twenty-sixth Street. The trains didn't run all the way down there. It was thought that engines were not fitted for climbing hills. So four horses used to take each car out from the station and draw it through the streets up to Forty-third Street. There the cars were made up into a train and hitched onto an engine which took them flying out to Brewsters'. By and by Vanderbilt got rid of that bothersome Murray Hill which stood square in the middle of his car line, by digging a tunnel right through the bowels of it.

This tunnel made the Commodore very proud of himself. A good many people had said, when he had begun the tunnel, that it was too big a job — that he couldn't go through with it. But he had done it — had widened Fourth Avenue forty feet in order to make room — and now was so vainglorious that he planned a still bigger scheme. He would take that street-railway end of his Harlem Railroad and continue it down from Twenty-sixth Street to Fourteenth, there turn the corner over into Broadway, and then run it all the way to the Battery. By this time Broadway had become a much-travelled thoroughfare. A street-car line through it would be a money-maker. Here is where, by means of taking the Common Council into our partnership, Tweed and I got in our scheme.

I set to work. I bought some more of the Harlem stock. (The price had got away beyond that eight-dollar figure.) Then, when I and the rest of us who were on the deal had got pretty well loaded up with Harlem, we got the Common Council to pass an ordinance permitting Vanderbilt to go ahead and lay his rails down Broadway. The Mayor signed it. Instantly, the stock went soaring. The Legislature up at Albany were mad as hornets. They saw all  the good fat pickings going to the Aldermen and Councilmen of New York City, rather than to themselves. But they couldn't do anything; because there was the clause in Vanderbilt's old Harlem Charter, permitting such a thing to be done whenever the New York City authorities gave their consent. The "Chancellorsville Rise" came along just at this moment and also helped. Hooker, with what he called "the finest army on the planet," had for months been watching

the rebels. At last he had crossed the Rappahannock and advanced against the enemy. We in
Wall Street began to hold our breath for fear lest
he'd end the war then and there, and our period
of prosperity come to an end. But he retreated
and now was on this side the Rappahannock once
more. It was a great relief. Stocks rose all along
the line. For we saw now that we'd have a longer
spell of war-time speckilation. Harlem went up
along with the other stocks.

With Harlem's stock up at a high figure, and
continually soaring higher, I saw what seemed
the favourable moment to make our move. So
we began to sell the stock short. In order to start
a Bear campaign, you must first balloon the stock
sky-high. Because when you are a Bear you sell
when the stock is high, and deliver when the stock
is low (that is, if the deal turns out right). Your
profit is the difference between those two figures —
the greater the difference, the greater your profit.
Besides, it is usually easier to put out a line of shorts
when the market is high. Through some kink or
other in human nature, the ordinary run of people
are bullish and hopeful towards a stock when it's
high. The stock has gone up so finely, they suppose
it's going to keep on going up, and you usually find
them ready buyers of your short sales.

This was true in the present case. The stock
never looked to have better prospects than it did

just now. The Harlem Railroad was already earning money, because it went through the rich Harlem Valley. And now, with the Broadway franchise added, the road was bound to roll up big dividends for everybody who owned anything in it. So, at least, most of the people figured. Thus, when our Bear crowd began to sell the stock short, people snapped at our offers of the stock like a pike bites at a shiner.

Then we told the Aldermen and Councilmen that the time had come to touch off the fireworks. So they met. Tweed was a master hand, anyhow, in manipulating a legislative body. He could make them do 'most anything he wanted. He was a big, overgrown chap, full of spirits, and could boss men around like sheep or cattle. The Board and Common Council took our orders. They passed an ordinance reconsidering their former decision as to the Broadway franchise. Then they rescinded the grant.

Harlem dropped like a shot partridge. Vanderbilt and his crowd thought, when the Aldermen had finally been brought to pass the measure, that the franchise was then as good as gold. He didn't realize that there were some of us who had inside power with the City Fathers and could turn a trick or two. Vanderbilt, who believed in getting a thing done and then let them howl, was starting to dig up the street and lay his rails. We got an injunction from the Court of Common Pleas prohibiting the laying of the track. We thought now that the stock, which had been at seventy-five, would drop to fifty. But something happened. The court dissolved our injunction. Vanderbilt sustained the market. And, do the best we could, the price refused to sag below seventy-three. The city politicians were for the most part men of small means. Their margins were soon exhausted. They were sold out. I had been a heavy owner of Harlem in my own right, so I myself got out of the hole in fairly good shape.

Then the battle-field shifted to Albany. A favourable report was purposely given out from the Legislature as to the prospects for a Broadway franchise for the Harlem Railroad. Harlem jumped from seventy-five to one hundred and fifty. Knowing something of what was to happen behind the scenes, I, in the face of all these appearances, went and committed myself heavily to the short side. Because this favourable report which had been sent out was only a blind; as soon as the stock, in obedience to it, jumped up, the legislators at Albany sold the stock short, for a decline. Then they out with their trick — they turned and defeated Vanderbilt's bill. In two days the price fell fifty points. But just as I was beginning to count my profits, the ticker began to tell another story — the stock turned. It went up to 127; to 140; to 150; yes, to 185. I saw at once that our boat, which had been sailing so prosperous, had struck some kind of a snag. And the nature of it wasn't very long coming to light — we had sold short 27,000 more shares of stock than there were in the whole capital of the road. We were in a corner. Our efforts to wiggle out only raised the price of the stock still higher. It touched 285. Even at that figure we couldn't buy any. Vanderbilt had us tight.

It was a case of compromise. When delivery time came, I went up to see him. He had his office on Fourth Street. We had a long talk together. I said there was no use beating around the bush — I was cornered — I couldn't make my deliveries — I might as well own up first as last. I told him that in this particular deal he had been too smart for me. We had oversold the market. I wanted to make terms. I told him that I looked to lose some money in the affair, and asked him to make it as small as he could. I showed him that customers are like fiddle-strings — you mustn't screw them too tight. Anyhow, he was in a position to let me off scot free, if he felt so inclined. Because he was squeezing loads of profit out of the other fellows in my crowd, and so could afford to let me go free. I reminded him how he and I had been old friends; in fact, I had named my boy "William Henry," after his boy.

But Vanderbilt didn't soften. "Drew," said he,

"this isn't a game of croquet that we are playing. It's man's business, this thing we call Wall Street. And it isn't going to do you any good to chat about old steamboat days. You tried to corner me, and you've got your fingers caught while you were setting the trap. If Harlem had dropped to 75, instead of rising to 285, would you have helped stand my loss? You are cornered tight, and now you've got to pay up. Turn over to me all of your personal property — I'll let you keep your real estate — and we'll call the thing settled."

I saw then that I was in for it. But I kept up a bold countenance. I said: "All right, Cornelius Vanderbilt. If you are so hard-hearted as to forget a friend, I won't speak of that any more. But I want you to understand that you haven't got your money yet. My contract with you merely reads that you can *call* upon me for so many thousand shares of Harlem stock. It doesn't say anything about my *delivering* the stock to you. *Call* all you wish. If you want to wrestle this thing out in the courts, we'll wrestle it." I thought maybe that threat of litigation would scare him. But it didn't.

"After this, never sell what you haven't got, Dannie; never sell what you haven't got," was all the answer he made. "Don't put it in any man's power to ruin you. By-bye."

I left him. But the truth is, in that threat I'd made, I had appeared braver than I really was. I thought for a spell of laying down on my contracts and telling Vanderbilt right to his face that I didn't care how much paper of mine he held, he couldn't collect it and that's all there was to it. But the trouble is, that would have given me a black eye on the Street. Wall Street conducts its deals on a "Pay-up" principle — when you've made a contract, keep it. They don't look with favour on any one who tries to squirm out. The Stock Exchange Board jacks you up good and quick if you don't live up to your word. I didn't want to hurt my future in the Street. As to the law courts, they also didn't offer me much help; because they hold that the paper you have given to the other fellow makes a legal contract, which you must live up to.

So there I was. I thought of turning to Tweed. He controlled many of the judges, and I might get off in that way. But just now I wasn't in very thick with Tweed. This whole affair of the Harlem corner hadn't helped him hardly any more than it had me. We had started out to squeeze Vanderbilt; and, unfortunately, we had got squeezed ourselves. So that Tweed just now was in a bad humour. Besides, his pride had suffered a fall. At Henry Clay's funeral, Tweed's oration in the Board of Aldermen, a kind of a funeral sermon over the life and death of Clay, was something he had taken a great pride in. It was the first public speech he had ever made. And, as it now turned out, it was his last. From becoming a great statesman and a moulder of public opinion, Tweed, because of this Harlem affair, had suddenly taken a fall. For when he and his Aldermen passed Vanderbilt's Broadway franchise measure, it had been in violation of Judge Duer's injunction, and Duer got so mad that he up and put the whole Board of City Fathers, Tweed along with the rest, in jail. Tweed was terribly worked up over it. He saw that he couldn't be a statesman and a leader of public opinion, after such a mishap as that; and he got almighty sore about it. To mention Harlem to him now was like a red rag to a bull. He sputtered and swore so profanely, when I'd try to talk with him about it, that I saw it wasn't much use.

Nevertheless, I used it as an argument with Vanderbilt. Going to the Commodore again, I told him that I had come to make a settlement if he was in the mood for it. I hinted that I had more or less of an inside track with the law courts of New York City, since I knew some of the politicians pretty close; and that if he wanted to fight it out to a finish, I could make a peck of trouble for him. He knew that I was more or less in with Tweed, the Street Commissioner of New York City, and his crowd, and Vanderbilt's future plans had a whole lot to do with the use of New York City streets. We came to a settlement. Vanderbilt had a lot of enterprises under way, and didn't want to get into litigation if he could help it — he said he didn't have time to bother. So we hit upon a figure at which I could settle my contracts. I wrote my check, and the thing was finished. It cost me well-nigh half a million. But I was glad to get out even at that figure. Because it left me something, and for a time it looked as though I might be stripped of all my goods. When you're cornered in selling shares short, you are in a terrible fix. The fellow who has cornered you, if he is so minded, can take every last cent you've got. Because, as I have put it in the form of a poem (I'm not much of a rhymer, but I suppose I could have turned my hand to verse-making if I had set my mind to it):

> "He that sells what isn't his'n,
> Must buy it back, or go to prison."

This Harlem corner did me more hurt than just the loss of the money. To hand over a half-million in cold cash did me lots of damage. And I couldn't blame it on anybody else, either. I felt like a cow that had stuck herself. Besides, it hurt me in the Street. They snickered at me now when I was coming to my office, or going home at night — would nudge each other when they saw me passing, and whisper: "He went short of Harlem." In fact, that got to be a saying on the Street, to mean any kind of a hard-luck blow.

The poor legislators at Albany also were hard hit by the corner.   Some of them had to leave Albany at the end of the session without paying their board-bill.   As for me, I spit on my hands and took a new holt.

## XX

THE Harlem loss made a big hole in my heart. And some might suppose that I was so in the dumps by it that I became sour and backslided from religion. But they would be mistaken. I know there are people who serve God only so long as they are prosperous. When an unlucky stroke falls, they curse religion. But I don't. It doesn't do any good. Spit against Heaven, and it will fall back into your own face. Besides, the Lord doesn't guarantee to make a man prosperous in each and every undertaking. It isn't all butter that comes from the cow; only a part is worked up into butter; and in some churnings the butter won't come at all, no matter how hard you work the splasher.

Besides, I have found that religion is often most needed just in the times when you are in the dumps.

"From every stormy wind that blows,
From every swelling tide of woes,
There is a calm, a sure retreat;
'Tis found beneath the mercy seat."

More than that, I had by this time invested a

whole lot of money in my church, and couldn't afford to lose it. The trustees of the old Mulberry Street Meeting House, when they saw the people moving up town, wanted to move the church up also, and be in the heart of the residential district. I helped this plan along. It wasn't fit, now that I had become one of the money kings, that I should worship in a dingy building down on Mulberry Street. I told the trustees I would help them build a new meeting house. They jumped at the offer. That big marble structure on Fourth Avenue, at the corner of Twenty-second Street, is the result.

We had big doings when the new church was finally dedicated. It happened, I remember, on a Sunday morning in early May. Dr. Durbin preached the sermon. His text was: "Behold the Lamb of God, which taketh away the sins of the world." Dr. Durbin was a master hand at theological exposition. He knew as much about the fine points of doctrine as 'most any man I ever met. He was learned in the Scriptures. He was an advocate of free grace, and could argue for hours, for he was a man of strong convictions. He felt the importance of right theological thinking. In fact, he never seemed so happy as when he was upholding the true Faith and attacking dangerous forms of doctrine. He was a positive man; so much so that in matters of theology he and I didn't always agree. But I had to admire his courage. The Prophets of the

Old Testament times, I suppose, were not always loved by everybody. Prophets often have to speak plain truth and hurt people's feelings. So, when Dr. Durbin's ideas didn't just jibe with mine — say, in the matter of Justification and Holiness, concerning which we had some little difference of belief, for I have always held that the witness of our conversion carries with it justifying grace and will of itself, in time, sanctify every unhallowed affection — I didn't hold it against him; he meant all right, anyhow.

On the present occasion, however, his views agreed with mine to a T. There haven't been many discourses from the sacred desk that have done me more good than this one. For he outlined the plan of salvation. He showed how wonderfully we, the converted, had been delivered from our lost and fallen estate. In picturing the sin-sick soul, he didn't use any lady-words. It was a soul, he said, that had no light, either above or round about; and in that state, said he, all of us who were there in that congregation had at some time or other been. God's wrath had burned against us while we were in that state of rebellion, so that Justice, in its righteous anger, had come near to sink us into Hell. But Free mercy performed the great transaction, and had plunged us into the crystal stream. The blood of sprinkling, which speaketh better things than the blood of Abel, had availed to cancel all our

iniquities.  Justification  by  faith  alone — how
the speaker brought out the wondrous comfort in
those words! — sealed the vow.  Pardoning mercy
ratified the convenant; and now, said he, our ransom
has been paid.

> "Salvation, oh, the joyful sound!
> What pleasure to our ears!
> A sovereign balm for every wound,
> A charm for all our fears."

Our High Priest, in his all-engaging charms, has
expiated our sins.  We are under the blood.

When he got to his main point, of how we are
freely justified by grace through faith, the great
congregation became roused.  "Hallelujahs" began
to be heard here and there.  I could well see why
they were so moved; because the preacher was not
only showing great intellectual power in this dis-
course of his; he was full of emotion as well, and
there was a light beaming from his eyes.  Once or
twice he got the unction; and then the words wouldn't
come fast enough.  Our own righteousness, he went
on to say, is but as filthy rags.  Faith in the all-
cleansing fountain, that is to be our crown of glory
and alone our sign and seal of salvation.  And so,
we, clothed in imputed righteousness as in a wedding
garment, are summoned to the marriage supper of
the Lamb.  And, being thus clothed, we dread now
no condemnation.  Our surety is on high.  The

blood that has been so freely shed has paid the debt — all the debt I owe. So that, with unfeigned sincerity, we rest in our glorious advocate. Filled with his righteousness, the sin-convincing spirit now passes by our door, as it did the Israelites in Egypt of old. For it sees the mark of the blood on the lintels, and visits its doom now only on the homes of the unregenerate. The pearly gates swing wide. Glory to the Lamb!

When the preacher was through, the hymn that followed was sung in a way to show that the earnest words of the speaker had not been spoken in vain. There was a volume to it and a glory that doesn't come as a tribute to mere human efforts.

When it was all over, and the benediction had been pronounced, I waited for Dr. Durbin to come down to me. Since it had been my money which had really made this large and beautiful meeting house possible, this dedication service was one in which I naturally felt a personal interest — yes, even a responsibility. I was, therefore, not only pleased but greatly relieved that the service had gone off so prosperous. Now at the close I didn't use many words in expressing my sentiments to the preacher. Sometimes the greatest feeling is put into the fewest words. I took him by the hand, pressed it warmly, and looking him in the eye, said: "Brother Durbin, I thank you for that sermon."

The many peaceful and soothing hours I have spent in this church since that opening day, have repaid me all the money I gave to it.  To be sure, they didn't call the church after my name; but city churches don't often do that.  Up in Carmel they did.  And I don't know a finer kind of a monument for a man than to have his name engraved on the front of some fine church.  Any one who goes up to that town to-day will see it — carved in solid stone, right over the doorway: "Daniel Drew Church."  Some of the people in Carmel have got to calling it the "St. Daniel Drew Church."  But I always regarded that as more of a nick-name than anything else.  It's a caution, anyhow, the way that the younger generation in this here land of ours, gives nick-names to things.  They don't seem to have reverence, the way that young people used to have in my day.

Then again, there is the Ladies' Seminary of mine, in Carmel.  Raymond, the circus man in that village, named it first after himself.  It looked for a time as though he would plant his family name into the life of the town deeper than my own could be planted.  Every man wants his family name to be remembered, at least in his native town.  You can stick up a gravestone, with your name carved on it.  But that's a dead thing.  But put the money into some institution — that will go on living year after year; you have hitched yourself now to something that's alive. The monument would have let your name remain unspoken, for marble is dumb. But institutions last from generation to generation, and speak out your name constantly. It is worth a man's while to build two or three of them during his lifetime, even though they are pretty costly at the time. Therefore, I was glad when the way opened for me to take Raymond's school and make it into "Drew Ladies' Seminary." About the only thing Raymond has got up in Carmel now is "Raymond Hill," where there's a burying ground. A burying ground is a dead thing, but seminaries are living things. Over at Brewsters', also, they were building their church. I gave to it $7,000. In this case they didn't put my name on the church. In fact, the church doesn't bear the name of any person at all. But the people around there all know that if it hadn't been for me giving a plumb half of the cost, the church might never have been built. Perhaps they will put a memorial window in, after I am gone.

But I don't boast. My gifts to religion and such like are not altogether gifts. They are a sort of an investment. I have always held that what you give to the Lord comes back to you. God has a long memory. For a time he may not seem to have noticed your gift, and you think most likely he has forgot all about it. But he hasn't. Such things never slip his mind. Soon or late, he will even it up with you.  God keeps a full set of books.  He always balances his accounts.  I trust his book-keeping.  Sometimes I have given money to him and have let the affair slip from my mind altogether; because I knew that he had put it all down on the right side of his ledger and would take care of the account.

I calculate there are lots of business men who don't prosper, because they don't give to the Lord a slice of their profits.  They try to hog it all.  When he sees that sort of thing going on, he contrives to put a spoke in their wheel.  They may think he doesn't know what they are doing, but he does.  God wears gum shoes when he comes down here upon earth to spy.  He doesn't let anybody know he's coming, least of all the man whom he's to spy out.  These men are like Ananias and Sapphira.  They think they can fool the Lord as to how much money they have, and so cut him down on his share.  But he isn't fooled.  To give a percentage to the Lord is just as good business policy as to pay the taxes on your house and lot.  In either case, if you don't  pay  up  good  and  prompt  you'll  sweat for it.

I haven't had to get out and look up all of the money-making things I have gone into.  Some-times they have come knocking at my door, as though they had been mysteriously sent.  And often these have been the very ones that have turned out most profitable. There's that affair with the man Parker, from the West— "California Parker," they called him, because he came from the Pacific Coast. I made a fine penny out of the dicker I had with him. But it wasn't altogether my own doings. I didn't look him up. It was as though I sat in my office and he came and made me a present of his money. I guess it was his father who had accumulated the fortune; and now the son had got it and had come to New York City, to swell it bigger, as he thought. A fat calf makes the sweetest veal. Seeing he was anxious, I took him into a pool which I was carrying on just then for the purpose of Bulling Erie shares. Parker came to me.

"Mr. Drew," said he, "I'm willing to take charge of this, if you say so. You have so many irons in the fire, you ought to be glad to have a partner help you out with one of them. I am willing to take this particular stock campaign off from your shoulders. But I will probably need your help before I get through. I think I can boost the stock a number of points. But in order to get it to the notch where it will stick and take care of itself, I will need more funds than I individually have. Therefore, at the right time, will you help me out?"

I said of course I would; I'd see him through. And at the time I meant it. Because I owned a large block of Erie shares just then, and was only too pleased to have some one boost them for me.

He thanked me and went away, saying that he would get to work at once.

I soon saw that he was carrying out the plan with energy. A flood of buying orders poured into the market. Erie rose point by point. I was glad. Each point of rise meant a dollar more in my pocket for every share I held.

By and by, however, I became less Bullish than I had been. Parker's buying now had boosted it from 100 clean up to 123. I thought it a good time to get rid of my holdings. It never does to overstay a market. Wait one day too long, and you will sometimes miss it altogether. In Wall Street the secret of success is to know when the iron is hot and then strike. Parker, when he entered into this dicker with me, had almost three hundred thousand dollars. So I issued an order to my broker (unbeknownst to anybody) to sell.

I didn't dump the shares onto Parker all at once. That wouldn't have been good policy. With too big an amount to take care of all of a sudden, he'd have become discouraged. So I fed the stock out to him by driblets, so to speak — didn't want to destroy his absorbing power. I offered it only in thousand lots, and even in lots of five hundred shares each.

I was glad to see that he took them; and this, too, without suspecting anything. The blocks being so small, he like as not thought they were coming from scattered parties throughout the country, here one and there one. Towards the end, however, in order to get rid of all my holdings whilst the price was at the top-notch and before the market broke, I dumped rather heavy blocks of it onto him. At one time I was scared. I feared I had overdone the thing. Because the price sagged like old Sambo. It looked as though I had unloaded onto Parker a jag of the stock that was too heavy for him. But he must have got under the load like a plucky fellow; for the stock was taken, and still the price held up fine.

He came in to see me soon after. He was pretty well het up by this work of supporting the market. He wiped the sweat from his forehead as he sat down in my inner office. When I saw him come in I was anxious first along. I feared he had discovered who it was that had been feeding all of that stock to him. But I was quickly put at ease. He was still friendly towards me. I saw that he was not of a suspicious turn of mind.

"Well, Uncle," said he, as he sat down (everybody called me Uncle); "I've been pounded pretty hard the last day or two, as you probably have seen from the tape. But I didn't let them break my lines. Once or twice they had me pretty near bushed. But I pulled myself together each time. And I think I have held my own."

"Why, what is it?" said I. "I haven't followed

Erie stock for the last few days as close as I do sometimes. I've been busy with other matters. Anything special turned up?"

"Why, no," said he; "that is, nothing disastrous; because I was able to take care of it. But some good-sized blocks of Erie have been coming onto the market the last two days. In fact, the market developed softness several days ago. At that time a whole lot of small offerings came in, brought out, I supposed, by the tempting prices at which the stock now stands. These lots didn't trouble me much. But the blocks which have been coming in the last two days have given me lots of bother. I took care of them. But it has cost me a pretty penny. I saw that it wouldn't do to fall down now, when we must have absorbed pretty near the whole floating supply of the stock, and have got the thing pretty near where we want it. I have accepted every share that was offered. But it has drained me dry to do it. I find I will have to call on you for that help which you promised. I was hoping at one time that I wouldn't need to. But I now see that I will, and have come to ask for it."

I had expected this call from Parker. I had been sort of dreading it. I knew he would be miffed when I told him what I would have to tell. I never did like a scene. In fact, I didn't know but what he might even get mad and try to do something rash.

"I'm sorry, my son," said I, when he had finished

his speech. "But I don't know as I can let you have that money, after all."

He looked up at me with a start, like a colt when it's suddenly frightened. I was glad that I had a clerk just outside the door of my private office, within easy reach if I should need him; because you never can tell what these Westerners will do when they get excited.

"What's that?" said he. "I don't believe I understood you."

"Why, it's just as I said," I replied. "I find that I'm not able to let you have that money." I saw that it was best to have the thing over quickly. Bad news to a man is like pulling a tooth. If you fool around with the forceps sort of tender-like, it will make it all the harder. The kindest course is to be stern-hearted just for a minute; yank the tooth out, then it's all over. That's what I did now. I handled him without mittens. I plumped the announcement out at him in straightforward fashion: "Couldn't possibly do it. My money is tied up just now tight as a fiddle-string."

"But," said he, and his voice got very low and quiet, "Mr. Drew, you promised."

"Tut, tut," said I; "just a mere word thrown out in casual talk. I didn't intend it to be in the nature of a hard and fast agreement. There wasn't anything put down in writing."

"I know that," said he; "but between men, a

gentlemen's agreement is even more binding than documents plastered over with seals and a notary's stamp."

"Well," said I, "you'll have to excuse me from going into a discussion of the matter with you. I haven't the time just now. I have some important business on hand that I've got to see to." And I arose, to bring the interview to an end — I never believe in handling a nettle tenderly. I didn't want to get into an argument with him. Didn't know what he might do if he got worked up. Hot-headed fellows sometimes get very sudden if they are het up by an argument. "I'm sorry, my son, if you are disappointed. It's unavoidable. I can't help you with any money. I shall have to bid you good morning."

He bit his lip. His face turned white all of a sudden. "Of course, Mr. Drew," said he, "you'll give me a chance to say this: That I am by this act of yours a ruined man! The earnings of a lifetime have been swept away! Unless you keep your promise, I and my family are at this moment reduced to beggary! Do I understand that your answer is final?"

"It's final," said I; "if you've lost any money, go and begin earning it back. Every time a sheep bleats it loses a mouthful." (This hope I held out to him was of course a rather small plaster for a big sore. But it was the best I could do.)

I started at once to the door to let him out. I could see that he was bothered considerable. For he sort of staggered as he walked across the floor. And his eyes glazed over, something like a steer just after he has been hit. He didn't say good-bye. He stumbled out through the office door and went away.

I was glad when the interview was over. I knew that I'd have to go through it; and now was relieved. Parker took it in a different way from what I had looked for. Instead of flaring up, he took it so quiet-like that I kind of felt sorry for him. But I wasn't in Wall Street for my health. If he thought I was going to lose money in order to help him, he had come to the wrong shop, that's all. Business is business. When I had told him some days before that I'd help him out with the money, I was in a different position from what I now was. For I had now disposed of most of my Erie stock. So that I'd have been a fool to loan Parker any money to keep the price of the stock up. When I have sold out my shares it isn't to my interest to keep the price up. It's to my interest then to have the price of that particular stock tumble just as fast and as far as it will. Because I can then buy it in once more.

And that is what happened in the present case. It wasn't an hour or two after Parker left my office, before Erie fell off several points. For Parker having now been taken out of the way (I guess the Street hasn't seen hide nor hair of him since), was no longer there to support the market. The price fell rapidly. The slump was also helped by Secretary Chase, who came into Wall Street just now and borrowed $35,000,000 for the Government. Erie dropped to ninety-nine. Thus I was able to buy back dog-cheap the shares I'd sold at the top of the market. I took a slice out of Parker on this deal which helped my fortune considerable.

## XXI

ONE day, about this time, I was in my office at 22 William Street, when the boy came in and said there was a man in the outer office by the name of Fisk. "He wants to see you on a business matter."

"Send him in," said I. I said it to the boy sort of careless-like, not expecting anything much. It was a name that didn't mean anything to me. Thought it was some stranger coming to see me on a small affair or other. I turned to the stock ticker once more, and to reading the quotations. The door opened. A man came in.

"I'm Fisk," said he. He stepped up and took my hand. He was as brisk as a bottle of ale. "James Fisk, Junior, of New York and Boston. 'Jim Fisk,' the boys call me, where I'm known. But I suppose here I'll have to put on all the lugs. Mr. Drew, I have come to sell those Stonington shares of yours."

I got my hand loose from his, and sat down. I got my breath after a minute. Not that I was mad. Somehow or other, you couldn't get mad at the fellow — he had such a hearty way about him. And he was so almighty sure of himself, he made every-

body else sure of him, too.  He was a big man,
heavy-set, with blond hair, and a moustache the
colour of a Jersey cow.  He wore a velvet vest, cut
low, so as to show well-nigh half of his shirt-bosom.
His hands were fat, and had rings all over them.
I could see he was a fellow to scrape up an acquaintance on short notice.

"And may I ask who is this Mr. James Fisk,
Junior?" I managed to inquire, after I had got my
breath again.  (I always did have a knack of being
very cold and dignified when I wanted to.)

"Of course, you can ask," said he.  "I'll give
you the whole pedigree, if you want it.  I'm from
Vermont — one of your Green Mountain boys.  I
was a peddler up there.  Got to be the Prince of
Peddlers.  That's what they called me.  My father
was a peddler before me.  Everybody around Bennington knows my father.  But they know me a
mighty sight better.  I put my father in the shade
before I'd been a peddler six months.  I'm one of the
go-ahead sort.  Never was cut out to be a moss-
gatherer.  It's push with me — all the time.  And
if you want to entrust me with the sale of this railroad stock of yours, I'll prove it to you.  Up there
in Vermont I had hardly started out before I had
a peddler's wagon with four horses.  'Jobber in
silks, shawls, dress goods, jewelry, silver-ware and
Yankee notions' — that's the way my sign read.
To see me come into a town, you'd have thought the

circus had arrived. In fact, I got the idea from a circus I used to travel with, Van Amberg's — that was before I became a peddler."

"What?" said I; "did you use to travel with Van Amberg's Menagerie?"

"Well, I guess. I got to be assistant doorkeeper in that shebang. Ever hear of it?"

"Ever hear of it?" said I. "Why, old Ike Van Amberg started that show of his from my part of the country, up in Putnam County. I know something about the menagerie business myself."

"Is that so?" said he. "Shake again, pardner! I didn't know when I came in here that I was getting among my own kith and kin."

"Why, yes," said I; "I was in the circus business before you was born. Came near being in it yet, for that matter."

"I want to know!" said he. "Say, did you have the wild mule, same's they do now, for the farmer boys to ride 'once around the ring for five dollars'?"

"No," said I. "We nadn't thought of that back in my time."

"Then you don't know what fun it is," said he. "Lord, it used to split my sides with laughing! In our show we had a mule picked up somewhere in our travels. Picked him up for a song, for that matter. He was so wild, the farmer we bought him of couldn't do anything with him. But we broke him. That is, we broke him enough for one of the clowns to ride, provided he backed him in the right way, and sat just right all the time. But as for anybody else — might as well have tried to ride a cyclone. At every performance we would take that mule, lead him into the centre of the ring, and then — 'Whoa there, January! Offer five dollars to any person in the audience who will step down and ride this mule once around the track!' You'd have hurt yourself laughing, to see the country clodhoppers try to earn that five. Sometimes, if the farm hand was uncommonly clever, he would manage to get on top of the beast and actually ride a few paces. Then the fireworks would begin. The show has got the five dollars yet —— So you worked under canvas, too?"

"No, not exactly under canvas," said I. "Truth is, back in the early days, the menagerie didn't have any tent. All they had was a lot of six-foot poles which they stuck up in the ground, and stretched canvas around them, leaving the top unroofed." And I went on to tell of circus life back in my day.

This sort of broke the ice. We got talking about old menagerie days. Before I knew it we were good friends. Fisk told me that after he'd got into the peddler business, he pushed it so hard that before long he had several wagons out. They would all meet in a town, pitch their camp and have half the population around them inside of an hour. In fact, he did so well, bought dry goods in such quantities, that the house in Boston which supplied him, Jordan, Marsh & Co., began to notice him, and before long gave him a job as travelling salesman. No sooner had he moved to Boston than he got acquainted with a woman there, who was influential with some of the Massachusetts politicians in Washington (Jimmy always did have a way of getting around women). The house he worked for had a lot of blankets they couldn't get rid of. Fisk said he would do the trick. So he got this woman to give him letters of introduction to one or two big men from Massachusetts in Washington. He went down there — it was just when the War was getting under way — kept open house for a few days, got some Congressmen in with him, and sold the whole batch of blankets to the United States Government at a high figure. He persuaded Uncle Sam that they were just the thing for the soldier boys.

Fisk, also, it seems, made some money on the side while he was in Washington, smuggling cotton through the Union lines. The blockade on the Southern ports had by this time got so tight that cotton was bringing war prices. "Nothing like knowing an opportunity when you see it," said Fisk, in telling me this part of his life. "There down South was cotton stacked up in great piles — perfectly useless and waiting for a chance to get to market. On the other side was the North, hungry for cotton. Says I to myself: 'Jim Fisk, Junior, you

are to be the middle-man between these two needs.'
So I set to work.   I got the cotton through."

"How did you do it?" said I.

"I'm not telling," said he; "but I got it through.
This war is a great thing for business, anyway,"
said he; "don't you think so?"

I said that depended.

"Of course," said he; "I mean for business of the
right kind.  You stock-market riggers here are bag-
ging money hand over fist.  If the War lasts long
enough, you won't have vaults big enough to store
away your coin.  I always did think, anyhow, that
John Brown was a bully fellow, for starting this war.
Tell you what, Drew, those soldier boys in blue are
our best friends.  'Tramp, tramp, tramp, the boys
are marching,' and you Wall Streeters rake in the
shekels."

I answered that I thought Uncle Sam's soldier
boys were indeed earning their wages.  And although
it would cost an almighty big sum in taxes to pay the
bills when the War was over, still, take it all in all,
perhaps it was money well spent.  For it certainly
was making good times in Wall Street.

Well, Fisk's success in selling the blankets to
Uncle Sam gave him a handle over Jordan, Marsh
& Co.  He went back to them while the sale was
still hanging fire, and said: "I've got the contract.
Now I want you to take me into the firm."

They didn't appear very anxious.  But Fisk said

he had some of the contracts signed in his own name, and unless they took him in, they couldn't have the orders. So they had to give in. He became one of the "Co." of the firm.

"But," continued Fisk, "our partnership didn't just turn out very scrumptious. Those Boston merchants are so all-fired respectable. They are too conservative. They think the good name of the house with smaller profits is worth more than a smaller name with bigger profits. We didn't hit it off well together, and the upshot was, they very soon asked me to leave. I did — for a remuneration. They paid me sixty thousand dollars to get out. I started in the dry-goods business myself, at the corner of Summer and Chauncey Streets, Boston. But it didn't go. Came to New York with what money I had left. I started in as a Wall Street operator. Result, lost every cent I had. This was a year ago. Had a silver watch — nary another thing. I was as flat as a nigger's nose. Am yet, for that matter. But I'm going to be a rich man yet. They can't keep me down. And I have come to you, Uncle, with this Stonington proposition. It will help make you richer, and it'll bring something to Jim Fisk, too."

I asked him how he proposed to go about the deal.

"I'll tell you," said he. "I learned that there is a Boston crowd that would like to buy out your interest in the Stonington Railroad. I have found out who they are. Give me the business. Let me handle it for you. I'll go down there and sell one or all of your shares of that road, in a way that will make your eyes open."

We talked it over this way and that. The visit ended by my naming a figure at which I'd let the stock go. He went out. In a few days back he came — had the papers all made out, bill of sale, contracts, blank receipts — everything. I turned over the stock to his Boston people. They paid the money. I got the cash. Fisk made a nice little amount as his commission.

This is the way Fisk and I got acquainted. He handled this sale of Stonington stock so knowing, I saw he was a gumptious fellow. I said to him that if he wanted to start in again as a stock broker, I'd help him along — would turn a good share of my business in his direction. He jumped at it. So the firm of Fisk and Belden was formed. Belden was the partner that I put in with Fisk, in order to accommodate his father, Henry Belden, an old friend of mine. Brother Belden's preaching and testimonies at the camp-meeting grounds outside the village of Sing Sing were, before he got the paralytic stroke, full of power and of the witness of the spirit. He was a camp-meeting shouter, old Brother Henry. To hear his "Glory Hallelujahs" in a love feast would have done your heart good. When I can do a good turn to a man such as that, I feel like doing it. So I gave his son, young Belden, a chance.

Very soon I was using this firm of Fisk & Belden for most of my important deals. A big operator's business has to be done on the quiet. The relationship between a Wall Street operator and his broker is a close one. In order to manipulate the market, you must keep mum while you are doing it. The broker is the only one besides yourself who knows what you're doing. He is in a position to give you away if he wants to. So I was glad to have a brokerage house that I could be confidential with. Pretty soon Fisk and I were in a lot of deals together, and in Erie most of all.

## XXII

THE Erie war was now about to open. It was the biggest fight I was ever in. So I was glad I had got an able helper like Jim Fisk; for I was going to need partners now as never before.

It was a fight, as anybody might know, between Vanderbilt and me. Pretty much all our lives we have been fighting each other. When he had a good thing, it always kind of seemed as though I wanted it, too; and when I had a good thing, he never slept easy till he had a finger in it. That had been the case with steamboats, and it was now to be the case, also, with the Erie Railroad.

Vanderbilt's make-up and mine were different. I suppose that accounts for our everlastingly crossing horns. His way was to break down opposition, by rushing straight through it; my way was to go around it. He was the dog, I the cat. A cat believes in going soft-footed — in keeping its claws hid till the time comes to show them. A dog goes with a big bow-wow; my plan has always been to go at a thing quieter. A cat won't spring at a dog from in front — 'tisn't good tactics. She gets around on the flank, claws the dog from behind, and so does a lot of damage without being in any danger herself.

The Commodore was a lordly fellow. He used to drive a team of horses, and would go riding up Fifth Avenue as though he owned both sides of it. His house was down on Washington Square among the silk-stockings. In winter he would wear a fur-lined coat and a stove-pipe hat; was very proud of his person. As for me, I was never a hand for vain-glory. Top-boots, such as I used to wear in drover days, have always been good enough for me. And I never could see the use of paying expensive prices to a tailor when you can get a suit ready-made for less than half the sum. As for cutting a wide swath, I never did take to it. My turn-out of one horse and a doctor's gig was good enough for me. When the Broadway stages started in, they were cheaper yet; so I used them.

Some of my friends used to scold me because I didn't dress up. They'd say: "Uncle Dan, why on earth do you walk around with such an old stick as that for a cane?" But I told them I wasn't proud. That stick had once been the handle of an almighty good umbrella. And now that the umbrella part was of no use any more, I felt it would be a shame to throw away the stick; because the stick was in just as good a condition as when I had bought the umbrella years before.

Another difference between the Commodore and

me was that he was by make-up a Bullish fellow, whereas most of my life I have been on the Bear side of the market. It used to be one of his mottoes: "Never sell short." Even in the darkest hours of the Civil War, he had lots of faith in the future of the country. He seemed to think that in America 'most any kind of stock would go up and be valuable if he only waited long enough. "I bide my time," he used to say to me, when I would tell him he'd better sell such and such a stock and get it off his hands. "Get it off my hands?" he'd exclaim. "Not by a jugful! I bought that stock as an investment; it's going to reach par some day, and don't you forget it."

Yes, he was a natural-born hoper. I have always been more conservative — have never allowed myself to paint the future in too bright colours. The Commodore made most of his money by stocks going up. I made most of mine by stocks going down. I wish now I'd been a Bull instead of a Bear. Because a Bull makes money when everybody's happy, that is, when stocks are on the upward move; so that people are willing to see him get rich. But a Bear makes his money when other people are unhappy. Because, in order for him to make, others have got to lose; for him to get rich means that there is a line of bankrupts in his train; and people cuss him so for taking money away from them, that his fortune doesn't give him so very much satisfaction.

Vanderbilt's faith in the future of our country sometimes led him into reckless expenditures. During the Civil War he was willing to have that conflict come to an end, even though it was making good business for us operators in Wall Street; because he figured that, with the country prosperous once more, he would be prosperous also. He even gave a million-dollar boat outright to the Government, for use as a gun-boat, to help hurry the War to an end. He seemed to think the country's interests and his own were one and the same — a position which leads a fellow into all kinds of extravagance. It's all right to love your country; but a fellow ought to love himself, too. I loaned some of my Stonington Line boats to the Government during the War; but I charged rent. In the year '62 alone, Abe Lincoln paid me $350,000 for the use of the boats. So I was really sorry when the Civil War was over. For then an era of prosperity set in; and prosperity isn't good for a Bear operator.

The Commodore gave a million dollars to Vanderbilt University — right out of hand. He didn't seem to have any fear of losing his fortune and dying poor. I have believed in giving sort of cautious-like. I gave a quarter-million as an endowment to found Drew Theological Seminary. But I kept the principal in my own hands — only paid over the interest each year — that is, I paid the interest as long as I was able. I have always believed that a man should be handier with a rake than with a fork.

Well, the Erie fight was between Vanderbilt and me. I had been the ruling spirit in Erie now for ten years, and had made so much money out of that road that other people got jealous. Part of those ten years was Civil War time. Stocks were bobbing up and down like a boy's kite. I was on the inside and could take advantage of these jumps.

The Civil War was over; Vanderbilt now vowed that he would get control of the Erie Road and put me and my crowd out of business for good and all. He said we were nothing but a nest of gamblers, that we were unsettling the entire market by our specki-lations, and that he wouldn't feel safe for his other properties until the Erie Railroad had also been placed in what he called safe hands. So he set out to buy a controlling interest in the stock.

I guess what made him so mad was a "Convert-ible Bond" scheme that I worked about this time. The Erie Road wanted three million dollars to make some improvements. I loaned her the money, and took as security for the loan three million dollars of bonds which were convertible into stock; and also twenty-eight thousand shares of unissued stock which the road just then had on hand. This pro-vided me in all with fifty-eight thousand shares of stock. Thus fortified — and when the Street didn't know that I held these shares — I went onto the

Exchange and sold Erie heavily short. Erie was then at 95, and promised to go still higher. People reckoned that I was a reckless plunger. The weeks ran along. Pretty soon it came time for me to deliver. The price held strong at 95. My enemies began to snicker. They said I was cornered. But I took the twenty-eight thousand shares I had kept up my sleeve, and dumped them into the market all to once. It was probably the biggest surprise Wall Street up to that time had known. Prices were knocked into a cocked hat. Erie gave one plunge — fell to 47. Which means, I made the other fellows pay me $95 a share for stock which was costing me now only $47. So I cleaned up $48 on every share dealt in. It was the finest scoop I had ever made. It is true, those 58,000 shares had been intrusted to me only to hold as security until the road should pay back my loan. But in a business deal, you can't stop for every little technicality.

Vanderbilt said that sort of thing had to stop. And he was going to be the one to stop it. So he started in. He didn't try to conceal his moves. He let everybody know. He went out in the open market and made his bids. He said that the Erie Road, in spite of all the dirty water — as he called it — in its stock, could be made once more into a dividend-earning property; and that it would be worth money to him and to the public generally to make it into a good road once more. At least he was willing to put his fortune into the attempt.  So he gave his brokers unlimited orders.  "Buy Erie," was what he told them.   "Buy it at the lowest figure you can; but buy it!"   And he swore an awful oath that the moment he got control of the road, there would be such a cleaning out of the Erie stable as it hadn't known for years.

One of his first moves was to get in with a Boston set that owned a large block of the stock — the "Boston, Hartford and Erie" crowd.   Almost before I knew it, he had worked up this combination among the directors, so that I was likely to be defeated for reëlection to the Erie Board.   I went to the Commodore to soften him down.   I said I'd try to do better from now on, if he'd let me stay in the Board. Besides, he needed me, even though maybe I wasn't just the kind of an Erie manager that he'd like to have.   He thought I was a selfish director; but there was a set of men now getting in who were really and wilfully thievish.

"You think I'm a director who is working only for my own pocket," said I.   "Well, I'll promise from now on to work for the interests of the road. But there is a set of bad men now getting in, who are unregenerate.   Commodore, you can't fight them alone.   What you need is a partner who is on the inside, and who can, therefore, fight those fellows for you better than you can do it yourself."

"Yes," said he, "but where in time could I find such a man?"

"I'm the one," and I spoke up good and prompt.

He laughed a great big laugh. (Vanderbilt had a hearty way of laughing, as though he wasn't afraid of anything or anybody. He used to poke fun at me — on the occasions when he and I were on good terms — because I didn't laugh a good loud laugh like he did. "Why in thunder, Dan, don't you laugh when you set out to do it," he used to say, "and quit that hen cackle of yours, which is no nearer a real laugh than one of my old Staten Island periaugers would be to a modern paddle-wheel boat?") He gave one of those laughs of his now.

"That would be a bully good idea!" he said. "You are just the fellow to take in as confidential friend and partner. Drew, you're as crooked as a worm fence. You'd betray me inside of twenty-four hours."

"I wouldn't betray you at all," said I. "I guess I haven't forgotten the time when we used to be friends together in the old steamboat days. Why, back there in that *Waterwitch* affair ——"

"Yes, yes," said he. "I remember old steamboat days. We have known each other quite a while, haven't we? I don't know but what I might give you one more trial." He thought for a spell. "Do you really think, Dan, if I took you back, that you could play fair?"

"I don't believe anything about it," said I. "I know I could. And I'm in a position to do you a whole lot of help."

"I declare, I believe I'll try it," said he. "But wait. I gave my promise to put you out. The Boston crowd wants to get rid of you. And I told them that at this next annual meeting I'd see to it that you were not re-elected."

"Yes," said I; "but you can tell them you have changed your mind."

"That isn't the way I do things," said he. "A promise is a promise."

"Well, if that is the way you feel," I answered, "why not work it this way? We'll go ahead and hold the election. I will be left out. We'll put a dummy in the place instead of me. Thus you'll be keeping your promise with the Boston crowd. Then, after the election is over, the dummy can resign and I will be appointed in his place."

"That's certainly a fruitful noddle you've got there, Uncle," said the Commodore. "I don't just take to that way of getting out of the difficulty. But maybe it's as good as any. We'll call it settled."

The election was held. My name didn't appear in the list of those reëlected to the Board. It looked as though I was out of Erie for good and all. But the next day the dummy resigned — said that on further thought he was not able to take it and would have to be relieved. We relieved him. I stepped into his shoes. I was back into my old place.

Now, I was ready for work. I started in. There was no time to be lost. Vanderbilt would soon have complete control of Erie unless I blocked him. Already I had Fisk with me as a partner. I needed another man. This other man I found in Jay Gould.

Jay had been worming his way inside of Erie for some time back. He had given up writing histories — had also sold his tannery business out in Pennsylvania. He had come to New York with a patent rat-trap to sell. Then he got into the Street. First along he dealt in small railroads. But when he saw what a bag of money I was making out of Erie he began to invest in its stock. He got in with some of the stock-holders, and by now had become a director himself and one of the powers in the road. I took him now as a partner. He was at the head of a clique in the Board of Directors that I needed in my fight against Vanderbilt. So he and Jim Fisk and I now stood together like three blood-brothers against the Commodore, our common foe.

Gould was just the criss-cross of Fisk. He was an undersized chap, and quiet as a mouse. I never liked his face. It was dark, and covered all over with whiskers so you could hardly see him. As to Fisk, you couldn't help but like him. Jimmy did me one or two dirty deals before he died. However,

I could take it from him, he was that big and warm-hearted in it all.  But Jay was so almighty silent. And he wasn't a healthy man, either.  He was as lean as a parson's barn.  Never seemed to me that he ate enough.  Jimmy used to put his purse into his belly.  Jay put his belly into his purse.  So that, though he himself was thin, his purse was fat as a porker.  Jimmy used to say:

"The difference between Jay and me is, I have more trouble to get my dinner than to digest it, and Jay has more trouble to digest it than to get it."

As I said, I couldn't help but like Fisk, no matter how wicked a man he was; and he was wicked.  He was very carnal.  The way he used to carry on with women was something scandalous.  He used to bring them right down to the office.  Didn't make any bones about it.  He would drive down in a barouche with a darkey coachman and four horses, and have two or three ladies of pleasure in the carriage with him.  Sometimes we would be in the middle of a hard day's work.  A carriage would drive up; a couple of ballet dancers would get out, bounce into the office where we were, trip up to Fisk and say, "Hello, we've come to spend the day."

I'd look up as much as to say: "You're going to put them out, aren't you?"

But he would answer my look and say: "Uncle, I've got a previous engagement with my Sweet-lips here, and this railroad matter will have to wait over until to-morrow. And this other female charmer here — Mr. Drew, allow me to make you acquainted with the prima donna of "Mazeppa" and "The French Spy." Then he would send out for a restaurant man, have victuals brought in, and would serve up a banquet to his ballet dancers right in his private office. He wouldn't care what the expense was; and he didn't mind whether he had known the girls before or not. Sometimes they would bring in another girl, one he had never met, and say:

"We've brought Annie along. You must meet her. They all say she's the sassiest queen in town."

"That's fine," he would answer; "and she's a lu-lu, too; she shall enjoy the carousal with us. The more the merrier. The world can never have too many girls of the kind that are toyful and cuddlesome."

I used to scold Jimmy for these wenching bouts of his; but my scoldings didn't count for much.

"That's all right, Uncle," he'd answer. "You're old and dried up. There's no fire in your veins. But for a gay young buck like me, a little spice in the midst of a hard day's work is needed. I never was one of your Josephs — woman-proof."

So I didn't have much peace of soul with either of these partners of mine. Gould, quiet as a clam; and Fisk, the devil's own. But both of them were handy in a stock-market dicker; and that was what I needed just now. The Erie war was rapidly coming on. I had to have partners that could help.

# XXIII

WHEN you set out to ride a colt, see that
your saddle is girt good and tight.
That's what I did now. I didn't want
to tackle the Commodore before I had first made
good and ready. This is the way I set about it:

At one of the meetings of the Erie Board of Directors I got the matter of steel rails to take the place
of the old and unsafe iron rails acted upon by the
Board. Our road, further, was being hurt because
it had a six-foot track, whilst the other railroads
were being built with only a narrow, that is, the
present standard-gauge, track. Their cars couldn't
go on our road, nor ours on their road. It had been
proposed that the Erie lay a third rail inside the
other two rails, in order that narrow-gauge rolling
stock could run on the track in the same train, if
need be, with our own broad-gauge cars. This,
and the steel rails to replace the iron ones, were two
such needed improvements that I now made them an
excuse for getting the road to issue some new shares
of stock. By means of my control of the Executive
Committee, I got them to vote to issue ten million
dollars of convertible bonds, the proceeds of which

— so they supposed — were to go into these improvements.

The advantage of convertible bonds was this: There was a provision in the charter forbidding the Erie Road to issue new stock except at par — which wouldn't have suited my purpose. Bonds would have been equally useless, seeing they are of no value in stock-exchange dickers. Bonds convertible into stock, however, were just the thing. Because it was only another name for an issue of stock at the market rate.

So now I had one hundred thousand shares of stock at my disposal, whenever I should care to turn the trick. Of course, legally speaking, these shares were not just at my disposal, either; because they were meant as a means of raising money to be put into the improvements and repairs that the road then needed. But all's fair in love and war. And in this particular case I felt that I was more in need of this nine or ten million than the Erie Road was. The road was under my management, because I controlled the Executive Committee, and, therefore, the finances. I felt that I was entitled to a few pickings, as it were. It's an ill cook that can't lick his own fingers. So, instead of using the money to buy steel rails, I had the old iron rails turned, in order to bring the unworn outside edge onto the inside now. Of course, this wasn't altogether as safe as new steel rails would have been. But I needed in my stock-market operations the money which this new bond issue was raising. And inasmuch as I had put in a good deal of valuable time as treasurer of the Erie Railroad, I felt I had a right now to sluice off some of her revenues into my own pocket. When you own a cow, you own her milk also. As to legal objections, by getting one of the judges on my side — as will be seen later — we got the law courts so jummixed up that they didn't know where they stood; and so the law couldn't touch me.

Whilst in the midst of these busy preparations, I had to cease operations for a couple of days and go out to the formal opening of my theological seminary at Madison, N. J. It was an occasion of great spiritual refreshment, and I'll write about it later. Just now I must finish telling about this Erie Railroad affair.

Supplied with ammunition in the shape of this fine, big issue of stock, I was now prepared for war. And I wasn't a moment too soon, either. Vanderbilt was already at work. He was out in the open market buying Erie with the boldness of a lion. I guess he was figuring that I was on his side, or he might never have been so bold and confident. Anyhow, he was going ahead as though there was nothing now that could stop him. I didn't say anything. I thought I'd let him go ahead, and sort of take him by surprise when the time came.

Vanderbilt wanted to buy Erie shares. All right. I was willing he should buy all he wanted. In fact, I thought I would help him in the matter. So I went onto the market, and sold Erie short in enormous quantities.

My friends thought I was going it wild. "What in the world, Uncle, are you up to?" they said to me. "Don't you remember those luckless Bears that went short of Harlem and got their feet caught in the trap? That's just what you're doing now. The Commodore is going to corner you tight as a fly in a tar-barrel." But I only smiled.

The Commodore now learned that I was against him, and got very much het up. His crowd taunted me.

"You're already beginning to count your profits?" said I to them. "Don't boil the pap till the child is born, that's all." And I went on selling the stock short.

Vanderbilt now made a move which he hadn't tried before. He went to the law courts and got out an injunction forbidding me and my crowd to issue any more shares of Erie stock. This last was a proceeding I was not willing to stand for. As chief director of Erie, I had a right to operate her as I saw fit. But here was Vanderbilt going to the law courts and putting a higher power over Erie's affairs than I was. He was tying my hands. So I went into the law-court business, too. I called a council of Gould and Fisk. We decided, since Vanderbilt had got a judge of the Supreme Court on his side to issue injunctions for him, that we'd get a judge too. So we went out to Binghamton, and got a judge there. Vanderbilt's judge had enjoined us from issuing any more Erie stock. This new judge of ours now got out an injunction commanding us to issue more stock. He wasn't a New York City judge. But he had as much power, so far as his legal standing was concerned. Because these Circuit Court judges work side by side. Any one judge has power extending over the entire state. Ordinarily they are supposed to stand by each other; but this was just after the Civil War, when things were topsy-turvy. Johnson was being impeached. The legal machinery of the country was that unsettled, we could do with it 'most anything we wanted.

When Vanderbilt had got out his injunction, restraining us from manufacturing any new certificates of Erie stock, he thought that he had all the leaks corked up at last good and tight. He supposed, therefore, that in issuing orders to his brokers to take all the Erie that was offered, he wasn't in any possible danger. I went onto the Exchange as though nothing had happened, and proceeded to sell more Erie. I sold all that I could — didn't set any limits — agreed to deliver all the stock I could find buyers for. Of course, in the Commodore I found a ready buyer.

People now thought me plumb crazy. "Uncle Daniel has gone clean off his head," said they. "It's got to be second nature with him to sell stock short. He goes onto the Bear side by force of habit. In this deal he hasn't any more chance than a grasshopper in January. The Commodore has got him this time. He's fixed it so that Drew and his crowd can't manufacture any new stock, and he has roped in all the floating supply that is still on the market. And yet here is Uncle Daniel still offering to deliver the stock in unlimited amounts. Where's he going to get it when these contracts mature? Drew is daft. He's going it blind, and will run his head against a post." Thus they talked. I let them. I was still able to find my way around in a Wall Street transaction — as they soon found out.

By and by the time drew near when these short contracts of mine would mature. (I say "mine." Of course, Fisk and Gould were with me. But I was the leader of the party, so I speak of it in my own name.) Jimmy came to me and said: "Guess it's about time to play our ace of trumps, don't you think so? We'll make Rome howl." I said I guessed he was right. So we called in Jay. We held a council of war. We decided that the time had come to set off the gunpowder.

Accordingly, we went to a printing-house and got them to print a hundred thousand shares of Erie. (It was those convertible bonds now being turned into stock.)  Of course, the printer could turn out only the blank forms; but since we were the officers of the road, or controlled the officers, such as the Secretary and such-like, we could get any amount of printed blanks signed in legal manner and made thus into good financial paper.

It was a helpful sight to see that printing press work so smooth and fast.  For we had only a few days more in which to make our deliveries.  All the Street thought we were cornered.  In fact, Vanderbilt himself was beginning to tell around that he was going now to clean up the Erie stable inside and out — wasn't going to leave so much as a grease spot of us behind.  It was an exciting time.  The Street knew that big things were about to happen.  For this was a battle of the giants.  Vanderbilt and I were the two biggest men in Wall Street.  When the two big roosters on the dung-pile cross spurs, there's going to be some feathers flying.

Gould and Fisk stood with me watching the printing press as she turned out for us the bright, new stock certificates.  Each one of those sheets of paper was of enormous value to us.  Not just because of the amount of money it would bring in dollars.  But this was a war, and each of these crisp certificates was a cannon ball, so to speak.  If we could pound the Commodore hard enough that he wouldn't have time to recover between the blows but would be forced to knuckle under, then we'd have him at our mercy, and all of his property also. Besides, with him busted up, there would be a great smash in values, and we on the Bear side of the market would then profit all along the line. It's far more important in a business war to break down the man himself, than to break down any particular piece of his property. Because when the man goes under, all of his fortune is at your disposal. So these bright new sheets of paper looked very beautiful to us. They were just so many additions to our ammunition supply. I could almost have hugged that printing press, she was that friendly to us. Jimmy, of course, had to have his joke.

"That injunction of the Commodore's," said he, "was aimed against the freedom of the press. As freeborn Americans we couldn't stand for that. Give us enough rag paper and we'll hammer the everlasting tar out of that mariner from Staten Island."

"Oh, come now," said Jay; "let's don't get rambunctious. We're not out of the woods yet. Our contracts to deliver the stock are rapidly maturing. We have engaged to hand over to the Commodore such enormous blocks of it that I can't sleep nights, thinking of it. And something may happen yet to get in our way."

"Happen!" said Jimmy, and he was as calm as a cat with kittens; "I'd like to see anything happen! If this printing press don't break down, we'll give the old hog all the Erie he wants."

I scolded him. But in my heart I was glad to have a partner who was so cock-sure. For we were in a ticklish place. If any hitch should come, we would certainly find ourselves in the tightest corner a man was ever in, and got out alive. Jimmy's spirit kept us in heart. Fortunately, the printing press didn't break down. It kept on with its klickety-klack, smooth as clock-work. As fast as the blank certificates were turned out and the printer's ihk had dried, Fisk took them and made them valid by putting in the proper signatures. "The Devil has got hold of me," he remarked; "I might as well keep on signing." Soon the entire issue was finished, and tied up in a neat bundle at the Company's office. The stock was now good financial paper.

But there was still a danger. And because the amounts at stake were so high, we determined to take no chances. The Commodore might hear that our printing press had been once more at work, and get his judge to enforce his injunction, by attaching this new bunch of Erie shares. In which case we wouldn't have time to print any more; for our deliveries were maturing the very next day. The Commodore's judge was in New York City, right at the seat of war. Whereas our judge was way out in Binghamton; so that the Commodore could act more quickly than we; and this was a time when minutes would count.

So we took measures. The new stock was over in the Erie office on West Street. We tied up the books of newly printed certificates in a neat paper bundle. Then we called the office boy and told him to take that bundle over to the Transfer Office on Pine Street. He started out with it. When he was just outside the door, something happened. He returned empty-handed, and white as a sheet. He said that a man — a big blonde individual, with a yellowish moustache and a large shirt front—had rushed upon him whilst he was in the hall, grabbed the bundle from him, and had whisked off with it before he could say "boo."

"Dear, dear!" said the Secretary (he was the one who had been enjoined from issuing this stock) "that's too bad!" But he told the boy not to mind; he had done his best, anyhow; it wasn't his fault; and sent him back to his desk. We all pretended to be het up over the matter; but we were pretty calm inside. Because we could have made a pretty close guess as to who had grabbed the bundle away from the boy. But, of course, if it had come to the taking of evidence in court, the Secretary could now clear his skirts; because the stock had been snatched out of his keeping. That same afternoon those shares turned up at the office of our broker. He parcelled fifty thousand of them out to his sub-agent in ten-thousand share lots. Now we were ready for operations.

The next morning the Stock Exchange opened calm and clear, as though it was a time of perfect peace. The president of the Board called out the shares of the various railroads in usual order: "Union Pacific!"    "Wabash!"    "New York Central!" — no response. He met with a dead silence. Then he called out "Erie!" Things broke loose at once. One of our brokers jumped out onto the floor and offered a block of one thousand shares of Erie; he followed this up with another thousand that with another; until he had offered five thousand; shares of Erie — wanted to sell them right then and there. Vanderbilt's brokers took the first two or three thousand-share blocks cheerfully. But it was noticed that they looked surprised. Then, almost before our first broker had got through, another sprang forward and offered blocks of Erie for sale — ten thousand in all. Our first broker followed up his previous offerings with five thousand more (that made up his ten thousand.) Still another of our brokers came and helped push along the landslide. He yelled out: "A thousand shares of Erie for sale! A thousand more of Erie!  A block of five thousand shares of Erie!" And so on until his ten thousand shares were offered.

By this time the Vanderbilt brokers were scared out of their wits. They got into communication with their master.  "Hell has broke loose," they sent word to him.  "Thirty thousand shares of

Erie have come raining down on us in the last half-hour, with more coming out every minute. What shall we do?"

All the answer he gave was: "Support the market."

As he didn't seem at all flustered, his brokers got courage, went back and took our offerings. They succeeded in absorbing the whole fifty thousand shares without letting the market sag more than a point or two.

But now came the death stroke. These deliveries of stock were made right away. As soon as the Exchange saw that these certificates were crisp and new, with the printer's ink hardly dry on them, the secret was out. In defiance of Vanderbilt's injunction, we had set our printing press to work.

The landslide then broke loose. For if we had been able to cut the legal red tape with which Vanderbilt had tried to tie our hands — had found a way to start the printing press to work once more — why, it was good-night to the Commodore. Because there is no limit to the amount of blank shares a printing press can turn out. White paper is cheap — it is bought by the ream. Printer's ink is also dirt cheap. And if we could keep on working that kind of deal — make Vanderbilt pay us fifty or sixty dollars for little pieces of paper that hadn't cost us two cents, we would very soon have all of his cash ladled out of his pocket into ours.

It was, I guess, the darkest hour in Vander-bilt's life. He had staked his reputation and a good share of his fortune on this Erie fight; and now we had suddenly unmasked a battery that was pouring hot shot into his ranks thick and fast. No wonder his followers began to desert him. They fell off by twos and threes. There was a small-sized panic all through the Vanderbilt party. Until now they had looked upon their leader as able to take care of them. Some of them had begun to think that he was a sort of supernatural person, one that couldn't be touched by mortal hands. But now his career seemed to have come to an end. He was no longer the high and mighty one that he had been.

This was the moment we had been waiting for. In war it is good generalship to know when to strike. We now dumped the other fifty thousand shares onto the floor of the Exchange all to once. The price, which had been at 83, dropped like a dead heifer. It was as though the bottom had fallen out — nothing was left to support things. Down and down and down it went, clean to 71. Consid-ering the number of shares involved, and the size of the transactions, it was the biggest stroke Wall Street had ever seen. The Commodore himself wasn't able to stand out any longer. The price rallied a little before the day was over, for it was seen that the Commodore wasn't as yet entirely swamped — he took all the stock that we offered, even the last fifty thousand, and paid over his good cash for it.    But the market had made a fatal break. Nothing he or his friends could do would bring it back again.    And the day closed with me and my crowd gloriously on top.

# XXIV

THIS was Tuesday, early in March. The next day, Wednesday, we met at our Erie Railroad office on West Street, to count our profits. It was a happy hour. Seven million dollars of Vanderbilt's had been scooped out of his pocket into ours. Four millions of it was in legal-tender notes, good crisp greenbacks. We hardly knew where to stow the money. We set to work tying it up in bundles. We were in high spirits. Jimmy couldn't get over laughing and talking about the "green goods." He said how the Commodore was all right for Staten Island, but he ought to have stayed down there along with the other farmers; because the streets of New York were not safe for people who didn't know the game. We were all in good heart.

Just then a messenger came and said something that made us sing another tune. He told us that processes for contempt of court were being issued against us, and we stood liable to arrest at any moment. That would mean the Ludlow Street Jail. I was that flustered I didn't know which way to turn. I thought of our Supreme Court judge out in Binghamton, and wondered if we could get him to issue an injunction enjoining Vanderbilt's judge from sending us to jail. But I was afraid we wouldn't have time to reach him. For the message went on to say that Vanderbilt was hopping mad, and was swearing by all the gods he could think of, that he would clap every last man of us behind the bars before the sun went down that night.

"There's no sun to go down, anyhow," said Jimmy, looking out of the window; it was a foggy day, and seemed to be getting worse.

"For heaven's sake, shut up!" said Jay; and I spoke up too. I said: "Jimmy, this is no time for your fooleries. In tackling the Commodore it kind of looks as though we had woke up the wrong passenger. We have got to do something, and do it almighty quick."

"I'm agreeable," said he. "I'll tell you what I'm going to do. I'm going to get my share of this swag over to Jersey in about two jerks of a lamb's tail; also, I'm going to live there myself for a while. Up in Brattleboro, in my kid days, I used to see individuals whom the sheriff was very anxious to interview, scoot through the covered bridge which there straddles the Connecticut; and, once on the New Hampshire side, snap their fingers at the Vermont sheriff. I have been feeling the need of a change of air for some time back, and think that the climate of Jersey would suit me to a T."

"Just the thing," I remarked, jumping up. "Once across the ferry we will be out of York State's jurisdiction. Vanderbilt's processes and writs couldn't touch us there. I think we'd better be getting over there at once."

"Not until we have packed up these souvenirs of the Commodore," said Jimmy. "It was very kind of him to send us so many birthday cards"; and he began to get the bundles of greenbacks together.

"And there are the account books of the Erie Railroad and the other records, including the transfer books," put in Jay. "Never would do in the world to leave those things behind for Vanderbilt's lawyers to get hold of. The Erie Railroad is packed within the books and papers right in this office. If the Commodore got them, inside of three months he'd have the road reorganized. Besides, we can't tell how long our stay may be over there. The road will have to be operated while we are there." Jay was always a thoughtful sort of chap. He could look a long ways ahead.

"Guess you're right," said Jimmy. "And the Commodore's idea of reorganization for the road, would reorganize us out of it into the nearest mud-gutter."

"Or into the Ludlow Street Jail," said I. "It's

my feeling in the matter that we ought to be moving right away." So we set to work. We got together all the papers, books, and other valuables which we could easily move, and carried them into a dray, for carting over to the Jersey City ferry.

The policeman on the West Street beat, between Chambers and Cortlandt, saw us rushing out of the Erie office with our pockets and arms jammed with bundles of greenbacks, with bags, packages — moveables of all kinds. He hurried over. He called to us to halt.

"What's all this muss about?" said he. On account of the mist, he couldn't make out very well who we were, and so was very stern in his manner. "Hold your horses a minute. I guess I'll take a hand in this."

But we called out to him that it was all right; that we were the officers and Executive Committee of the Erie Railroad, and had been compelled to make a hasty move to other headquarters. As he was closer now he saw who we were. He apologized for his mistake. He said he was sorry, but through the fog, as he saw us hurrying out, he thought we might be thieves.

"Guess again," said Jimmy; "you were wrong that time. We're not thieves. Why, bless your stars, we're the owners. Only, a certain individual in Wall Street with whom we had a little misunderstanding yesterday, has kind of struck up the jig before we could tune our fiddles.   We're moving over to Jersey for a temporary change of scene." The officer let us go.   A five-dollar greenback seems big to a policeman, and was a small amount to us just then.

We held the ferry-boat whilst we were getting the stuff on board.   We saw that it was going to be too slow to carry all the money by hand, so we got a carriage.   We bundled over four million dollars into the coach.

By and by we had the stuff on board.   Gould said: "There!  We'll have our men put this stuff over in the Erie Depot for us; then we can go over to-night or to-morrow ourselves.   We can get our home affairs straightened out by that time, and be ready for a sojourn in foreign parts."

But I spoke up at once.   I said that as for them they could remain on York State soil as long as they wished.   But I wasn't going to shilly-shally there another minute.   I was going to leave the State by the same ferry-boat that took the stuff. Because Vanderbilt wanted to get hold of me the worst way, and would have liked nothing better than to hear the gate clang that should coop me up in the Ludlow Street Jail.   I wasn't going to take any chances.

"But, man alive," said Jimmy, "aren't you going to say good-bye to your home and native land? And pack up some of your personal belongings — a clean shirt at least?"

"I'm not going to say good-bye to anybody," I replied. "I'm going to leave on this here boat; you fellows can be as foolhardy as you wish. I'll notify my home when I get onto another soil." So I went onto the boat and gave orders to the captain to push off. Even then I didn't feel safe until the gates had been shut, the engine started, and a fine strip of water spread between me and Vanderbilt's process-servers. In fact, I couldn't be altogether sure even then, because the jurisdiction of the York State courts reaches to the middle of the North River; I didn't know but what he might have some of his sheriffs concealed on the ferry-boat, to nab me before the boat got into Jersey waters. So I didn't move around much. I didn't want to attract attention. This was ten o'clock in the morning. At that time of day there isn't much traffic on the river in the Jersey direction. There were only a few on board. I didn't have much trouble keeping out of sight. When the boat reached the middle of the river, I got my spirits up; and when at last she bumped into the slip at Jersey City, and I was on foreign soil, I felt more like my old self. Vanderbilt now could get me only through extradition papers from the Jersey officials. And when it came to that, I thought I could have something to say.

We had arranged that Taylor's Hotel, which is a stone's throw from the ferry terminal in Jersey

City, should be our headquarters. So I had our goods taken over there, and went there myself. That afternoon was a busy one. In moving from New York City we had moved also the Erie Railroad head office. The trains were running as usual. We had to establish some kind of headquarters in Taylor's Hotel. I got from the landlord the use of several rooms which connected with each other, and told him that I expected some more of my party over at any time.

All day long I looked for Fisk and Gould. But they didn't come. I began to think they had decided to stay over in New York for the night. But shortly after dark, in they came. And they were a bedraggled pair of men.

"What in the world!" said I. "You didn't have to swim over, did you?"

"Pretty near," said Jimmy; "in fact, it looked for a spell as though we weren't going to get here at all. It's a beast of a day. We came over in a row-boat."

"A rowboat?" said I. "How's that?" And I looked at Jay. He pointed me to Fisk.

"You tell him," said he.

"Why, nothing special," said Jimmy. "Only we were taking a bite together at Delmonico's, after a hard day's work, when a message came that the sheriff was after us. We decided to scamper. We didn't dare trust the ferries. Because after the news of your departure and of the moving of the books and the headquarters of the Erie Railroad got out, Vanderbilt was so thundering mad we thought he might have watchers now at every ferry terminal. So we went down to your People's Line dock. The *St. John* was in the slip. We told her captain who we were, used your name, and said we wanted him to help us over to the Jersey shore. He let down one of the life-boats, and sent two of his men to row us over. I said: 'Row up stream, so as to keep out of the track of the ferries.' We got along all right until we got to the middle of the river; when I'll be blasted if the fog wasn't so thick and with the night coming on, we got lost! We couldn't do anything but row around in a circle. We came deuced near being run down two or three times, but managed to dodge. By and by one of the Pavonia ferry-boats came along. She looked as though she was going to run us down, sure-pop. We called out. We made them hear just in time to veer their boat off. Then we got hold of her guards and hung on. We came mighty near being swamped from the swash of the paddle-wheels. It was as slippery a job as a man ever had. But we managed it. And here we are, a little the worse for wear, but hale and whole. At least, I am. Jay over there looks as though he'd cave in. Cheer up, my hearty! Nothing is lost save honour."

"That's just what I'm thinking of," said

Jay. "What will this do to our reputation at home?"

But Jimmy laughed at him. "We've got the coin right here with us. That's all we care about, isn't it, Uncle?" and he looked towards me. "So we have the chink, we'll bear the stink."

# XXV

IT WAS a great inconvenience to me to have to move so suddenly into another state, and my feelings towards Vanderbilt in it all were not the most friendly. I missed my home a good deal. I was at this time nigh onto seventy years old. A man of those years can't pack up and move so suddenly as he had made me do, without being put to a lot of hardship. And I was accordingly in hopes that Vanderbilt wouldn't be able to live through the pounding that we were giving him. Because if he should bust up, we could go back to New York at once. But if he should manage to keep his head above water, he could work it so as to make us stay in Jersey — nobody knew how long.

And for a time the prospects were bright. It looked as though Vanderbilt would go under any minute. He had staked his fortune on this Erie fight; and now, when he had thought he had me cornered tight as a bull's knot, I had up and given him the slip. And I had saddled onto him a hundred thousand shares of fresh Erie stock at over seventy dollars a share — stock which hadn't cost me anything more than the paper and the expense of printing. It was a critical moment for him. His friends and followers, whose fortunes depended on his, hung round him to watch his actions. They wanted to see if he was equal to the strain. Because the market was in a panicky condition. Our fight had been on so big a scale that it had sucked all the rest of the Stock Market into it. It looked as though the biggest crash in the history of Wall Street was about to come. Because Vanderbilt was likely to keel over. And if he went, all the stocks that he was interested in would go. A flood of selling orders would pour into the market, and an enormous panic would follow. So his followers hung on his every movement. I believe if he had weakened so much as by the quiver of an eyelid, a moan or the twitching of a muscle, it would have been immediately whispered abroad that the Commodore was giving way, and then the landslide would have come.

But, unfortunately, he didn't weaken. He had paid over seven million dollars for the stock we had saddled onto him, without a murmur. Further, not only had my manœuvre hurt his reputation for success, but it had withdrawn from Wall Street seven million dollars in cash. This withdrawal tightened the money market. Money rates went up, stocks went down. Larger margins were demanded of the Commodore for the carrying of his investments, at the very moment when it was hardest for him to get ready cash. But he managed it.

Where in the world Vanderbilt got the money to support the market at this time of times in his life, I never found out. Where in the world, also, he got all that strength of nerve to stand up under the strain, not showing so much as one sign of weakening, is more than I can see through. Why, I heard afterwards that, even whilst he was being pounded the hardest, he would drive his span of horses along the Avenue to the Park, calm as anything; frequent the theatre, dances and such like vanities, or spend a whole evening playing whist with his friends. As for me, I never indulge in worldly amusements, which the Discipline forbids, or so much as touch cards — those Devil's playthings. How it was that he dared do those things, and at the very time. too, when it looked as though he might go under, the time of all times when he ought to have been mournful and fasting and propitiating the Wrath, is past understanding.

But he did. And he weathered the storm. He even kept up a show of spirits, as though nothing had happened. Just when things were at their most critical, one of his brokers went to him and asked:

"Mr. Vanderbilt, will you sell some Erie stock now?"

He answered in a thundering tone: "Sell? You fool, no! Take every share offered."

It was too bad that we weren't able to break down the Commodore's iron nerve; because it meant that he was left in a position to hit back and do us a power of harm. For Vanderbilt over in York State was as cross as a bull with a sore head, when he saw that we were out of his reach. I fancied I could see him, a big lion pacing up and down the shore line, roaring over at us and getting madder all the time. The thought of it hurt my sleep. To be sure, he couldn't get at us; but it's a fearsome sound to have a dog bark at you through a fence, even when you know he can't get out. Thinking of him in the night would give me goose pimples; I'd get the creeps all over, like when you take a dead man by the toe.

We settled down for a long stay at Taylor's Hotel. "We might as well make ourselves comfortable," said I; "because we'll probably be here for quite a spell."

"Of course we'll be comfortable," said Jimmy. "I never did just take to this town as a permanent residence. For one thing, I don't think her girls can hold a candle to some of the Madame Light-skirts over in New York. I guess also the theatres are sort of third-class over here. But what's the difference? We'll be so busy we couldn't gad about even if we wanted to."

So we began to make ourselves at home. We got the landlord to let us have Room No. 3 — it was the Ladies' Parlour — for our offices.

"I kind of like the name," said Jimmy. "It always did seem to me that a 'Ladies' Parlour' was just the kind of a room for a business office."

We had the rooms leading off from that for our sleeping quarters. Our dinner at night was served in a private dining room. Jimmy laid in a store of wine and told the landlord to put himself out on his bill of fare. We got a line of messengers arranged between our hotel and the Erie Terminal at the Long Dock. Soon we had an office for the Erie Railroad set up in Taylor's Hotel that, for the time being at least, was as good as the one in West Street.

The Jersey City people were mightily pleased to have us with them. They felt that our presence there was an honour to the city, seeing that we were the head and front of the Erie Railroad. For now they had not only the main depot of the road within their city limits, but the business headquarters as well and the presence of its Executive Committee. We encouraged this feeling in them. It's a good thing to have the people who are round about you favourable to you. And in the present case I had reason, very soon after, to be thankful for it. Because this Erie war (and it was a real war, too, as will be seen, even though it has never got into the histories) soon got to the point of open violence.

We came over to Taylor's Hotel on a Wednesday, in the month of March (just two years after the close of the Civil War). Things ran along more or less smooth for a day or two. But I feared that everything was not going to be right for long. Because the Friday following fell on the thirteenth of the month. That's always bad. I was afraid something would happen on that identical date. But it didn't. The next day also passed off calm. Sunday I went to church in the morning, because I felt as never before the need of comforting words. Besides, I wanted to set an example to the rest, in the matter of attendance on the stated preaching of the gospel. Because (and I grieve to state it) I was in the midst of an ungodly set. Besides myself, I don't know as there was another Christian in the party. They were all, for the most part, profane men and breakers of the Sabbath. They knew that I was a professor of religion; so now I wanted them to see that I didn't leave my piety behind when I was away from home.

The Sunday kind of made me feel more at ease — seemed to take away some of the fear that had come over me when Friday fell on the thirteenth. So when the next morning, Monday, dawned, I was more or less calm. I was seated with my feet in a chair in our Hotel Taylor headquarters, thinking how nicely we were getting along in spite of the sudden change from home life to life in a strange state. When suddenly news came that a band of toughs had come over from New York City. They were collecting on the Long Dock and around the Erie Depot; and, as the day wore on, their numbers increased.

I at once gave out my explanation of it. I said that Vanderbilt was trying to kidnap me. He couldn't get me in his clutches by legal means without extradition papers from the Jersey authorities. And we were so in favour with the Jersey people by this time — since they began to hope we would make Jersey City the permanent headquarters hereafter of the Erie Railroad — that Vanderbilt in his rage was determined to get me by fair means or foul; so he had collected a lot of hoodlums from the Washington Market district, by offering a reward of fifty thousand dollars to any one who would bring me over to New York City and into his hands alive. Because, as soon as he had me on York State soil, he could serve a summons on me for violating the injunction of his judge, Barnard. He'd clap me behind the bars in the Ludlow Street Jail, and then have me so at his mercy that in all likelihood he'd squeeze out of me the fifty thousand he had paid for my capture, and perhaps a whole lot more.

Jimmy tried to "pooh-pooh" me out of my scare. He said Vanderbilt wouldn't go about a thing in so clumsy a fashion as that. But it was all right for Jimmy to be at ease. He wasn't the one the Commodore wanted. I was the big fish he was angling for. If he could strike me down, me, the head of the enemy's forces, he could round up the rest of them easy. So it stood me in hand to protect myself. A general ought never to expose his own person.

He ought to keep in the background, out of the reach of danger. So much depends upon him. He's got to look out for himself, not only for personal reasons — and I had personal reasons, goodness knows; for if those Washington Market toughs had once got me in their clutches, they'd have given me a shirtful of sore bones — but, also, for the good of the cause that he stands for. So I sounded the alarm good and strong.

I soon got Gould to see the thing as I did. When the news came that the tough characters were gathering in the neighbourhood of our hotel, Jay got very thoughtful. He began to snatch off the corners of a newspaper and tear them into bits. I had come to know Jay by this time. I knew that when Jay gets to snipping off corners of newspapers, it is a sign he is mighty uneasy over something. By and by he out with it.

"It's this way, Jim," he said, turning to Fisk. "It isn't that our persons are in danger. But I'm thinking of the money. Here we've got over seven million dollars, a lot of it in greenbacks. All of it belonged to the Commodore, and we've taken it away from him. What more natural than that he should try to get it back, by hook or by crook? At a time like this, when things are in all kinds of confusion, possession is nine points of the law. The Law Courts are all tangled up. Vanderbilt has on his side the Supreme Court in the New York

City District, we have on our side the Supreme
Court in the Binghamton District. The judges
are issuing so many injunctions back and forth that,
so far as the law stands, there isn't a lawyer at the
New York bar can unravel the snarl. At such a
time the fellow who has the cash right in his own
fist is a sight better off than the fellow who techni-
cally has the law on his side, but without the cash.
With the money in our fist, we have nine-tenths of
the Law; and Vanderbilt is welcome to the other
tenth," Jay added with a grin. It was seen by
Jimmy also, after we had held our council of war,
that my suspicions as to Vanderbilt's hand in this
move were not so crazy after all. The thought of
putting on a uniform and of having real soldiers
to command, sort of appealed to Fisk, anyhow.
We decided to take immediate steps of defence.

I called Chief of Police Fowler, and he got fifteen
picked men from the Jersey City police force to guard
the approaches to Taylor's Hotel — "Fort Taylor,"
as Jimmy now called it. Then we summoned
Inspector Masterson, who was General Superintendent of Police for the Erie Railroad. He organized a force of the Erie Railroad employees to patrol
the Long Dock and the streets around our citadel.
Three twelve-pounders were mounted on the dock
dividing the ferry from the Cunard wharves, with
the Hudson County Artillery in reserve.

Inasmuch as it promised now to be a state of war,

we detailed ourselves, each to have charge of some particular part of the defense. Masterson was under my charge, because I could supervise him and his men without going out from the "Fort"; and I thought it best at this particular crisis not to expose myself unnecessarily. We had a small navy hastily gathered. It consisted of four life-boats, manned by a dozen men each. These we armed with Springfield rifles. Jimmy took charge of the navy.

"I'll take care of that end," he said, as soon as a fleet of armed boats had been suggested. "I wish I'd thought to bring over one of my uniforms."

Jimmy liked to be in command of boats, soldiers and such like, where he could give orders with a loud voice and wear a sword. (He used to like nothing better than to go up the Sound on one of his steamboats, walk up and down the decks covered with gold lace, and then, when he had got the boat some distance up the Sound and the passengers were all to sleep and couldn't look at him any longer, he would have another boat come and take him off and back to the city.) So now, as soon as a real navy was under way, Jimmy said that he'd take charge of it. That was the place of greatest danger, he said, and he wanted to be on the firing line. So he became the "Admiral." It was a name he liked, anyhow. Fisk was a vainglorious man. Still he wasn't a timid person — wasn't afraid of anything, for that matter. He could face a street full of sheriffs without scaring. "There's no gallows built high enough to hang Jim Fisk," he used to say.

Besides the guards around Fort Taylor, we sent over a dozen detectives to watch the ferry terminals in New York City and also on the Jersey side. These were scouts, so to speak, to let us know of the advance of the enemy, before they got within dangersome distance. We set five other detectives to watch the hoodlum neighbourhoods in New York City, and find out if there was any recruiting going on. We had a dozen couriers to run back and forth from "Fort Taylor" to the Erie Railroad to carry our messages. Because the business of the Road had to be cared for, even during the state of war in which we then were. Gould was in charge of this, the Business Department. For freight agents, division superintendents and such-like were reporting to us now at Taylor's Hotel, instead of at the offices in West Street. Jay was always a good hand at business details. With Fisk as Admiral of the navy, and Jay in charge of running the railroad, that left me free to superintend the land forces for our defence. As night drew on, I had Chief Fowler and Mr. Gaffney, president of the Jersey City Police Commissioners, over at "Fort Taylor" to a council of war. It was seen that the night was the time of greatest danger. Should the enemy charge down on us in the middle of the night, they might over-power any ordinary police guards and whisk us and our cash over to the other side of the river before the Jersey City people knew it. So, as darkness settled down, we agreed upon a set of signals whereby the whole city could be alarmed if the attack should come — fire signals if the attack came by night, and an alarm with guns if the attack came by day. Fur-ther, a force of a hundred and twenty-five citizens of Jersey City came and surrounded the "fort," and they agreed that in case of need they would summon the entire city to our rescue.

A pair of double doors, with a transom above, led from the business office into our sleeping rooms. These doors didn't offer as much protection as I should have liked. They were not built for an assault. A force of prize-fighting toughs might break them down, or perhaps get in at me by means of the transom, whilst I was asleep. So we had a force of guards stationed in the big outer room by night.

Winds blow hard on high hills. For once in my life I had trouble in going to sleep. Commonly, I have been a good sleeper. Even in the most excit-ing times of my life I haven't lost a wink of sleep over business matters. But now it was different. Over there in Jersey City everything was so strange. It wasn't like what I had been used to at home. And I told some of the others of my uneasiness.

"Now, see here, Uncle," said Jimmy, finally,

"don't you get to snivelling. You'll be taken care of all right. My navy is on guard. If Vanderbilt tries to come over, we'll swab the deck with him. I have mounted some artillery on the docks. The military forces of the city are aroused. You and the money will be looked after."

"Yes," said I; "I believe you care more about guarding the money than you do about guarding me. I almost believe you would like to have me caught and taken over there into Vanderbilt's clutches."

"Bosh and tommyrot!" said he; "don't you know we are just as anxious to keep you away from the Commodore as you are yourself? A pretty broth you would spice up for the rest of us, if you and he got your noddles together."

"Well, then," said I, "if you are so set on taking care of me, why don't you do it, and increase the guards? Why, a thousand of those hoodlums from Cherry Hill might come over here in the middle of the night in rowboats — no one knows. They'd be enough to carry off this whole hotel, lock, stock and barrel, and us inside of it!"

"As to crossing that North River in rowboats at night," said Jimmy, "rest your boots that if any of them tried it, they'd be out of commission by the time they got to this side. It's the gol damnedest river to get lost in that I ever saw in all my born days. While as to guards — just step out here a minute." He took me out through the double doors into the big outer room; there he showed me the watchmen. They were sleeping on beds made of blankets spread on the floor. As we came in they arose and saluted us — real military style.

"Mr. Drew," said Jimmy, "these are the men who are protecting you, and they look well able to do it, don't they?"

I had to say something. I answered that they did look to be strong men, loyal and true, if the time came to fight. And I had no doubt they would be willing to give up their lives, if need be, at the call of duty. The men saluted once more, and we went back into our own rooms.

Even then I didn't get a good night's rest. The trouble was, I couldn't be sure of the kind of treatment I would get at the hands of those toughs, if they once got me into their clutches. In fact, I thought I'd rather have fallen into Vanderbilt's own hands than into theirs. Because they were a violent set of men. I tossed on my bed considerable. But I had some company in my misery, because Gould was even worse off. Jay wasn't anywheres near so good a sleeper as I. Even amidst ordinary business worries, Jay used to have nights when he'd lie awake for hours. Why, he even had a cup of hot milk by his bed, for him to drink in the night when he couldn't get to sleep any other way.

The night wore away without any attack. The next day, the news of our preparedness got over to

New York. Then we knew we were less likely to be disturbed. Because in war, when your enemy knows you are ready for him, he isn't anywheres near so likely to come at you. After a few days the threat of violence passed away. But we still kept up our guard, particularly at night.

# XXVI

WE NOW got a bill introduced in the Jersey Legislature which was then in session, incorporating the Erie Railroad under a New Jersey charter, with headquarters in Jersey City. The bill proposed to give to the road all of the rights which it held as a York State corporation.

Vanderbilt, as soon as he heard that such a bill had been introduced, got a lobby to work at Trenton and fought the bill tooth and nail. So long as we were in Jersey as a visitor, he knew he would have a handle on us. The Erie charter was a York State thing, and didn't look to any moving of the headquarters permanently out of the State. So if Vanderbilt could defeat us in getting a home in Jersey, he would be able to get us back onto York State soil soon or late.

But we also set a lobby to work. And here we had two or three things in our favour. We were nearer Trenton than he was. In the next place, we had a lot of ready cash, whereas he was scant of cash by precisely the amount which had been put into our pockets. And in the third place, it was a welcome thing to Jerseyites, this prospect of moving the headquarters of the railroad to their soil.

We worked this last lever all we could. We wanted at least the appearance of a settled abode in Jersey City, so that the Commodore would give up the job of waiting for us to come back, and go to something else. We made believe that we liked it in Jersey even better than we had over in New York. In fact, we even went so far as to get Jay to buy a beautiful house in Jersey City, and to give out that he would move his family there shortly. With these helps we got the bill jammed through both houses of the Legislature at Trenton. The Governor signed it. This was notice served on Vanderbilt that we were in this fight in earnest. He was boasting that he would keep us over there until we fried in our own fat — "till we stewed in our own juice" was the way he put it. So now we showed him we could stay in Jersey just as long as was necessary.

At Taylor's Hotel, Jimmy was all the time getting off jokes. At the dinner table at night, he was full of mirth. He started a kind of a camp fire to take up our time after dinner was through. "We'll hoist the flag of No-surrender at this citadel," he used to say, and he would get some of the people about him of an evening to sing war songs. He was getting to be high-cockalorum in one of the militia regiments over in New York City, and liked to keep up the military idea. I used to laugh at his jokes, even when I didn't see much fun in them, he had such a hearty way of getting them off. He would joke me by saying that the Commodore was of more use in the world than I was. "Vander built and Dan drew," was the way he used to put it. Still I was glad, first along, to have him and Gould with me at Taylor's Hotel. For I felt the need of partners in the fight I had on my hands. It's a fine thing when friends do each other a good turn. You scratch my back and I'll scratch yours, as we used to say in drover days — help me and I'll help you.

But after a few days at Fort Taylor, our relationships became a little strained. And this got more so as our stay lengthened. Because I had brought over with me a big sum of money — the proceeds from the sale of stock to Vanderbilt — and Jimmy and Jay wanted some of it. They kept pestering me to divide up with them. Until that sum of money came in among us, I can truthfully say that we had been as friendly together as anything. Like dogs which play together free and happy, until there's a bone thrown among them. I was almost sorry I had the money, they pestered me so for it. From the time they got their eyes on those greenbacks, we agreed like three cats in a gutter. I was anxious to have the war come to an end, and get away from them.

We tried in several ways to hit back at the Commodore and lay him out. For no one must think that in this war we were only on the defensive, and that Vanderbilt was doing all the attacking. We soon came to see that the best way to fight fire is by starting a back fire. We had Vanderbilt already on the rack, because of the money he had lost to us, and because of the stringency caused by the withdrawal of that money to the Jersey soil. Now we started in to push the fight still closer home to him, by attacking his property, the New York Central. We announced that the Erie was going to cut by one-third both its passenger and freight rates from New York to Buffalo. We actually made a start by cutting the passenger rate so low — from $7 to $5 — that the New York Central couldn't possibly meet it. (In fact, the Erie Railroad couldn't afford the rate either; but then we as its Executive Committee were in a tight fix and thought it no more than right that the Erie should come to our rescue.) We also let it be noised abroad that we planned to start a fifty-cent-fare line of boats from New York to Albany, which would hurt Vanderbilt's Hudson River Railroad.

We got in an attack on him in still a third way. We got our agents to introduce in the Legislature at Albany, which was then also in session, a bill legalizing the $10,000,000 issue of stock that our printing press had turned out. Some scoffers called it "A Bill to Legalize Counterfeit Money." But

I have made it a rule all through my life never to mind what scoffers say. Vanderbilt fought the bill hard. And now he was in a better position than we. Because though we had been nearer to Trenton, he was now nearer to Albany. More than that, he could go and come when he wanted to; while we were hindered by our inability to cross even onto York State soil. It began to look as though our bill there would be defeated.

Finally, after the bill had been reported out of the Committee, we found we lacked one vote of the number necessary to pass it. We saw something desperate would have to be done. I called a council of war. I showed how that one of us would have to run the risk and go up to Albany. When they proposed me, I said I couldn't do it nohow. I was the big toad in this puddle. Vanderbilt would pounce onto me before I got half-way up to Albany, and fix me up so quick that my legislative usefulness would be over before it had begun. Fisk would have been a good one, only he was such a dashy fellow. As soon as he got there just like as not he would start in to cut a splurge and drive around in four-in-hands, with half the chorus girls in Albany. He wasn't fitted to do a work softly, as this had to be done. Gould was the man. So I told him that he just had to go and represent me there in the fight at Albany.

"All right," said he finally. "We'll send out

word to the press that I have started off to Ohio, to push the completion of the eighty miles of broad-gauge track from Akron to Toledo, to give us that connection with Chicago we have been talking about so long. Also draw off a half-million dollars from the Erie treasury — (charge it up to sundries) — as my ammunition." So we told the newspaper reporters that Gould was off on the Ohio trip. We gave him a trunk full of greenbacks, and started him off to Albany sort of quiet-like.

We hadn't worked it any too softly. The moment he got to Albany and had set up his headquarters at the Delevan House, Vanderbilt got wind of it and had his New York judge summon him to New York City right off to answer a writ. Gould went back to New York in response to the writ. He then got the case put off. The judge said, "Mr. Gould, I'll postpone the trial. Further, I'll put you under the personal charge of an officer who will see that you don't escape us." So the judge detailed an officer to be with Gould every minute. He said to him, "See to it, officer, that he doesn't get out of your sight." Gould went back to Albany. The officer went along as a kind of valet. At the Delevan House Gould very soon had the senators and assemblymen coming to see him by ones and twos and threes. Now and then he went up in person to the Capitol on the hill.

He carried on my business there so successfully

that Vanderbilt began to scare and got word sent to the officer who was in charge of Gould. So the officer hinted that Gould's presence was very much desired back in New York. Gould answered that he was sick and couldn't possibly stand a railway journey to New York at this time — would have to wait for a few days.

"Now see here," said the officer; "you don't come any such game as that on me. You were well enough just now to go up to the Capitol in a snowstorm. If you can do that, and if you can spend the day and half the night in your secret conferences with committeemen from the Legislature, I guess you're strong enough to make the trip to New York with me, when the Court orders it.",

Gould said he couldn't think of it — it would be too great a strain on his strength — it was inhuman for any law court to ask him to do it. So the officer had to come back to New York alone and report to the court that his prisoner was virtually a runaway, for he had refused to obey the Court's command. This gave Gould a few days longer to be at liberty, which he employed in fixing up some more legislators. Finally he got enough to secure the bill's passing.

But it had been costly work. Those fellows at Albany were a slippery lot. To keep one of them, even after you'd got him, was like holding a wet eel by the tail, they were that untrustworthy. When you have secured a Senator to vote your way, at a price of $15,000 and then have him flop to the other side for $20,000 — well, it shows the kind of people I had to deal with in these transactions. The *New York Independent* called this Legislature of 1868 the "worst assemblage of official thieves that ever disgraced the Capitol of the Empire State." And there were times in the conduct of these negotiations when I thought that that editor was right. In the committee of investigation which the Senate appointed afterwards to look into the charges, they tried to cover up themselves by attacking me. One of the senators said that my conduct in these matters had been what he called "disgraceful," and he expressed his belief that Gould and Fisk "were concerned, and probably interested with Drew in these corrupt proceedings." I give his exact words, because they have found their way into the official documents of the State; otherwise I wouldn't have noticed them.

The ups and downs of the Bill as it was on its way through the Legislature was the means of all kinds of rumours on the Stock Exchange. The whole market was unsettled. Vanderbilt didn't like that state of affairs. The fight was hurting him considerable. His New York Central slumped from 132 to 109. He had said he would support the market if he had to mortgage every dollar of property he possessed. But the job was too big. Furthermore he was exposed to fresh issues of Erie stock, and we threatened 'most every day now to start our printing press going once more. His friends were getting scary, and more and more were leaving him. The Commodore began to see that in trying to oust me and my crowd from the Erie management, he had roped a heifer that he couldn't hold. So about this time I got a note from him looking to a settlement. Most likely he thought of me as the one through whom he could best start the negotiations. Because he and I had been friends in former days and I had named my son after his.

I was glad to get the note and to see that the war was coming to an end. I didn't like it over in Jersey. It wasn't home. I used to take a walk around the city two or three times a day; I tried to be at ease. But it wouldn't go. There wasn't any snap in me. Each morning I'd start into the day's work limply, like a horse that's got corns. I couldn't do much else than sit, sometimes for half a day at a time, with my feet up in a chair, thinking. Over in my big house in New York, and busy every day in Wall Street, I had been as happy as pigs in peastraw. I was tired of being away from home. A man at my age misses the comforts of family life. I wanted to sleep in my own bed, be with my own family, sit in my own pew on Sunday, go to the Wednesday night class, and such-like.

It had been hard for the letter to get from Vander-

bilt to me, Jimmy and Jay were so all-fired suspicious
of me. They were afraid I was going to betray
them and make terms with the Commodore with
them left out. "I'll stake my back teeth you're
planning to flop," Jimmy said once. And he issued
orders to the landlord to tell all the servants that no
mail matter or bit of paper of any kind was to be
delivered to me without his seeing it first. He
wouldn't even let me get a telegram, but he must
open it before it got into my hands.

But the Commodore was clever and worked it
very shrewd. He got a detective to come to Taylor's
Hotel and put up there as a commercial traveller.
This detective slipped a note to the head waiter —
for we ate in a private dining room, as a precaution
against process-servers — and told him to hand it
to me. The head waiter said the orders from the
proprietor were so strict that he was like to lose
his job if he took any note to me.

"That's all right," said the detective; "Vanderbilt
will give you another job when you lose this one."
So the note was handed to the waiter and he slipped
it to me on the sly.

The note was short. It read something like this.

"DREW: —
    "I'm sick of the whole damned business.
Come and see me.        VANDERBILT."

I tried to make away with the paper at once.

But I wasn't quick enough. The rest had spied it, and now were furious at the head waiter. They went to the proprietor and stormed around so that the poor fellow lost his job — as he said he would. But Vanderbilt made it right by taking him into his employ.

I decided to meet the Commodore's offer of peace. Not that I felt any great love towards him. He had been calling me all kinds of names during my stay in Jersey — said I was no better than a batter pudding; that I would turn tail on my partners any time he wanted me to; that I had no backbone and such-like. And whilst I was starting rumours about him through Wall Street, in return for the mean things he was doing to me, he up and said to friends, "This Erie war has taught me that it never pays to kick a skunk." It hurt me considerable when these remarks of his came to my ears. I had half a mind to resent them. But I now concluded to forgive him. He didn't know me, that is all; he said those hard things about me ignorantly. I decided I'd go over and see him. But I would do it on a Sunday. Because on that day process-servers can't ply their trade. During those twenty-four hours, those who are hounded by the law have a day of freedom — neither the sheriff nor his deputies can touch you.

So when Sunday came I set out from the hotel, supposedly for an afternoon's walk. When I was out of sight I changed my course, and slipped over to New York.  I found Vanderbilt at his house on what used to be the Potter's Field, but was now called Washington Square.  It was a fine big house, red brick with white trimmings.  I was very cordial in my greetings to him.  I thought it best to show a friendly spirit and act as though nothing had come between us.

"How do, Commodore," said I, and I grasped him by the hand.  "The sight of you is good for sore eyes."

"Come in," said he.  He was short as pie crust. I saw that those convertible bonds were sticking in his gizzard.  But I made up my mind that I'd keep sweet, anyhow, let him be miffed as much as he pleased.

"You've got a fine house here, Commodore," I remarked, sitting down in an easy-chair and crossing my legs in a friendly sort of a way.  "It beats all creation how this city is a-growing.  Why, back in my 'Bull's Head' days, this here place where you've got your fine house used to be called Shinbone Alley — the graves around here were as thick as bugs on a pumpkin vine.  Those were great old days, anyhow.  I often think of the times when you and I were in the steamboat business together."

But Vanderbilt puckered up tighter than chokecherries.  "Now see here," said he; "let's don't get gushy.  Of course I'd like to be affectionate and chat with you about old times. No one knows how my bowels yearn after you, Drew. But as I understand it, this is a business interview. So, if you'll wipe that tobacco juice off your chin and draw up here to the table, we'll talk." I wiped my chin and drew up close to the table. We talked the thing over.

We didn't come to any settlement at that time. When a great war has been waging, the first time the two sides meet for a conference, about all they can do is to shake hands and become friends once more. That is enough for one interview. The details of the treaty of peace are settled in a second conference. So now with us. We talked the thing over in a general way and decided that it was better to be at peace with each other than to be fighting. Anyhow, I was then in no frame of mind to go into the matter in cool and careful fashion. I was on pins and needles. I was all the time looking at the clock to see if I could be sure of getting back on Jersey soil before twelve o'clock midnight. Because my freedom would expire at that time. If I allowed myself to be caught napping, Vanderbilt might have a process-server in hiding, and nab me. So we appointed a time for another conference. I bid the Commodore good night, hastened to the ferry, and got back onto Jersey soil before the Sabbath came to an end.

I was glad that a treaty of peace was in sight.

It had been almost a month now since our move to Jersey, and I had got heartily sick of it. Besides, there was another side to the thing. During the legislative contest which we were waging in Albany, each turn in the tide of fortune up there had been followed by hundreds of speckilators in Wall Street, to take advantage of the turns in Erie stock which the rumours from Albany caused. One day it would be noised abroad that Vanderbilt was sure to win; and Erie would go up. Then a day or two after it would be reported: "Uncle Dan'l and his crowd have got control of the Senate; they are going to pass their bill, and rivet their hold on the Erie Railroad forever." Whereupon Erie shares would go down. Thus outsiders were getting just as much speckilative advantage in Wall Street as we were, because their guesses as to the outcome at Albany were as good as ours. We insiders didn't have any better chance than they.

I began to see that it is poor policy for big men in Wall Street to fight each other. When I am fighting a money king, even my victories are dangersome. Take the present situation. I had scooped a fine profit out of this Erie deal, and it was for the most part in solid cash. But — and here was the trouble — it had all come out of one man, Vanderbilt. Naturally it had left him very sore. And being so powerful, he was able to fight back. As has been seen, he did fight back. He had put me and my party to a lot of inconvenience. That always happens when you take money from a man on your own level. On the other hand, if I had taken these profits from outsiders, it would in the aggregate have amounted to the same sum. But the losers would have been scattered all over the whole country and so wouldn't have been able to get together and hit back. A thousand dollars of my total profits would have come then out of a lumber merchant, say in Oshkosh; five hundred dollars from a coal dealer in New Haven; eight hundred dollars from an undertaker in Poughkeepsie; a thousand dollars or two from a doctor in Syracuse; and so on, here a little and there a little. Many drops of water make the mighty ocean, and many small profits, added together, make the big profit. Thus, by making my money from people on the outside, an insider like myself could make just as much in the long run, and not raise up any one enemy powerful enough to cause him discomfort.

So, as the time for the conference with Vanderbilt drew nigh, I made plans to be there good and punctual. I thought it best to go there alone. Gould and Fisk would probably want so much for themselves, when it came to a settlement with Vanderbilt, that I was afraid, if they were there too, the thing wouldn't go off smooth. We had set the conference for the home of Ex-Judge Pierrepont. Gould and Fisk knew that something was in the wind. So, in order to put their heads in a bag, I made believe that I was going to let them be a party to the affair.

"When the final settlement is made, you must be there," said I.

"You bet your giblets we'll be there," Jimmy remarked. "Won't we, Jay?" Jay grinned and said he'd try to make it convenient to attend. "Don't get the kink in your head," Jimmy added, "that you're going to see the Commodore alone when it comes to dividing up the swag."

I saw from this that I was going to have a job on my hands to get the thing fixed up without their knowing it. So I hit upon a scheme. On the night of the conference I made the appointment with Fisk and Gould, but I fixed it at the Fifth Avenue Hotel in New York. Then when we started over I made an excuse and said for them to go on up to the Fifth Avenue Hotel ahead and wait for me. They agreed, and started off. I then skipped over by another way, and went to the house of Judge Pierrepont.

I was glad to find that Vanderbilt had kept the appointment. We went into Pierrepont's drawing-room, drew up around the table and were soon busy with our treaty of peace.

"Now let's understand one thing first of all," said Vanderbilt. "This ten-million batch of Erie that I've paid good money for, has got to be taken off my hands. So, Drew, set your wits to that end of the thing first. Otherwise, there won't be any settlement." I told him I thought it could be done. I'd take the money from the Erie treasury and use it to pay him for the stock he had bought of me.

Vanderbilt replied that it was none of his business where the money came from, so long as he got it. We were getting along in the conference fine as anything. When suddenly the front-door bell rang. Fisk and Gould walked in. Pierrepont went out into the hall to meet them. Gould engaged Pierrepont in conversation. Jimmy edged over towards the drawing-room door and suddenly bust in on us. He was in high spirits, as usual. He took on as though he was mighty glad to see me.

"Hello, Uncle," said he; "put her there! Can't tell how glad I am to find you here. Jay and I were afraid we might not be able to get here in time. We waited down at the Fifth Avenue Hotel, but in some way or other missed you down there. Then the man whom we had set to follow you came and said that you were up here at Pierrepont's house, and spoke as though you wanted us. So we set aside everything else and have come. Hope we can be of some assistance in drawing up a treaty of peace with our honoured adversary here." Vanderbilt broke out in a loud roar of laughter. I wasn't in any mood to join him. I didn't feel at all like laughing. I tried not to show it, but the truth is, I was very much put out. They had bust in on me just at a time when the thing was going smooth as anything.

However, I made the best of it. I told them that I had been planning to look out for their interests, whether they had come or not. I hadn't thought it necessary to invite them to this particular conference, because often the early stages of a negotiation can be handled better by one person acting for all, than by them acting for themselves. But that was no matter now. If they chose to be present, as far as I was concerned, they were welcome. We made places for them at the table, and got once more to work.

"This is where we'd got to," said Vanderbilt. "The nine million dollars worth of stock that was saddled onto me is to be bought back, and we're going to call the thing quits."

"But where is that nine millions to come from?" asked Jimmy.

"Why, Drew here says he proposes to take it out of the Erie treasury."

Jimmy gave a long whistle of astonishment. "By the Lord Almighty!" said he, "that's a corker. Commodore, I'm an ungodly man. Wall Street sucks the conscience out of a fellow, anyway; and I don't know as I had any large amount of it even before I went there. But there are some things that even I can't stand for. And this almighty robbery of Drew's against the Erie Railroad is one of them."

"I'm not saying anything, myself, as to the equity

of this thing Drew proposes," said Vanderbilt. "It's none of my business, anyway. In these matters every man must chew his own meat. But, however you arrange it, some way has got to be found for taking this dirty batch of stock off my hands, or by the Lord God, I'll hound you curs from now to Kingdom Come."

I tried to persuade Jay and Jimmy to consent to the plan. I showed them how they had made some money in their short sales. And though, of course, they wouldn't be cleaning up so much on this deal as I, still I was older; they had lots of time yet. I told them I couldn't stand it much longer at Taylor's Hotel. Those quarters were so cramped, compared to what I'd been used to, I felt about as comfortable there as three in a bed. A man at my age, I told them, needs to be home and enjoy his friends. I pleaded with them until well on towards midnight.

At last Jay spoke up. He had been silent a good share of the evening. He never was much of a fellow to talk, anyhow. I used to wish I could be silent like him, for it's the still hog that eats the most. He now had a few words with Jimmy on the side. As soon as it was over he spoke up; Jay took a masterful tone at that moment, which I had never seen him take before. In fact, Gould was a different man from that time on, a leader rather than a follower.

"Mr. Vanderbilt," said he; "we are willing to come to some such arrangement. We will allow Drew here to keep the profits he has made in this deal, and to draw the money out of the Erie treasury. But,"— and he spoke now in so positive a tone that I had to open my eyes to see if it was really the quiet-mannered Gould I had formerly known — "there's got to be one condition attached. Dan Drew has got to get out of the Erie Railroad for good and all."

I began to speak up at once. I didn't like the idea of letting go my hold on Erie. One of my ideas in coming to a settlement was that I might get back into Wall Street as a railroad manager and so as an insider. I started to explain the thing. But they wouldn't let me talk.

"Now, see here," broke in the Commodore. "I suppose I'll have to preside at this meeting. Your arrangements as to the Erie Railroad are something that don't exactly concern me. I'm not responsible for that road. Don't know but what, all in all, I am just as glad that I'm not. But we must conduct this meeting in parliamentary fashion. All in favour of the basis of settlement as just stated, namely, that Drew is to be left in possession of the money he has made and himself to get out of the road from this time forth forevermore, say 'Aye.'" And then, "All opposed say, 'No.'"

The vote was put, and of course I was voted down. I knew perfectly well that if it came to counting noses, I'd be out; and I tried to get some other way of deciding it. But they carried the day. A treaty of peace was drawn up along those lines. Judge Barnard fined the smaller directors of the Erie Company ten dollars each for contempt of court. Us bigger fellows he let off scot free. Thus the legal snarls and tangles were got rid of. And the war came to an end.

After it was settled, I was more contented than I had thought I would be. My profits in ready cash were big. In this deal I had certainly brought my hogs to a fine market. To be sure I had lost the Erie Railroad. That goose was gone that had laid for me those big eggs. But with the nine millions now sluiced off from her treasury, I thought the Erie Road wasn't really a valuable enough property to squabble over. Jimmy, I guess, had something of the same feeling.

"Yes," said he, as the conference was coming to a close, "the pirates have gone off with the swag, and have left us nothing but the confounded hulk."

"Don't you mind," said Jay; "there may be some service left in the old vessel yet."

"Drew," said the Commodore to me as I started to leave, "I dare say you will chuckle a heap, with that hen-cackle of yours, over this thing which you'll call a victory. Most likely you'll tell all your friends how you downed the Commodore. Well, I don't know but what you have downed me, after a fashion.

But I don't want you to think it was because I didn't have money enough. If I wanted to, I think I could raise the cash to buy your crowd, body and breeches. But I confess that I haven't money enough to buy up that printing press of yours. In the present state of our country's jurisprudence, there doesn't seem to be any limit to the amount of certificates of stock that you fellows can manufacture out of white paper. I'm willing to own up, Drew, that here's a case where you fooled me. Good night."

I said, "Good night," and was glad to be out into the street a free man once more.

Anyhow, Vanderbilt had only himself to blame for this trouble he had got himself into. He had no call to mix up in Erie matters. If he thought I was going to submit tamely and let him push me aside without fighting back, he had the wrong sow by the ears, that's all. The trouble with Vanderbilt was, he had an idea that the law is the highest power in the land. He now saw his mistake. He never stopped to think that law is no such wonderful thing after all. Law is like a cobweb; it's made for flies and the smaller kind of insects, so to speak, but lets the big bumblebees break through. I showed him in this affair that I was the bumblebee. Where technicalities of the law stood in my way, I have always been able to brush them aside easy as anything. In this Erie war we had judges from New York, Binghamton, Albany and Brooklyn, issuing contrary injunctions. It has been called, "The darkest scene in the history of American jurisprudence." I don't know anything as to that. When you're in business you can't split hairs, or bother over technicalities.

But, anyhow, with the settlement that had now been reached, Vanderbilt had been taken care of; the loss had been saddled on the outside people. That is always the safe way; because, as I guess I've already wrote, the outsiders are so numerous they can't get together and hit back. It must have been one of these outsiders who wrote a poem about this Erie war. I never thought much of the poetry of it. It has always seemed to me no better than a string of foolish jesting. For my part I like hymns better:

> Cornelius, the great Cornerer,
> A solemn oath he swore,
> That in his trouser's pocket he
> Would put one railroad more.
> And when he swears he means it,
> The stout old Commodore.

> But brooding o'er the Erie sat —
> In fact, on the same lay,
> A bird that, feathering his nest,
> Affirmed, by yea and nay,
> Before he'd budge he'd see them all —
> Much further than I'll say.

Said he unto the Commodore:
"Your bark is on the sea;
But do not steer for Erie's isle,
Since that's been struck by me.
Go, man of sin, and leave me here
To my theology."

The dearest ties on earth to some
Are plainly railroad ties;
So little wonder that he spoke
In anger and surprise —
Tears would not flow; the Commodore,
It seems, had dammed his eyes.

Such "Erie" sights, such "Erie" sounds,
Came from this Erie crew,
It seemed indeed a den of lines
Prepared for Daniel — Drew;
Not strange that he at last resolved
To make his own adoo.

Fleeing from jars — perhaps the jug —
Dan looked to foreign lands,
And to his brethren said, "Arise!
These Bonds put off our hands;
We will unto New Jersey, where
My Seminary stands."

Just how the joust may terminate,
Nobody knows or cares.
No need to ask how fares the fight —
They'll ask us for our fares,
And whichever side may win, will plow
The public with its shares.

So we will sing, Long live the Ring,
And Daniel, long live he;
May his high school confer on him
Exceeding high degree,
Doubling his D's until, indeed,
He is D. D., D. D.

# XXVII

THAT "Seminary" spoken of in the poem was Drew Theological Seminary in Madison, New Jersey. My founding of it came about in this way:

I had been spoken to several times by the preachers who used to visit at my house when they came to New York, say during Conference week or for other occasions, about how fine it would be to establish a great theological institution. I had let them know that I might be willing, when the time should come. Because this was just when the Civil War was over. I was then Treasurer and Managing Director of the Erie Railroad, and was making money so fast I could afford to give some of it away.

So one day a couple of preachers, Brother McClintock and Brother Crooks, came and saw me at my house. I knew what they were coming for, and was there to meet them. It had to be done more or less in formal style. I let them in and had them take seats.

They said: "We have come to see what spirit you are in, Brother Drew, in reference to the Centenary Movement that is about to be inaugurated.

What offering are you willing to make in token of your gratitude to God for your connection with his Church?"

I answered right up: "I am willing to donate two hundred and fifty thousand dollars for the endowment of a Theological Seminary."

It didn't take long to clinch the thing. After five minutes the interview ended. I never shall forget their handclasps and their hearty "God bless you's," as they said good-bye at the door.

We had other interviews. The committee began to suggest to me that this would be a great monument to Daniel Drew, if the school should be established on a large enough scale. I answered that when I put my hand to a thing, I usually did it in proper fashion. In fact I couldn't afford to have my name connected with any institution, if it was to be only a one-horse affair.

"Supposing we should call it 'Drew Theological Seminary,' Brother Drew?"

"Why, brethren, I have just said that if my name is going to be attached to it in so out-and-out a fashion, I shall have to take care of the school and see it through, no matter what it costs." So I said I would give, first, the ground and buildings. Second, as the foundation of a library, twenty-five thousand dollars. For a permanent endowment fund of the Institution, two hundred and fifty thousand dollars, as soon as the charter should be secured the following winter. And I would swell the amount finally to half a million.

It was so big a gift that a public meeting was needed in order to celebrate it. They were setting out to raise a million dollars in all, as a fund to celebrate the one-hundredth anniversary of the church in America. The brethren felt it would give the whole movement for this Centenary Fund a big boost, to announce right at the start a gift of a quarter of a million dollars from me. So a meeting was arranged to be held in my big church on Fourth Avenue. I looked forward with a good deal of pleasure to the time when the gift was to be publicly announced.

Finally the night came around — a Thursday evening, late in January. It was a stormy night. But big preparations had been made for the meeting and the church was filled. All our churches in the city had joined their choirs into one, which now filled the back gallery of the church. A great choir it was — well-nigh two hundred voices, I should judge. The congregation was so large, I said to myself, "If the weather had been fine to-night, this church wouldn't have begun to hold the people." Brother Crooks opened the meeting, since he and Brother McClintock were the ones that had seen me in the interview at my house. The opening hymn was that well-known one, which is so full of praise; and when the enormous choir began it, we in the

congregation joined in and there was a volume of
sound that must have reached to the Pearly Gates.
I was one of the vice-presidents of the meeting, and
so sat in the front pew.   I'm not much of a singer,
but I couldn't help joining in the hymn:

> Before Jehovah's awful throne,
> Ye nations bow with sacred joy;
> Know that the Lord is God alone;
> He can create and He destroy.

There was prayer by Dr. Durbin, and an address
by the chairman of the meeting — a man from somewheres out West.   Then another hymn.

This second hymn fitted into the present occasion
fine.   Because my gift was to be made a kind of
missionary agent, to coax gifts from other men all
over the country:

> See how great a flame aspires,
> Kindled by a spark of grace.
> Jesus' love the nations fires,
> Sets the kingdoms on a blaze.

> To bring fire on earth He came;
> Kindled in some hearts it is.
> Oh, that all might catch the flame,
> All partake the glorious bliss!

As we got into the hymn I felt as though all eyes
were upon me, even though only a few as yet knew
of my offer of a quarter of a million dollars.   I

looked upon my gift as a kind of seed, that was not only going to do good in itself, but was going to unlock the purse-strings of other rich men:

When He first the work began,
Small and feeble was His day;
Now the word doth swiftly run,
Now it wins its widening ray.

More and more it spreads and grows,
Ever mighty to prevail;
Sin's strongholds it now o'erthrows,
Shakes the trembling gates of Hell.

Saw ye not the cloud arise,
Little as a human hand?
Now it spreads along the skies,
Hangs o'er all the thirsty land;

Lo! The promise of a shower
Drops already from above;
But the Lord will shortly pour
All the spirit of His love.

When the turn of Bishop James came to speak, he said that in this Centenary Celebration the authorities had proposed that it be not only a spiritual one, but also take a financial character. And these two features, the spiritual and the financial, were combined in Dr. McClintock's speech, which closed the evening. He went on to show the supreme importance of the doctrine of holiness in this life.

"Our Church," said Brother McClintock, "has put forward as its very elementary thought, the great central pervading idea of the Holy Book of God from the beginning to the end: The holiness of the human soul, heart, mind and will. It might be called fanaticism, but, dear friends, that is our mission. If we keep to that, the next century is ours. If we keep to that, the triumphs of the next century shall throw those that are past far in the shade. Our work is a moral work. That is to say, the work of making men holy. There is our mission. There is our glory. There is our power."

Then he went on to show the importance of holiness in consecrating your pocket-book. Said he — and now came the public announcement:

"I think it right to say that one of your members has set you a noble example. I hope that Daniel Drew's life may be spared to see the erection of a Theological Seminary to which he has consecrated a quarter of a million dollars, and to which he will give as much more before it is finished. It is a grand start."

I wish I could put it down on paper, the applause. I sat quiet through it all. But I think I took more real joy out of the joy of those people when my gift was announced, than out of 'most anything else in my life. I felt as though I was doing a work which perhaps was bigger than even I myself could realize. It seemed as though I was no longer just a person, but was a great and mighty force, working for my fellow human beings throughout the wide world, for all ages to come.  For the speaker went on:

"God has given us, as you have been told to-night, mighty power.  We stand here upon our eastern coast and look over yonder; there is old Europe. We stand upon our western coast and look yonder to the west, again, and there's old Asia.  Asia, the land of population.  Europe, the land of ideas. And America — the land in which population and ideas are to come together.  Now think of that! Here is the field where the prolific energies of the Asiatic life are to be penetrated through and through with the sharp and living ideas of a vital Christian civilization.  Are we up to the grandeur of that thought?"

This was the closing speech.  Of course nothing but the doxology could bring such a meeting to a fit close.  And the swing which was given to those grand old words will be remembered, I suppose, by every one in that congregation:

> Praise God from whom all blessing flow:
> Praise Him, all creatures here below;
> Praise Him above, ye Heavenly host;
> Praise Father, Son and Holy Ghost.

The weeks which followed this meeting were busy weeks.  They were busy for me, because I was just getting into the Erie war (which I have wrote about). In fact I was just at that moment in the campaign where I broke the market by dumping onto the Street those fifty-eight thousand shares, when nobody thought that I would dare do it. I also had my reëlection to the Erie Board to look after, when Vanderbilt was going to put me out. The campaign which terminated in the scampering to Jersey City followed.

They were busy weeks, also, for the Committee of Preachers which had my theological school in charge. Because I put upon them the work of carrying out the details of the school's establishment. My first idea had been to locate the school at Carmel. I thought it would be well to sort of centre my institutions in the region where I had first seen the light of day. But, to put up new buildings would take too long. Besides, a location nearer New York might be more favourable. Out at Perth Amboy, New Jersey, was a place called Eagleswood School. This had been a boarding school, and I made the owner an offer for it. He wouldn't sell at the figure I named.

My attention was then called to the old Gibbons estate, "The Forest," out at Madison, New Jersey. Thomas Gibbons, as I guess I have wrote, had made his home there. He was the one who owned the steamboat that Vanderbilt had worked on when he came up from Staten Island. Gibbons had also been the one to fight the Fulton-Livingston monopoly, which opened the Hudson River and made my entrance into the steamboat business possible. His son, William Gibbons, was now owner of the estate. I looked over the place. It was in a beautiful part of the country. The town there has since got to be known as the "City of Roses." The country place which Gibbons had built at the Forest was large. There was a carriage-house, a horse-barn, and the owner's residence — a big building with six white pillars in front. Gibbons and I dickered for a while. We came to terms. The money was paid over. A deed was secured.

We were in a hurry to begin the school. So we fitted up the buildings just as they were. Gibbons's mansion was made into the main hall of the Seminary. I got it called "Mead Hall" (after my wife's name, before I married her). The carriage- and horse-barns were fitted up for "dormitories" — that's what the professors called them; it means places to sleep in. And in the month of November, 1867, came the exercises which opened the school.

## XXVIII

IT WAS a red-letter day in my life, the day that
I went out to Madison, N. J., to attend the
opening of my seminary. All the big men
of the church were present. Great preparations
had been made for the event. I was the central
figure. But my walk and conversation that day
were modest, as becomes a Christian. In fact my
church paper, in describing the celebration, used
these exact words:

Of all the company present at Madison on this
opening day, the most modest and unassuming
person was Mr. Drew himself. A lady who
expressed a desire to see the founder of the Seminary
was told in our hearing that the most unpretentious
elderly gentleman she saw would be Mr. Drew.
The description was perfectly exact. Though
grateful to the church for its recognition of the gift,
there is in his manner no trace of self-consciousness.
Mr. Drew has been happy in a great opportunity,
and has had the wisdom to use it well. His example
will inspire our men of means to go forward in the
same direction.

It was a Wednesday. By ten o'clock that morning the main street of Madison was filled with people, guests from nearly all the Eastern states, going to a neighbour church which had kindly opened its doors for the services. At ten-thirty the service began. Dr. McClintock gave out the opening hymn. While it was being sung, I couldn't help but think of the privilege that was mine in here founding a school that was to send forth young men year by year to build up the walls of Zion and to dispense the sincere milk of the word:

> With stately towers and bulwarks strong,
> Unrivall'd and alone —
> Loved theme of many a sacred song —
> God's holy city shone.
>
> Thus fair was Zion's chosen seat,
> The glory of all lands;
> Yet fairer and in strength complete,
> The Christian temple stands.
>
> The faithful of each clime and age
> This glorious church compose;
> Built on a rock, with idle rage,
> The threat'ning tempest blows.
>
> Fear not; though hostile bands alarm,
> Thy God is thy defence;
> And weak and powerless every arm
> Against Omnipotence.

Then the speakers began. Dr. Johnson, from

Carlyle, Pa., was one.  He referred to the little group of young men who were forming the opening class in my Seminary.  He talked about the kind of training which they ought to have.  He said:

We don't want them "to draw their materials for preaching from philosophy, from science, from anything outside of this Book as its foundation.  Look at that inventory of the Christian's panoply that Paul gives!  While armed from helmet to greaves, there's but one defensive weapon, and that is the Sword of the Spirit which is the Word of God.  We want to be able to wield this Sword of the Spirit aright.  You remember that John, in that picture he draws of the great city that he saw in his vision, tells us that the sons of God were victorious through the blood of the Lamb.  Now no Christian warrior is qualified to fight until the blood of the Lamb has renewed his heart.  And in connection with the blood of the Lamb is mentioned the word of their testimony.  And what is the Christian's testimony but that of the experience of the great truths of this Book which David calls God's testimonies?

I couldn't help but feel, while those words were being spoken, that young men trained in such truths would become mighty powers in the world.  And I was glad to think, as I looked upon that band of young men, that I was the one who was making it possible for them to go forth as tongues of fire in the midst of a dark world.

If I was inclined at that moment to forget my modesty just a little, I don't know but what I really did forget it when the last speaker on the morning's programme, Dr. North, got up. After expressing his admiration for the beautiful scene which we were there enacting, he said that other gifts from other rich men were also greatly needed. Then, with an outburst, he exclaimed:

"Oh, that we had one more Daniel Drew!"

This closed the morning's exercises. I have wrote about the thing in full, because it was an historic occasion. Not that I remember out of my head all the words that were spoken and the things that were done. It's all here before me, in clippings from my *New York Christian Advocate*.

At the conclusion of the morning exercises, we repaired, several hundred strong, to the Seminary grounds, a short distance west of the village, where, in the edifice heretofore known as the Forest Hill Mansion, and now lavishly reconstructed, the guests found, in the room which is henceforth to be the chapel, a sumptuous entertainment provided by my liberality for their refreshment, and beneath whose savoury burden the tables literally groaned; while others were as bounteously provided for in the town hall, turned, for the time being, into a tastefully garlanded refectory. (Refectory means a place to eat.) After doing ample justice to the viands now spread before them in prodigal profusion, the visitors, many of them distinguished divines who had come from afar to grace the occasion with their presence, and whose eloquence signalized the inaugural and has made the event memorable, were invited to examine the buildings and ground, to which they promptly responded, and concluded their inspection with the most unbounded admiration of the premises, profuse felicitations to the donor, and unqualified approbation of the judgment of him and his advisors in the selection they had made.

In fact, the meal that day wasn't any of your nose-bag feeds — no snatch-and-go kind of a thing. We had moved tables into the big room of what had been old Tom Gibbons's house. The meal was a rib-tickler. A restaurant man had been hired for the occasion. He had got orders from me to put up as costly victuals as he could find, and send the bill to me. And now, as I looked over the crowd, and saw them stowing the good things away under their belts, I was glad I hadn't been stingy in the matter. I remembered how, in my old drover days, I used to get hungry enough sometimes to drink pig's milk. We didn't have any such viands as these to eat, back in those days.

The exercises in the afternoon began at half-past two. This wasn't a Sunday. Yet the services were almost like what they are on a Lord's Day. We started off by singing that hymn which is so fit when young men are setting forth into the beautiful life of the Christian ministry:

> Go, preach my Gospel, saith the Lord;
> Bid the whole world my grace receive;
> He shall be saved who trusts my word,
> And he condemn'd who won't believe.
>
> I'll make your great commission known,
> And ye shall prove my gospel true,
> By all the works that I have done,
> By all the wonders ye shall do.
>
> Teach all the nations my commands —
> I'm with you till the world shall end;
> All power is trusted in my hands —
> I can destroy and I defend.

Philip Phillips was there, and sang in a sweet voice: "There Will Be No More Sorrow There." In the morning he had also helped out with his beautiful hymn: "I'll Sing for Jesus." After the solo, Dr. McClintock made a speech in which he told about the school and its plans. Said he:

The full extent of Mr. Drew's gift was not announced at the beginning. He is one of those men who do more than they promise. You should know that he founded a Young Ladies' Academy at Carmel. That gift was entirely apart from and in addition to the Centenary gift involved in the Theological Seminary. What will be the extent of these two donations, I do not know. This much I do know, that Mr. Drew is not in the habit of putting his hands to any object and letting it go unfinished or half accomplished.

When he finished, I felt that even if I hadn't been of a mind to help the school in a big way, I ought to do it now.

Dr. Porter represented the Newark Conference at the exercises. The announcement of the "Drew Theological Seminary," he said, had made his heart leap for joy. He was persuaded that God in his providence was leading the Church to adopt those measures and take steps from time to time that were calculated to meet the exigencies of the times and advance the interests of His cause. He added that it was the mission of the Church to arouse the public mind with regard to experimental and practical religion, and this it had done.

Dr. Cummings was there, from Middletown, Ct. His words were even more personal. Said he:

Among the thoughts that have suggested themselves to my mind to-day is that of the noble illustration exhibited on this occasion of the Christian use of money. We know that men often give liberally for worthy objects, and yet the influence of that gift is transient. It accomplishes a good work, but it lacks the element of permanency in its influence. The history of educational institutions is, in this respect, remarkably encouraging.

Nothing can be nobler than to give the funds and moneys which God himself has bestowed.

I wish I could give more of his talk. It was a very good speech. It made me better acquainted with his college up there in Connecticut; and I have helped it out also with some money.

The speech of Bishop Janes was one that I thought must do the young students for the ministry a lot of good. In fact, they were words that everybody ought to lay to heart. He said:

I assume that all the young men who come here for the advantages of this institution will be Christian young men; that, having received the grace of repentance they have been justified by faith and regenerated by Divine Grace. I assume, also, that they have been led to feel in their own minds that they were moved by the Holy Ghost to take upon them the work and office of the Christian pastorate; that they don't take upon themselves this honour, but are called to it of God, as was Aaron. I also assume that the church has been convinced of the correctness of the convictions by their natural gifts and Christian graces and the unction attending their religious exercises, and has recommended them to the travelling connection for pastoral work.

Now, with these assumptions, I ask, what is necessary for these young men? Knowledge and discipline. They are ambassadors of God. It is, therefore, all-important that they have a knowledge of God, of His mind, of His will, of His relation

to us, and especially of His mind and will concerning our salvation.  It is necessary that they should
understand human character, the condition of the
human mind and the human heart, the passions,
affections, aspirations, desires and purposes of
men.

Now our discipline says that we are to read
the Bible and such books as help to a knowledge
of the same; and the original languages of the Scriptures may be important to us in learning these
things, in giving us the different shades of meaning and enabling us more perfectly to understand
our translation of the word of God.  Now, having
this knowledge of God and man, we need drilling.
We propose to train our young men in the camp.
We expect men here trained to fight in the skir-
mishes of the Lord or to lead a forlorn hope.  Our
Government doesn't send men to West Point to prepare them to carry the musket, but expects every
man to be an officer.  And in the education of men
here, we don't expect those who go from this institution simply to stand in the rank and file of Immanuel's Army.  We expect every man to be competent
to be a leader and lead forward God's sacramental
hosts, and to lead onward and onward, until all
the cohorts of error are driven from the world, and
the standard of Immanuel is triumphant over all
lands.  And I charge the founder of this institution
and the trustees and faculty to see to it that the
young men under their care are not only informed,
but disciplined and drilled, until ready for camp or
field.

I call upon the authorities of this institution to
see that this place is our Jerusalem, where the

young men who tarry here shall be indued with power from on high and go forth in the name and strength of God to subdue this world to His authority. I now invoke the benediction of God upon our beloved brother, whose munificence has brought us together on this occasion. And I pray that God may command His blessings upon those who, from time to time, enjoy its advantages. That, being themselves blessed by it, they may be made a blessing to mankind.

The last speaker was Dr. Allen of Girard College. He spoke more or less off-hand. But his words were full of meat:

If there has ever been any prejudice in our church against our men of wealth, the donations of Mr. Drew would do much to cause it to disappear and to vanish forever. The church needs the money of its wealthy men. If more of them would give according to their means, as our worthy friend has given, no doubt this prejudice would entirely cease. I will only add that, in speaking of the eminent founder of this institution, we fear him not as a rich man. If my classical friend, Dr. McClintock, will allow me, I will put a negative in a classical description Virgil once used:

"*Non timeo Danaos dona ferentes.*"

(Those words tacked onto the tail end there, are from one of the dead languages. I don't just remember now what it was that some one told me they meant.    But it was something like: "A man is not dangersome, if he brings a gift.")

With the benediction, the services which opened Drew Theological Seminary came to an end.    I came away feeling, in the words of the benediction, the peace of God which passeth all understanding. The *New York Christian Advocate* said: "We most heartily congratulate the munificent founder and patron of the new seminary in view of its propitious inauguration, and also upon its fortunate location and the highly commodious buildings and ample grounds in which the nascent 'school of the prophets' begins its career."

## XXIX

I WAS glad that the opening of my theological School came just when it did. Because it fitted into a niche in the year's work when I had the time to attend it. If, instead of coming in November, it had come two months earlier, it would have found me right in the midst of my dicker to get back into the Director's Board and Treasuryship of the Erie Road. And if it had come three months later, it would have found me in the midst of the war with the Commodore. Maybe, just at the time when the opening services were being held, it would have found me at Taylor's Hotel. Of course, in that latter case I could have gone to Madison, it being also outside of York State's jurisdiction. Still, it would have been inconvenient for me; because those weeks at "Fort Taylor" were weeks of so much distress of mind, that I couldn't have entered into the spirit of the inaugural occasion as I felt it deserved.

These were months, anyhow, in which I was hard pushed by business cares. Just when the first year of my Theological Seminary was drawing to a close, a bad accident happened on the Erie Road, which enemies tried to lay at my door. An express train was coming along from the West one night. It had made the trip safely until it got to Carn's Rock, some sixteen miles west of Port Jervis. The road at that point is cut into the side of a precipice, over-hanging a gorge. It was the last place where a rail-road treasurer would like to have an accident. As bad luck would have it, just at that point is where the accident took place.

As the train was rushing along in the darkness of the early morning, the wheels in some way got off the rails and four cars were hurled down the embank-ment. They dropped eighty feet to the bottom and were crushed into a tangled mass. Twenty-two people were killed, and all the survivors mangled. The rear car was a sleeping coach. This was so smashed that the passengers inside couldn't get out. It caught on fire, and the people were burned alive. The shrieks of the passengers as they tried to get out of the burning car, were described in the newspapers the next day. Public feeling was aroused. The people out around Port Jervis held an indignation meeting. They got up an investigation to find out the cause of the "murder," as they called it. They seemed to think that some of us who were at the head of the road had set about to kill those poor passen-gers intentionally. It was the most unheard-of charge that a man ever had to stand up against. So I was glad when the investigation committee had got through and made its report. Because then it was seen very clearly that the horrible thing wasn't a "murder" at all, but had happened just by accident.

However, I was not altogether pleased at the way this committee worded its report. I had tried to give out to the public that the accident had been caused by the spring rains, and by the softening of the road-bed, due to the winter's frost coming out of the ground, causing the rails to spread under the weight of the engine. But the coroner's report said that the accident was due to the rotten condition of the rails. It said that an inspection of the track at that point had showed that some of the rails had been used so long that they were worn to rags. This increased the public clamour. The investigation went on further and dug up unpleasant points in connection with my management of the road.

The truth is, I had been obliged for some time back to scrimp expenses on the road-bed. The superintendent of that department had been pestering me for a long time back, because of the "worn-out and rotten condition of the rails," as he put it. He was a faithful fellow, one who took the welfare of the road very much to heart. But he was for improvements, no matter what the cost. I had the financial end to look after. New rails for five hundred miles of road-bed cost a sum of money which track foremen haven't big enough minds to grasp. I was constantly more put to it than the Erie workmen had any idea of, to keep the road even in as good a condition as it was. It is true that I had got the directors of the road several times to vote to borrow money for buying steel rails to replace the worn-out iron rails. But I had invariably found, as soon as the money was raised, that I needed it in my stock-market operations. However, I wanted to keep the road up. As a matter of fact, I had told the superintendent of road-beds to go ahead and order new rails — had given my full authority for the purchase. But, unfortunately, the manufacturer of rails sent the order back unhonoured — said that our last purchase hadn't been paid for as yet, and he wasn't going to send any more until we paid for those we already had. So, as the next best thing, I had got the old rails taken up and turned. A train wears out the inside of the rail more than the outside, because the flange of the wheel rubs against the inside edge. I figured that to have the rails turned was the next best thing to getting new rails altogether.

That's the long and short of the whole thing. I got lots of blame at the time for the killing of those poor people, and for their burning alive in that sleeping car. So I want to state my side of the case. The *New York Advocate* was very considerate and charitable towards me. But *Harper's Weekly* came out against me and my fellow operators of the road without any charity at all:

"The directors of the Erie Railway," it said, "deserve the moral reprobation of the community. Had they been in any degree as solicitous for the proper condition of their road and for the safety of the passengers whom they entrapped into their trains, as they have shown themselves for the personal advantages that might arise from speculating in the stock, this horrible catastrophe would not have happened. The Legislature is in session, and we hope that it will do something to protect the public against the mingled rapacity and neglect of the Erie Railway management; let it decide that travellers shall not be recklessly massacred."

But I didn't care what the papers said. No matter what you do, people are sure to put a wrong construction upon it. The best way is to be boiler-plated, so to speak, and not mind what the papers say. A bare-footed conscience would suffer considerably in treading among thorns. For instance, there was old Enoch Crosby. I guess I've wrote about him in these papers somewhere. He's the one that was a spy during the Revolutionary War, and now lies up in the Old Gilead Burying Lot at Carmel. That man, when he was working as a spy for the patriot troops in the war, had to tell stories now and then that didn't just square with the truth. Well, he was that prickly in his conscience that, after the war was over, he wouldn't join the church, because of those fibs he had been forced to tell. He was always present at meeting time. He was even treasurer of the church. But, for year after year, he wouldn't apply for membership, because he worried so much over those little lies he had told while he was a Revolutionary spy. People told him he was good enough to join any church. But he wouldn't hear to it. This lasted going on thirty year. All that time he was interested in the church and a worker for her. Finally, when he had got to be an old man, he up and said he would unite with the church if they were willing to take him in. Which they did. So he became a member. This was when I was a boy in Carmel. The people then were all talking about how Enoch Crosby had finally got into the church.

What I'm saying is, Crosby ought not to have been so thin-skinned. Those little fibs he told were when he was in active business. If he had told the gospel truth every time, he wouldn't have been so good a spy. He had to stretch the truth now and then, in order to get his work done. He was a fool to think that just because he had had to do that sort of thing in his business life, he couldn't get into the church. The church isn't so skittish as that. Some folks think she is. But she isn't. She's not squeamish in such matters. She takes a practical view of things every time. Why, there was that preacher I have wrote about, who got me to give the money for Drew Seminary. He didn't stickle over what my enemies were saying about me. He used to tell the story of the founding of the school, like this:

It was rumoured that Daniel Drew was disposed to found, as a thank-offering to God, a Theological School in or near New York. We were appointed by our denomination a committee to wait upon Mr. Drew and ascertain his position. I shall never forget the pleasant interview which we had with Mr. Drew in his home. With the utmost simplicity of manner he informed us that it was his wish to devote a quarter of a million dollars to the founding of a Theological School. Let me pause for a moment to give my impression of this remarkable man. To me he was one of the pleasantest figures in our fold. Reticent, no doubt, but loyal to his church, and sensible to his obligations to our denomination for building up in him the traits that had led to his prosperity. He delighted to think of the way he had been led on. For my part, I am glad this school bears his name.

If Enoch Crosby had been able to do his day's work, and always tell the full truth, then of course he should. But there are times when it isn't so easy. A business man has got to get along somehow. Better that my hog should come dirty home, than no hog at all.

# XXX

I WAS now one of the biggest men in the country. I had fought Vanderbilt to a draw. That meant much. Vanderbilt was by this time a man of power, so that ordinary people were scared of him. But I wasn't. He was rich. But so was I. My property at this time footed up to thirteen million dollars. (If I only had stopped to think, I'd have seen it was an unlucky figure, and would have dodged it in some way. If it had been twelve millions, or fourteen millions, I might have had better luck in keeping it.) My bread was buttered on both sides, so to speak. I had a great mansion at Union Square, had my own stable, and a servant to drive my horse and milk my cow. When I went down to Broad Street the people would point me out to strangers. I was one of the big men of the Street.

Maybe I hadn't had so much book-learning as some. But I had more money than many a man whose head was chock-full of book-learning. My clerks, who had more schooling than I, didn't dare to put on any of their bookish airs around me. They knew I could buy them out ten times over. One night on leaving the office I set the combination of the safe at the letters which spelled the word, "Doare." The next day I was kept at my house for some time. The clerks wanted to open the safe. So they sent up. I told them the combination was for the word "Doare." They didn't talk back. They were too much scared of me for that. They tried to open the safe. Pretty soon they sent again: "Mr. Drew, what was the word that you said was the combination for the safe this morning?"

"Doare," I said, "an ordinary house doare, barn doare, stable doare — any kind of a doare."

"But," they insisted, "there are five letters to the combination of our safe. Are you sure it's the word doare? We've tried it — several ways."

"Of course I'm sure!" said I. "Turn to those letters and it will work."

But they had trouble with the thing, and finally I had to go down and help them out. When I took the thing in hand, the safe opened as easy as anything. I turned to them:

"There," said I, "it opens as easy as an old sack. Just d-o-a-r-e."

I have found out since that the ordinary house doare is commonly spelled in a different way from that. And I dare say some of those clerks poked fun at me at the time; but it wasn't when I was around. Book-learning is something, but thirteen million dollars is also something, and a mighty sight

more.  Why, on the walls of my house out at Drewsclift, I had, framed and hung up, a cancelled check
of mine for one million dollars.  It used to make
the people out there stare their eyes out when they
came to see me and I would show them that picture
on the wall.

Then there were my steamboats.  I was now
president of the People's Line.  Isaac Newton had
been the first president.  But during the Civil War
the boat that was named after him got afire and had
to be sent to the bottom.  It was during one of her
trips up to Albany, and while she was opposite
Fort Washington.  It was found that the fire had
broken out because the back part of the arch of the
starboard boiler had blowed down, due to the shat-
tering of the pins which hold the braces in position.
The excitement and exposure was too much for poor
Newton (he was another of your thin-skinned men).
Nine of the passengers lost their lives in the accident
to his boat.  He sickened and died.

So I became president.  St. John took my place
as treasurer.  Then we built that great new boat,
the *Drew*.  I don't mean the old *Daniel Drew*.
That was a day-boat.  I never was very proud of
her.  She was too narrow.  When she had many
passengers aboard she would list over, like a horse
with a sore foot.  The *Drew* didn't list over.  She
stood up, her keel even, no matter how many passengers she was carrying.  For she was a floating

palace — and is even yet. Cost $800,000. She could sleep a thousand people. I was proud to have my picture at the head of the stairway leading up into the passenger saloon. Maybe people have wondered to see, as the owner of so great a boat, a plain-looking man, his face criss - crossed with wrinkles. But I started out as a boy so poor, I didn't even own a rowboat. And it's always the case, a wrinkled purse makes a wrinkled face. I suppose, too, that some people have thought Vanderbilt a much more stylish man than me, because he wears his beard on the sides of his face, whilst I wear mine under my chin. But those little points don't count. And I have seen people stand at that platform half-way up the stairs, and look at my full-length portrait there for as much as five minutes at a time.

I used to ride on the boat often. It was a pleasant way to take a trip on a hot summer's night; and didn't cost a penny. In going to Saratoga I used to take one of the bridal chambers for my stateroom, if there weren't any bridal couples on board. During the summer time, at this period of my life, I and my family used to have a tent up in the garden back of the Grand Union Hotel, taking our meals at the hotel table. I could go to Saratoga without its costing anything; and I used to like the air up there. That is the way I got acquainted with John Morrissey. He had his gambling house right opposite the Congress Park. So when I would go out in the morning to take a drink of the spring water, I used to meet him. But I never would go into his place. Gambling is a sin that I didn't want to countenance. But I used to have many good chats with Morrissey, and when he and I were going up the river in my boat, we would visit way into the night.

I also had a tent down at Ocean Grove (which was then just beginning to be settled). Before Ocean Grove came, Peney's Grove at Brewsters', and the camp just out of Sing Sing, amidst those great oak trees, used to be my favourite camp meetings. It was a refreshment both to body and spirit, when August set in, to get away from business cares, set up my tent at one or the other of these camp meetings, and receive a blessing.

In the summer time also, before the camp meetings opened, I would go out to my big farm, between Brewsters' and Carmel. I don't know but what I enjoyed myself raising fat beeves there almost as much as I did my work in Wall Street. I knew how to handle money, and I knew also how to handle critters. Western breeds were the ones I kept mostly on my farm. And I had fine luck with them. One year, out of a hundred and twenty head of cattle sold from my farm, a hundred weighed over a thousand pounds in the beef. My son, Billy, must have learned the trick of cattle raising from me. Because when he went to live on the farm, he surprised me one year by sending to the New York market a pair of oxen which took the prize. We had a big time down in Wall Street when those oxen were led through. One of them was called "Commodore Vanderbilt" and the other, "Daniel Drew." They were all fixed up with flags and trimmings and knickknacks. There was a band of music to lead the procession. When they came by my office, at 30 Broad Street, I looked out of the door and was proud to think I had a son that could raise a pair of cattle like that. Their picture was painted in oil, and is a witness to this day to the fine stock that these York State hills can breed, when a man knows how.

Besides my money and boats and farms, there was something else which made me one of the big men of the country. This was my position in the Street. It's a great thing to be an insider. Even a man with as much money as I, wouldn't have been so big as I was, unless he had been on the inside of the great operating cliques. We were so powerful that even the law couldn't get in and bother us with its technicalities. The *London Times* had to admit our great power. That paper come out with a howl like this:

The parties concerned have long ago shown that there is no financial iniquity which persons in command of money cannot commit in Wall Street with entire impunity, as regards legal consequence in the Civil Courts, and very nearly, also, as regards social position.

Of course this London paper was bound to be more or less bitter, and blow about "financial iniquity" and such-like.   Because the British stock-holders in Erie had for a long time back been trying to oust me from control of the road.   That is why this sheet of theirs kept slurring me as it did.

But I didn't care.   I was on top.   At this time in my life, all my eggs had two yolks.   Most every deal I went into turned out prosperous.   I was as contented as mice in a cheese.

# XXXI

I SOMETIMES wish I had stayed in the steamboat business and let Wall Street alone. I'd have made money in a more steady way and without the risk. Steamboats are not so liable to ups and downs as stocks are. And at this time I was earning from my steamboats alone enough money to have made me in time a man of comfortable means.

But the trouble with business of that kind is, there are so many little things to look after, which keep you on the go well-nigh all the time. Because the profits from a business line are made up of a lot of small profits; and each detail is liable to leak money unless you look out.

For instance, there was the one item of the bar, on my steamboats. Going into the bar one day on the steamboat *Drew*, who should I see there but the Captain of the boat taking a drink. I was going to be mad at first, and stood watching him in order to think what I should do. He stood very cool, finished his glass, put it down, and then paid the bartender a quarter. When I saw that, I wasn't so mad.

"Do the employees on the boat pay every time they get anything from the bar?" I asked.

"Always," said he; "at least I do. In fact, Mr. Drew, I find it a very good way to keep in check a natural propensity of mine which might otherwise grow into something inconvenient." I was glad to know that he always paid; but the incident merely shows the many leaks that could occur in a business as big as this steamboat business of mine, if a fellow were to follow it up as a life pursuit.

Then, also, there is the bother which small business matters bring you. I had a lawsuit hanging over my head for years over the sale of the steamboat, *Francis Skiddy*. It belonged to the line which went from New York to Troy. I sold it to the People's Line. In reality I was buyer and seller too. Because I owned a controlling interest in both lines, and so could make the seller sell, and the buyer buy. Well, some of the smaller *Skiddy* stock-holders got mad at the transaction and sued me for damages. Because on the last trip of that boat, just before she was going to be delivered to the People's Line, she ran on a rock off of Statt's Landing, and ripped a hole in her bottom sixteen feet long and three planks wide. This, of course, lowered now by a good deal the selling value of the boat. And yet gave me the thing I wanted out of her, the engine. This was still undamaged, and could now be transferred into another boat, and at a reasonable figure. I had been wanting the *Skiddy* engine for this other boat a long time back. I gave out that her running on the rocks just at this time when the sale was about to be made, was an accident which I hadn't had anything to do with. But her stock-holders made a big fuss. They went into court and sued me for sixty thousand dollars. The thing dragged and dragged, and now finally the court has made me pay it. It merely shows the vexations of spirit that come when you are in a business line.

I like Wall Street because you stand a chance of making money there so much faster than you can in the slow-poke ways of regular business. One turn of two or three points in shares will, if you are on the right side and have put out a big enough line, net you as much money in six days as an ordinary business would in six months. By this time I had got so that I knew all the ins and outs of Wall Street. There are trade secrets in every calling. The new-comer is always at a discount compared to the old veteran. I found that many times now I could turn this expert knowledge of mine to account. One morning, I remember, I was riding down to the Street in the carriage of a young stock operator who had taken me in with him, to save paying fare in the Broadway stage. He knew that I was on the inside of some of the big stock-market operations, and he thought he might get some inside tips. I had looked for something of the sort to occur. It's a caution the way outsiders hang around people who are on the inside. The flies get at you when you're covered with honey. Whilst we were driving down Broadway he pumped and pumped; but I was as dumb as a heifer. I made believe there were big things just then under way which we, who were on the inside, didn't want other people to get onto.

Well, when we reached the Street, and he had got the carriage stopped in front of my office, I opened the door and stepped out. In doing so, I contrived to bump my hat against the top of the doorway. It was a black felt hat. (I like black felt for a hat. It's so durable. You can wear one several years before it begins to show signs of wear.) My hat fell off, and some pieces of paper fell out. On those pieces of paper I had written what seemed to be orders to my brokers: "Buy 500 Erie, at 68." "Buy 1,000 at 67." "Buy 2,000 Erie at the market." "Buy 3,000 Erie at 67½," and such-like. Of course, as they spread over the floor of the carriage, he or any one else couldn't help but see what they were, and read them. I made believe I was awfully put out to have the secret given away like that. I made a scramble as though to gather them up before any one should see them; then I said good-bye and went into my office.

I calculated he would most likely act on the hint. And he did. He drove rapidly to his office. He told his crowd of the discovery he had made. "A

big Bulling movement in Erie is on! The old man"
(that's what they sometimes called me) "is buying
Erie! A campaign is under way. Boys, we
must get in on this!" So he bought a block of five
thousand shares of Erie. The rest of his crowd
followed him. Their combined buying forced Erie
up point after point.

That was what I had been looking for. I had been
wanting for some time back to find a buyer for some
of my surplus stock. Now it was coming my
way fine. I immediately dumped onto the market
all the Erie it would stand. I succeeded in disposing
of a large share of my holdings at the top figure.
Then of course the market broke. It sagged four
points in the next two days. My broker friend and
his crowd were badly caught. He came to me with
a face as long as your arm; said how he had been
led to believe that there was going to be an upward
movement in Erie; he had bought heavily; and now
it had all gone to smash. "Uncle, what in the
world shall I do?"

I told him he could do anything he pleased. And
I couldn't keep from chuckling at the fine way I had
got him to gobble the bait. In fact I always did
like a joke. So much so that they got to calling
me the "Merry Old Gentleman of Wall Street."
They had other names for me, too; such as, "the
Speculative Director," "the Big Bear," "the Old
Man of the Street" and so on. Some of these

names I didn't like. But "the Merry Old Gentle-man" — I kind of liked that. I believe in being merry when you can. A good chuckle, when you've got a fellow in a tight box and you watch him squirm this way and that, does more good than a dose of medicine.

As to this particular Erie deal, by thus making a market for my shares, I cleaned up a fine profit. That merely shows how an operator, if he is onto the tricks of the trade and has natural ingenuity besides, can make business in a sick market, where a newcomer would have to sit and twiddle his thumbs.

I have always had a natural bent for stock-market dickers. I suppose it's because I have been sort of humble in my manner. That puts people off their guard. (I never was proud, anyhow. People used to say: You couldn't tell from Dan Drew's clothing but what he was a butcher in a Third Avenue shop. But I let them talk. You can't tell a horse by his harness. And I have always thought a man should have more in his pocket than on his back.) I have found a spirit of humility very helpful. It makes the man you're dealing with think he is winding you around his finger; whereas you are the one who is doing the winding.

That's how I got the best of a lawyer friend of mine once. He was a young fellow. I had him do some legal work for me. He did it. Then he sent in a bill. It seemed an almighty big fee to ask for just a few months' work. I paid it. But I made up my mind I'd get it back. And I did. I was talking with him not long after. I turned the conversation to Wall Street matters.

"Sonny," said I, "you won that lawsuit for me, and I've taken a kind of liking to you. I want to help you. We fellows on the inside sometimes know what's going to happen in stock-market affairs before other people. It's my advice to you to take some of your spare cash, all the money you can lay your hands on, in fact, and buy Erie stock."

He held off. He said that his business was law and not the stock-market. He believed that a shoemaker should stick to his lasts. Fair words made him look to his purse. And such-like.

"Now, son," said I, "do as I say. I knew your father. And because of that friendship, I feel a kind of interest in you. I want to see you get a start. You buy Erie. Buy all you can of it, at the present market price. Trust me, you'll never be sorry." He thought for a while. He said he guessed he'd try the thing for once.

That was what I'd been waiting for. I went out and immediately gave orders to my brokers to sell all the Erie they could. Soon the ticker told me that my brokers were finding a buyer for the Erie they were offering. I thought I could give a pretty shrewd guess as to who was the buyer. I supplied him with all he would take. By the time

the market broke, I had saddled him with enough
Erie at a good high figure to sluice from his pocket
into mine all of that fee which he had scooped out
of me just a few weeks before.  I now called the
account even.

# XXXII

FOR a spell after settling up with the Commodore at the close of the Erie War, I got out of Wall Street. I was by this time over my scriptural allowance of three score years and ten. I thought I had earned a rest. I figured that I had made my wad, and now should begin to enjoy it.

> Let worldly minds the world pursue;
> It has no charms for me.
> Once I admired its trifles, too,
> But grace has set me free.

I seemed to myself to be now in a quiet harbour, like that fine big bay that dents in from the Hudson River at Fishkill. I could look out from that safe retreat onto the human vessels that were tossing in the billows outside. "From every stormy wind that blows" — that has always been a favourite hymn of mine. And that other tune, too:

> Oh, Beulah Land, Sweet Beulah Land,
> Where on the highest mount I stand;
> I look away across the sea,
> Where mansions are prepared for me,
> And view the shining glorious shore,
> My heaven, my home forever more.

But after two or three months of nothing to do, I kind of got tired of resting. I saw Gould and Fisk making money in Erie hand over fist, and I hankered to get back. I wanted to stick a finger in that pudding, so to speak. They had taken Bill Tweed and Pete Sweeney into the Board of Directors. This was giving them such a fine pull with the law courts and the New York City authorities that they could do most anything they wanted to, and not be troubled with suits or legal technicalities. Tweed became a director of the railroad, "to get square with Erie," as he put it. For he was still nettled over those old losses in Erie speckilations which he said I had caused him, and now he vowed he was going to get it back — was going to take it out of the road, no matter what it cost her. When I had got out of Erie at the time of our settlement with Vanderbilt, I figured that in taking my pay in cash and leaving Fisk and Gould the road, I had got the best end of the bargain. I was chuckling to myself to think how I had taken the horse, so to speak, and had left them holding onto the halter. But Jay's words were proving true. And although Erie seemed a badly waterlogged craft, there was a lot of service left in her yet. Therefore I wanted to get back on board, so to speak.

At the time of that settlement, a little feeling had arisen between me and the other two, Jay and Jimmy. But personal feelings don't count in Wall

Street.  Operators can swear everlasting vengeance
on each other one day, and be thick as molasses
before sundown the next.  In financial circles, it's
the money that counts.  No matter how mad you
may be at a fellow, if you need his money you make
up with him easy as anything.  Erie was still a
money-maker.  So I wanted to get on the inside
once more.  If I could have another turn or two
at the milking stool, so to speak, I felt I'd be willing
to retire from active business altogether.  Accordingly, before the summer was over, I was calling
on Gould and Fisk, and they were coming to see
me, just as though we hadn't had any differences
at all.  Before I knew it, I was back in the thick
of things, and busy as a pup.

We now set out on a Bear campaign — we three,
Gould, Fisk and I.  Being backed by Tweed and
his political crowd, it promised big returns.  But
it required a lot of nerve.  In fact, before it was
through, it raised more excitement than I had bar-
gained for.  It was the Lock-up of greenbacks.

It seemed a foolhardy thing to do — go short of
stocks just at that particular time.  Because it
was the fall of the year.  The Government reports
showed that bumper crops were to be harvested in
nearly all parts of the country.  A big traffic from
the West to the seaboard was promised.  The
election of General Grant as president was almost
a settled thing;  and if he was elected, the policy of

the Government would be an immediate resumption of specie payment.    Money was easy as an old shoe. When money is easy, stocks go up.    Because at such times people have got the means to margin large holdings and so are hopeful and Bullish.    It was about the last time in the world, one would have said, to begin a Bear campaign.    But that's really just the time in which to begin it.    Because the way to make money in Wall Street, if you are an insider, is to calculate on what the common people are going to do, and then go and do just the opposite.    When everybody is Bullish, that is just the time when you can make the most money as a Bear, if you work it right.    And we of our little clique thought we could work it right.

When money is easy the public buys stocks, and so the prices go up.    The way to do, we calculated, would be to make money tight.    Then people would sell, prices would go down, and we could cover our short contracts at a fine low figure.    In this work of making money tight we were helped by one fact. The Government, in order to resume specie payments, had adopted a policy of contracting the amount of greenbacks in circulation.    It was refusing to reissue greenback notes after it had once got them back into its vaults.

But that wasn't enough to tighten the currency to the point where it would serve our ends.    So we set about working it ourselves.    For this purpose we made a pool of money to the amount of fourteen millions. Fisk and Gould provided ten millions, and I agreed to put in four millions.

The banks, as everybody knows, are required by law to keep as reserve twenty-five per cent. of their deposits. This is in order to take care of their depositors. When their cash on hand is over and above this twenty-five per cent. margin, bankers loan money free and easy. As soon as their cash begins to creep down to the twenty-five per cent. limit — which can almost be called the dead line — bankers begin to get the cold shivers; they tighten their rates, and if the need is urgent enough, call in their outstanding loans. Knowing this we made our plans accordingly. We would put all of our cash into the form of deposits in the banks. Against these deposits we would write checks and get the banks to certify them. The banks would have to tie up enough funds to take care of these certifications. With the certified checks as collateral we would borrow greenbacks — and then withdraw them suddenly from circulation.

When our arrangements were complete, we went onto the stock market and sold shares heavily short. People thought we were fools, because of all the signs pointing to a big revival of trade. Soon these contracts of ours matured. We held a council. We decided that the time had come to explode our bomb. So all of a sudden we called upon the banks for our greenbacks. I remember well the scared look that came over the face of one banker when I made the demand. At first he didn't understand.

"Oh, yes," said he, after I had made my request; "you wish to withdraw your deposits from our bank? Of course, we can accomodate you. We shall take measures to get your account straightened up in the next few days."

"The next few days won't do," said I; "we must have it right away."

"Right away!" he said. "What do you mean?"

"I mean," said I, "within the next fifteen minutes."

He began to turn white. "Do you understand that a sudden demand of this kind was altogether unlooked for, and will occasion a great deal of needless hardship? A wait on your part of only a very short time would permit us to straighten out the whole affair without injustice to our other depositors and clients."

"I'm not in business," I said, "for the benefit of your other depositors and clients. I've got to look out for number one."

"So I perceive," he said; "and I suspect that you are willing to look out for that person quite regardless of other 'number ones' that are scattered somewhat thickly through human society. However, we will probably have to do your bidding. I will see what help we can get from some of the other banks."

As soon as he began to communicate with the other banks, his alarm increased. Because he found that their funds were being called on in the same way as his own (we were calling in the greenbacks from our chain of banks all to once). Then he got to work in good earnest. Because our fourteen millions (through the working of that law of a twenty-five per cent. reserve), meant a contracting of the currency to four times that amount, or fifty-six millions in all, besides the certifications. He called a hasty council of the officers of the bank. He ordered them to make up my greenbacks into a bundle, for me to take out to the carriage which I had brought along with me for that purpose. I started to thank him, but he seemed too busy to notice me. Messengers were being sent out on the double-quick to all the brokers who were customers of the bank, notifying them they were to return their borrowings to the bank at once.

As each of these brokers found his loans being suddenly called by the banks, he sent word in turn to his clients that they must put up the money themselves to carry their holdings of stock. Because the public in buying shares don't pay for them outright; they only pay a margin, say of ten per cent. The broker, therefore, has to put up the other ninety per cent., which he borrows from the banks, and charges his customers the interest.

The customers immediately sent back word to

the brokers: "We haven't anywheres near the cash to pay for our stocks outright. Borrow from the banks, even though you have to pay ten per cent. interest."

"But we can't get money at ten per cent.," answered the brokers.

"Then pay fifteen," said the customers.

"But we can't get it at fifteen," came the answer. "The rates for money have gone up to 160 per cent. There's a terrible tightening. No one was looking for it. We've got to have the cash, or we can't carry your stocks a moment longer."

"Then let the stocks go," came back the last answer; "throw them on the market, and do it before anybody else begins."

You can imagine, when a thousand people begin to sell, what a slump takes place. The money market is the key to the stock market. They who control the money rate control also the stock rate. Stocks began to tumble right and left. Many stop-loss orders were uncovered. Prices sagged point after point — thirty points in all. And every point meant one dollar in our pockets for every share we were dealing in.

People everywhere began to curse us. The air round about us three men was fire and sulphur. Men couldn't get money to carry on their business. Merchant princes, who had inherited the business from their fathers through several generations, lost it now in a night.  This was the time of the year when ordinarily money would flow out to the South and West to pay the farmers for the crops which they had been working all spring and summer to bring to harvest.  But now that money couldn't flow, and so these farmers in a dozen states also began to hurl their curses at us.  Many of them had been counting on the money from their crops to pay off mortgages.  Some were driven from their homes, and their houses sold.

In fact, the curses got so loud after a while that I kind of got scared.  I hadn't thought the thing would kick up such a rumpus.  It almost looked as though our lives weren't safe.  They might burn down my house over my head, or stab me on a street corner.  So I got out of the thing.  My shirt fits close, but my skin fits closer.  I told Gould and Fisk that I wasn't going to be with them in this lock-up deal any longer — my life was too precious. If they chose to be dare-devils and stand out against a whole country rising up in wrath against them, they could do it.  But for my part I was going to make my peace with my fellow men.  So I released the money I was hoarding, and was glad to be out of the thing at last.

## XXXIII

EVEN though I drew out of this lock-up deal, I got a good share of the blame. In fact, people seemed to curse me more than they did Gould and Fisk; because they said these other two were younger — were pupils of mine. And that I was chargeable for getting them into these plundersome habits, as they called it. If I had ever cared much for the speech of people, I suppose I'd have taken the thing to heart.

But I never cared what people were saying, so long as they didn't do anything but talk. Talking doesn't hurt. You can pass it by. This locking-up of greenbacks had netted us so fine a penny that we could afford to stand a lot of abuse. Besides, the people whose money we had got were not able to get back at us. We were protected from law-suits by means of our standing in with Tweed and his crowd. We were also able, because of this political influence, to show the people who were all the time reviling us that we were pretty powerful in New York City and were not to be abused.

There, for instance, was that man Bowles, who owned a sheet up in Springfield. He had been

333

picking at me and my Erie crowd for a long time
back.    A lot of the newspapers, anyhow, were now
beginning to snarl and snap at us:—"Erie Rascal-
ities," "National Infamy," "Railroad Burglary,"
"Drew at the Head of a Piratical Horde of Plun-
derers"—what not!  One of them, a Bill Bryant,
editor of the *New York Post*, got what he deserved.
Tweed's Judge, Barnard, right from the judge's
bench, called him, "the most notorious liar in the
United States."    And now this other fellow, Bowles,
was also to be taken down a peg or two.    For Bowles
had come out with a pitchfork article against us,
and against Jimmy in particular.  This time he
went too far, and we hit back.  Jimmy was the
last one of us, anyhow, whom they ought to have
hit.  Because he stood in with Tweed and his crowd
even more than Gould or I.

So one day soon after, this man Bowles was down
in New York City, attending a meeting of the New
England Society at the Fifth Avenue Hotel.  He
was standing in the hotel office.  There he was
approached by Jack McGowan, the deputy sheriff,
and another.  One of them passed on beyond
Bowles, then turned, seized him by the arms, and
began to shove him towards the street door, whilst
the other held a paper in his face, a warrant for his
arrest.  Once in the street, they pushed him into
a carriage which was in waiting, and drove rapidly
to the Ludlow Street Jail.  This was eight o'clock

at night.   Bail was fixed at fifty thousand dollars.
Bowles had so many friends that he could probably
have raised it.    But all the details had been arranged
so thoroughly that now the sheriff's office was closed
for the night;   and so bail couldn't be received.
Bowles asked a friend to carry the news of his arrest
to his wife, who was in poor health at the Albemarle
Hotel, and asked for writing materials to make
out the note;   but this was held back for a time.
Because the idea was to punish him once for all,
by some hours in solitary confinement.   By ten
o'clock the news of his arrest had got out and there
was a lot of his friends gathered at the jail, such as
Mr. Dana, Mr. Bond and General Arthur.   But the
jailer said he couldn't let any one see the prisoner.
They looked up the sheriff and found him at a party
which was being given at the house of Mr. Brown,
on Fifth Avenue, to celebrate a Tammany victory.
The sheriff excused himself for a minute, and getting
out of sight, didn't come back.   Bowles's friends
went over to the sheriff's house, but they couldn't
get anybody out of bed.   So the prisoner had to
spend the night behind the bars.   Of course, in
the morning his friends who had been up all night,
such as Mr. Dunn, Cyrus W. Field, and the others,
got the bail bond, and by eleven o'clock he was free.
But he had gone through an experience which must
have taught a lesson to the pen-and-ink fellows far
and wide.

Fisk was a fellow who carried out his plans when he once made up his mind to a thing — didn't mind the expense. He used to drive in the park with his lady-loves, behind six horses — three white ones on one side and three black ones on the other. He liked to make a splurge. He had a boat, the *Plymouth Rock*, that used to run down to Sandy Hook. Jimmy put canary birds all through the passenger cabins. One day Vanderbilt was going down on the boat and took Jimmy to task for it.

"Fisk," said he, "that is all very nice, those birds that are warbling so beautifully. But they have to be fed, every last bird in those cages."

But Jimmy was a fellow who didn't count the cost of bird-seed, or of anything else for that matter. When the *Plymouth Rock* was finally turned into an excursion boat, he would parade the decks dressed in an Admiral's uniform. He liked to swell around in his fine clothes and get the women to gaze at him.

The way he carried on with Josie Mansfield and those other bad women was a caution. I think it hurt our Wall Street business. Because it drove away from us some people who might have gone in with us on our deals. But it didn't do any good to scold Jimmy, he was that set in his way.

I tried it. I had a talk with him once or twice about his soul. Because in our class meeting over in my Fourth Avenue Church, soul-saving used to be a subject we brought up a good deal. Wednesday was class-meeting night in our church. I didn't feel right when I missed a meeting. I never was a regular leader. I didn't feel I could give the time to looking after the spiritual welfare of each and every member of the class, as a leader should. But I was often called upon to lead the meeting, when the regular leader was away. And at these times I used to direct the thought of the meeting into lines of practical religious work, such as soul-saving and the like. Of course, in our prayer and class meetings we didn't limit our testimonies and prayers to this one line; because religion has to do with personal growth in grace as well as to the practical work of carrying the gospel to others. More than once, when I've had to lead the class-meeting, the subject has turned to the subject of the Pentecostal blessing. I have in mind one night in particular. A good soul in the meeting who had once experienced holiness — she had come out as a Perfectionist — was now beneath a cloud because she had lost her sense of sanctification. As leader of the meeting, I asked her if she had also lost her sense of justification. She said, no; it was the second step which she had fallen back from. Then as leader I tried to get her to trust justifying grace and the smitten rock, as a fountain now of entire sanctification. Because, if we have the witness of our adoption and a faith that shows our sins forgiven, then the all-quickening word assures us of the further step into sanctity and into perfect liberty from the power of bondage.   Before the meeting came to an end that night, the victory had been won — she was once more firmly on the rock.   But the practical side of the gospel messages is not to be overlooked; and I thereupon took occasion, when she had got back onto the mountain summit, to turn her thoughts to the blessedness of working for the Master and of going forth into the vineyard and gathering precious sheaves.

This started me also.   I thought of those around me in business life, who were as yet unreached — who had never yet experienced regeneration and the cleansing gift.   Then and there I made a vow, with the cloud of witnesses looking down upon me from the battlements of bliss, that if grace should be given me for the task, I would try to save at least one soul in the year that was then before me.

One day, accordingly, when I thought the opportunity was favourable, because Fisk and I were alone in the office, I turned the talk to more serious things.   Without seeming to make it refer to him, I told of cases I had known, where unbelieving men had been mightily wrought upon — born again as it were in the twinkling of an eye, and given power over the World, the Flesh and the Devil. Because, "Whilst the lamp holds out to burn, the vilest sinner may return."

Jimmy listened.   Fisk could be serious now and

then, even though people who didn't know him used to suppose he was nothing but a boaster and a maker of jokes.

"No, Uncle," said he, when I finished; "there isn't any hope for Jim Fisk." (He used to call himself "Jim Jubilee, Junior!" That was when he was in one of his joking moods. But he didn't do it now.) "I'm a gone goose. No need of a fellow bulldozing himself. Might as well look the thing in the face. I am too fond of this world. If I've got to choose between the other world and this, I take this. Some people are born to be good, other people are born to be bad. I was born to be bad. As to the World, the Flesh and the Devil, I'm on good terms with all three. If God Almighty is going to damn us men because we love the women, then let him go ahead and do it. I'm having a good time now, and if I have got to pay for it hereafter, why, I suppose it's no more than fair shakes; and I'll take what's coming to me. As to the vain pomp and glory of the world, I have covetous desires of the same. So there you are."

I tried to tell him that he was not yet beyond redemption. He was despairing of himself more than was any use of. He was still on the mercy side of the Judgment, and cases had been known where an eleventh-hour repentance was efficacious. If he sought prayerfully, he would be given grace to mortify those corrupt affections.

He answered that he didn't want them mortified. He said that, though I might be one of those who were born to be saved — for theological mysteries were something he didn't know very much about — he was sure that he himself was born to be damned. And that it wasn't any use for him to try to be anything else.

For a spell after my talk with him, I don't know but what Jimmy was a little more sober than usual in his walk and conversation. But it didn't last long. A morning or two later, down he comes to the office in his great barouche, driven by a Negro coachman; and there on the seat beside him was that Josie Mansfield. She was decorated all over with the rich stuffs he had bought her. For, when buying things for women, money spilled out of Fisk like corn out of a broken sack. In fact, Jimmy was almost as proud of her fine dresses as he was of his own clothes.

"Before she met me," he used to brag, "Josie didn't have anything but a black-and-white silk gown to her name. And now look at her: I pay the bills for her to go down to Long Branch and drive along the Avenue. Oh, I tell you, Uncle, when Jimmy Fisk starts out to do a thing, he does it up brown!"

It got so after a while that he was spending almost as much time with Josie and her set as he was with us in the office. Why, he set her up in a house on

West Twenty-third Street, and used almost to live there. It was the same side of the street as his own house, and only a few doors beyond. He used to say that he himself didn't know which place to call home. Besides her and Nellie Peris and Bella Lane and the rest of them, he got to bringing over ballet dancers from Paris. (He bought an Opera House over on the corner of Eighth Avenue and Twenty-third Street, where he gave French Opera. He used to sit in a box, or behind the scenes, as Manager-in-chief.) And he made them into his concubines. He didn't have any more shame in it all than a cow does over a bastard calf.

I didn't give up with that one effort to show him the error of his ways. And when I think of the end those light women brought him to, I'm glad that I at least discharged my duty. I tried to tell him that those women were after him only for his money; that they were nothing but men-traps, and that these petticoat affairs of his would get him into trouble. I might as well have talked to the wind.

"Kissing is all right, Jimmy," I used to say to him, "in the calf time of a fellow's life. But when you're grown up, what you want is not those ladies of pleasure, but a good pillow mate. The right kind of women are not seen around opera houses and such places. Women," said I, "are like poultry; they shouldn't gad too far from the front gate."

But you couldn't argue with him. "I'm the

gander can take care of those geese," he used to say. "I travel on my shape, Uncle; and I don't make any bones of saying that I like these scarlet women — they're approachable. Some parts of your Bible suit me to a T. I worship in the Synagogue of the Libertines."

He wore his hair in fancy ways — "kiss curls," he used to call them — and had the idea that he was the buck to take a lady's fancy. The way he went on was something scandalous. I tried my best: "They that yield themselves unto sin are the servants of sin," said I. "Sin should not have dominion over you, Jimmy. Because you are not under law but under grace." It didn't do a speck of good. He might be serious whilst I was talking. But let one of those French light-heels come tripping along he'd up and after her in a jiffy.

He even boasted that it was for the sake of helping our business that he romped with those loose women the way he did. Such outlandish things as he used to think up! For instance, there was that deal with the new Knoxville Railroad, then starting up out West. Fisk said:

"Uncle, there's nothing like knowing how to do things. Just see what a fine combination we've got — our clique here — you, me, Jay, and the rest of our crowd. Because here, through our partnership with Big Bill" (he meant Bill Tweed), "we've got New York City under our thumb; we could even send a man to Abraham's bosom, if it suited our purpose, without risk of the hangman. And now through me we've got the power that comes through women! One hair of a woman, Uncle, will draw more than a pair of bay steers. Why, just now, though you fellows didn't know it, I'm getting a line on that Knoxville deal that's like to turn us a fine penny."

"How's that?" I asked.

"Why," said he, "you know that connection of theirs with the soft-coal district, which has been in the air some time. If that goes through, it would be the right thing to load up with some of the shares of that road."

"Well," said I, "is it going through?"

"There you are," he replied; "that's just where I'm getting in my fine work. Because there's a young chap in town, a nephew, or something or other, of one of the big men in that road. He knows what's what in that railroad, and whether this line into the soft-coal district is going through. It's up to us to corkscrew the news out of him."

"How can we do it?" I asked. "Money?"

"No, that would be inartistic. It's women that's the bait for the average man. Leave it to me, Uncle, leave it to me."

Some days later, in one of our councils together, Fisk came in, spry and merry. He told us he had got the news at last.

"News of what?" we asked.

"Why, news of that soft-coal connection with the Ohio River. It's going through," said he.

"Are you sure?" I asked. "How did you get it?"

"Oh, through my Josie."

"Josie?" I said; "who's that?"

"Why, my Twenty-third Street charmer. Not that she herself could handle a lad like this Horace — I guess his name was Horace; something like that, anyhow. Because, from what I gather, he was quite a shy lad — one of your 'mother's boys.' Josie is too plump to take the fancy of that kind. He needs the slender and artful lass, if he's going to be roped in. So she got Nellie to undertake the job. Nellie is the girl for an artistic piece of work. She's playful enough — after the ice is broken — and can give a fellow a lumptious time. First along, though, she has a bashful way about her that just takes with a certain type of man. And I guess this Horace was that type. Put Nellie in one of her neggledeegee gowns and the lights low all through the house, she could win over St. Anthony himself. She has a way about her of backing off at the start, that's very fetching. But once started, Uncle, she has got the prettiest way of saying, 'My nose itches' when she wants more kisses, of any girl I think I ever met. And I've met a lot. On Twenty-third Street they belong to the tribe of Amorites. And this dear young Horace, after the acquaintance was once made, didn't find any difficulty, I'll warrant, in making progress swiftly. In fact, Nellie herself helped the acquaintance along. She got him to stay at the house all night, on some pretext or other. Before the night was over he told her everything she wanted to know. The railroad into the soft-coal region is going through. He plumped the news right out at her. I don't blame him. I'd have told too. A nice pair of dumplings ——"

"Now see here, Jimmy," said I, breaking in on him; "if that railway connection is sure, it's time we laid in a line of the stock. A thing of that sort has a way of getting out, if you wait too long."

And it did. The point on that particular stock, which he had such pains to worm out of that young man, Horace, really didn't help us much. As I remember now, after taking out the brokers' commissions and so on, I don't believe any of us made a cent on the deal. The trouble was, another stallion had been whinnering around Fisk's mare, so to speak. That Josie of his was getting another lover, and wanted to let this other in also on the good things. As Jimmy said to Ned Stokes (he was the one), "two trains can't run in opposite directions on the same track." So when Josie gave away the same secrets to Ned which she gave to Jimmy and our crowd, it didn't do any of us any good. Because the advantage of inside information in Wall Street dickers is, that you and your clique are the only ones that know it.

"We're hooked by a cow," said I, when it was seen that this deal in stocks wasn't going to turn out well. "What did I tell you, Jimmy? They that are in the flesh cannot please God. For to be carnally minded is death; but to be spiritually minded is life and peace."

# XXXIV

LITTLE disappointments, such as the one I have just wrote about, always come in the life of a speckilator. In a big harvest there are always some weeds. And I had learned by this time to bear up when the market turned against me. The very night, when we found that our railroad speckilation in the soft-coal field was going against us, I was walking in my sitting room at home, my hands behind my back, humming out loud that comforting hymn:

"From every stormy wind that blows" —
Danck spoke up — I mean my grandson, Dan Chamberlain. I used to call him Danck, for short.

"Pop," said he, "why in the world are you everlastingly singing that, 'From every stormy wind that blows'?"

"Because it's true, Danck," said I, "It's true:

"There, there on eagle wings we soar,
And sense and sin molest no more,
And heaven comes down our souls to greet,
And Glory crowns the mercy seat."

I was happy, anyhow, these days. Because I was about to celebrate my golden wedding. I and my wife, just two years before, had been out to Drewville, two miles this side of Carmel, to the golden wedding of my brother Tom and his wife, on their farm. I said then, if the Lord would spare me and my wife to see the day, we too would celebrate, when the time came. Our lives were spared. The fine big house on Union Square was just the place to hold a big celebration in. And on a Friday night in March, the next year, I think it was, after the founding of my theological seminary, the great event came off.

I was sorry that it fell on a Friday. I think it brought some bad luck with it. For instance, some of my neighbours who lived in the aristocratic section around Union Square and Fifth Avenue — Robert Goelet lived across Seventeenth Street from me, on the upper corner — didn't come. They sent notes of regret. This may not have been altogether on account of Friday's luck, either. Some of the newspapers about this time were beginning to pitch into me. They were shameless in the things they said. There was the *Nation*, for instance. Just as I was beginning to make preparations for my golden wedding, and was straining the traces to make it a social success, that paper came down on me like a thousand of brick. Speaking of the operations of me and my ring in Wall Street, it said, soon after our campaign of locking up greenbacks:

These men in the course of these operations had ruined hundreds of men in and out of Wall Street, had arrested the whole business of the country for nearly two weeks, had brought the banks to the verge of suspension, and seriously threatened the national credit. Foremost among them is said to have been a wealthy gentleman of advanced years, of eminent piety, a builder of churches, a former treasurer of the Erie Company, and a fit colleague of the speculative Executive Committee. It is possible that the perpetrators of these outrages cannot be reached through our criminal courts; it is possible that the financial community will continue to allow itself to be dragooned and plundered by these organized robber-gangs; but it cannot be that respectable men will countenance such deeds by social recognition of the doers. It makes but little difference whether the fortunes thus acquired are spent in building of churches and endowment of theological seminaries — all good men should unite in treating the owners as infamous.

But though some of my neighbours around Union Square didn't come out the way I had hoped, still my golden wedding was a success. The reporters came. My house was big and on the corner of the street. More than that, I was a big man down in the financial district. So their write-ups of the affair the next day — some of them — were fine. I was particularly pleased at the nice way my *New York Advocate* described the affair. And it didn't have to stretch the truth, either. The golden wedding was celebrated at our residence in the presence of a brilliant assemblage. The very rare event was welcomed with the most hearty congratulations, costly presents were showered in from dear and intimate friends, and throughout the splendid festivities I and my wife, the aged and respectable couple whose conjugal days have been so happily bound in one for half a century, were the recipients of the most affectionate compliments. Not only were the drawing rooms of the mansion brilliantly illuminated, but also, suspended from the ceiling, were beautiful wreaths attached to the globes, the flowers indicating by letters thereon, that I and Mrs. Drew were married in the year 1820, and the attendance that night comprised many of the relatives of the honourable lady and myself, whom all assembled to honour. The toilets of the ladies were exceedingly handsome. The reception commenced shortly before ten o'clock. I and Mrs. Drew, the latter attired in lavender silk covered with white point lace, and both looking very hale and pleasant, warmly received our friends, who were profuse in their earnest congratulations. Reverend Dr. Ridgeway, of our St. Paul's Church on Fourth Avenue, on behalf of his congregation, presented in a feeling address a very appropriate gift in the shape of a gorgeous basket of flowers, of solid silver and gold, emblematic of the intrinsic and solid worth of the recipients, wrought with beautiful forms and adorned with exquisite tracery, symbols of those natures visited by grace, and wrapped with the flowers and fruits of domestic and religious fidelity. On the bowl were the words: "GOLDEN WEDDING" encircled with linden leaves, emblems of constancy, the gift being adorned with suitable monograms. The Reverend Mr. Foss said prayer, which being concluded, I and Mrs. Drew mingled with our numerous guests and proceeded to partake of an elegant repast. Altogether, the event was one to be remembered with pleasure.

But it wasn't over yet. When the speech-making was through with, I told the people to go out into the dining room. "I hope you're as hungry as a meat-axe — every one of you," said I. "I want you to put inside all the pork and potatoes you can carry away." I called it "pork and potatoes," just to surprise them, when they should get into the room and see the spread of eatables I had provided for the occasion. For it wasn't any of your "big boast and small roast" with me that night. The meats were all of the finest — none of your bull-beef on my table. And I, as host of the party, spurred up their appetites. For I was in such light spirits on that occasion, I didn't care how much they ate.

"I don't want anybody to be under my roof this night," said I, "who can't play a good knife and fork at meals. So set to," I added, in a cheery voice. "Get your nose in the manger, there, Brother So-and-so; let me see how much oats you can get outside of." I have always had a knack of getting people in a good humour.

I felt glad that the thing was going off so fine. Just the day before, my friend, Brother McClintock, had died. I had been afraid that this might cast a gloom over the affair. But I kept the people in good spirits by shaking hands and mixing up with them. And everybody said, when the hour came to go home, that they had had just a grand time.

The thing cost like sixty. But it was worth the money. Besides, I was by this time in a position where I could stand a big expense now and then without sweating. Why, during my Erie days, there was one item of profit alone, from the Buffalo, Bradford & Pittsburg Railroad deal, which amounted to a fine penny. We picked up that little branch line for a song, and then, as the Executive Committee of the Erie Railroad, rented it to the Erie at a sum which brought us in a hundred and forty thousand dollars a year clean profit. For another, there was my deal with the Lake Erie line of steamers. As head and front of Erie — I was not only its Treas-surer then, but also its Managing Director — I made the Erie road hire that steamboat line from me.    And the profits from that deal were six hundred thousand dollars.

I tell these things in order to show that I was one of the really big men in the financial community. I could foot the bill for one wedding celebration or for a hundred of them, and hardly know that I had spent the money.

## XXXV

B Y THIS time the boys down on the Street had got to supposing that I was more or less of a back number.

"Uncle Daniel," they said, "is a toothless old dog. He will growl, but his bite doesn't amount to much any more. From now on he's no good except to poke around the Street, his hands behind his back, and look wise."

But I showed them that I wasn't dead and done for just yet. There was still some fire in my brains. I had more tricks and dodges to show them. As Marsden, for one, found out. Billy Marsden had been one of my agents in Erie speckilations. He had made a nice sum of money for himself out of those deals. But I didn't intend that he should keep it. He had made that money by hanging onto my coat tails, so to speak. From which it really belonged to me more than it did to him. So I set about to get it. I got Marsden to head a buying movement in Erie. I went in with him in the deal. We bought well-nigh every share that was loose in the New York market. Then, whilst Marsden was still buying, I, all unbeknownst to him, began to unload my holdings at the nice figure the stock was then reaching. Marsden took my offerings of stock, until I had saddled so much of it onto him that his money began to give out. Then he got suspicious. He began to accuse me of playing fast and loose with him.

"Drew," said he, "some one is doing me dirt. You and I are now the only holders of loose stock in the market; and still it's being offered to me in large blocks. You snake-in-the-grass, I'll lay that it's you."

I tried to tell him that it wasn't; that he was barking up the wrong tree. The stock was probably coming from distant sources of supply that we hadn't reckoned on. If he would only keep on buying for a few days longer, it would probably all be absorbed and the floating supply exhausted. But he became more and more suspicious.

Finally one day he arranged a meeting with me in my office at an early hour. He said it might be a meeting that would last some little time, and that therefore we must be free from interruptions. I suspected he was going to try some scheme on me. So I thought up a trick that would meet him half-way. I told him to come; I'd be glad to see him, and would be with him as long as he wished.

On the day appointed, he came early to my Broad Street office. We went into my private office. He turned and locked the door. I asked him why he locked the door.

"I'll tell you why," said he, and he began to stamp like a horse that's got pin-worms; "I'm going to find out whether you have been playing me square or not. And I'm taking this means to find out. Just before coming over here, I issued orders to my brokers to go onto the floor of the Exchange and offer to buy Erie. Now I'm going to keep you here behind lock and key for a while, to see if the market is still supplied with Erie when you're out of it. You don't stir out of this room until my brokers have had a chance to see."

I made believe to be hurt by his unkind suspicions. I said I didn't want to leave the room, or issue any selling orders to my brokers; because I wasn't doing any selling. But it hurt me to think that my old friend and partner had lost faith in me.

"Drew," said he, "you lie faster than a horse can trot. It isn't going to do you any good to be soft-soapy. That door isn't going to be unlocked till I ferret this thing out."

I spoke back. He answered me. Soon we got all het up in an argument. I made believe to send home my remarks by pounding on the table. For I had suspected Marsden's scheme; and so, before he came, I had told one of my clerks to place himself just outside the door of my private office, and every time he heard me pound on the table, he should send word to my brokers on the floor of the Exchange to sell a thousand shares of Erie.

Marsden didn't suspect my scheme in the least. He was scampering around the room, nimble as a new-gelt pig. Every time I'd answer him good and hot, and pound with my hand on the desk, he got all the hotter, and spoke back. He kept the thing going. I was willing. It gave his brokers time to take all the Erie off my hands. Every once in a while I'd make believe to get all het up again, and hit the desk. This lasted well into the day.

By and by Marsden looked at his watch. "Well, it's pretty near closing time on the Stock Exchange; so I'm willing now to let you out of the room. I want to hear from my brokers, and see if they have had any offerings of Erie."

I told him he was welcome to go and find out, so far as I was concerned. I was glad I'd had the chance to prove my innocence. "You suspected me unjustly, you young spunkie," said I. "And now you'll find out. You'll see that it's been some-body else who has been unloading that stock onto you. Leastwise, you'll now see that it hasn't been me." Marsden went away.

The deal nearly broke him. In fact, my scheme was a little too successful. During that red hot argument, I had loaded his brokers with such blocks of the stock that when Marsden finally got back to the scene, it crippled him up. He couldn't take care of the purchases which his brokers had made. And when it came to settle the thing, I had to let

Marsden off with only part payment of his obligations to me. And in doing so I had to let the cat out of the bag. But I had a good chuckle over the success of my joke. I always did enjoy a joke, anyhow.

Speaking of jokes, I think one of the best funs I ever had was when I got the best of some of the church brethren. A number of them had got to coming to my house and talking Wall Street talk. They knew I was one of the inside operators, and that points from me were worth their weight in gold. (Everybody is kin to a rich man.) Even some of the professors out in my theological seminary in New Jersey were getting the Wall Street fever. On their visits at my house, whilst the talk of a winter's evening would be on matters of faith and doctrine, the subject in some way or other would get switched off to modern life and to the doings of Wall Street. First along, I was tender about having my business affairs brought into our conversation. But I soon saw that they were willing, if they had the chance, to try a flier or two in the Street.

So one time when a lot of them were coming pretty often, and seeing that I was starting out just then on a Bearing-down campaign, I allowed my talks with them to turn sort of gradual-like to present-day affairs, and to Wall Street. Then I'd say, in sort of an off-hand way, "I'm willing to tell one of the secrets of the Street if you'll keep it dark. An upward movement is just now being engineered. Of course, only those who are on the inside know it. The outside public thinks that the market is going the other way. Those who are on the inside take advantage of this ignorance. People who buy now will be in on the killing, when the butchering time arrives. Brother so-and-so, I have given you this little tip, because you and I have known each other so long. But don't tell anybody else!" Then a day or two later, when another one of the brethren would be visiting me, I'd say to him the same thing. And I was a good midwife at the business, being by nature patient and cool.

In this way there set in a good-sized buying movement in those particular stocks that I was selling short — Wabash, Quicksilver Mining Stock, and shares in the Canton Land Company of Baltimore. Because, when you give a fellow an inside tip on the market, and inform him that he's not to tell another soul, he's going to let at least three or four others in on the secret. Those three or four others tell their friends, also. And the thing spreads like a fire in the woods.

Well, a short horse is soon curried. When I had got the thing fixed up, I went and dumped onto the market some jags of stock big enough to break the price a few points. That was enough to start the fall. Because these brethren were not very plentifully stored with this world's goods. Their

margins were soon exhausted. They were sold out.
I covered my shorts at a nice low figure.

I think it was one of these fellows from my theological seminary that was meant in a little skit
that appeared in the public prints about this time.
I give it here because it shows that a person should
not go into Wall Street dickerings unless he first
knows the ins and outs:

He was a long, lank countryman,
　And he stoppeth one or two:
"I'm not acquaint in these yeere parts,
　And I'm a-looking fur Daniel Drew.

"I'm a stranger in the vineyard,
　And my callin' I pursoo
At the Institoot at Madison
　That was built by Daniel Drew.

"I'm a stranger in the vineyard,
　An' my 'arthly wants are few;
But I want some points on them yer sheares,
　An' I'm a-lookin' fur Daniel Drew."

Again I saw that labourer,
　Corner of Wall and New;
He was looking for a ferry-boat,
　And not for Daniel Drew.

Upon his back he bore a sack,
　Inscribed "Preferred Q. U.";
Some Canton script was in his grip,
　A little Wabash too.

At the ferry gate I saw him late,
With his white hat askew,
Paying his fare with a registered share
Of that "Preferred Q. U."

And these words came back from the Hackensack:
"Ef yew want ter gamble a few,
Jest git in yer paw at a game of draw,
But don't take a hand with Drew."

It beats all, how easy people get the Wall Street fever.   If folks will dance they must pay the fiddler, that's all.

## XXXVI

I WAS so busy these days, the Sabbath was well-nigh my only time of rest. Week-days were work days. Sometimes I even worked nights. After the Exchange closed on Broad Street, I used to go up to the Fifth Avenue Hotel, where a dealer had opened a kind of evening exchange in the basement below the office. Admission was fifty cents. Shares were bought and sold there from seven o'clock to nine. When Sunday came, therefore, I often got out of the city for a day in the country. But I made it a habit to go to church, even when I was away from the city. I remembered that in my early life my backslidings had come about when I had forgotten to go to meeting, and was breaking the Lord's Day. Sabbath desecration has been my besetting sin all through life, anyhow. Time and time again I have had to ask to be forgiven for it. So I now tried, like every watchful Christian should, to remember my weakness and to guard against it.

It was on one of those outings in the country, I remember, that I heard a sermon which made considerable of an impression on me. It was along a line that I had never heard before. The title of the sermon was: "Taking God into Partnership with You in Your Business." As soon as the preacher announced his subject, I pricked up my ears. It was new. Since then — and I'm sorry to say it — many of the sermons I've listened to have had a good deal of this new and strange doctrine in them — "A heaven here below," "A better world here and now," all that sort of stuff. I am missing more and more the good, old-time hallelujah message. The preachers seem to be preaching nowadays as though religion had to do with the things of this world, whereas, in the good old days, this very sin of worldliness was what we were warned against. I don't know but what my seminary for the training of preachers, founded with my own money, is taking to some of these new-fangled ideas.

Well, as I started to say, this sermon was about "Taking God into Partnership with You." It was a brand-new thought to me. I was struck with it. As I walked home that day from the church to the hotel where I was stopping, I talked about the sermon with a friend who was with me.

"Do you think," said I, "that there is anything in what the preacher told us this morning."

"Why, yes," said he; "I think there's a great deal in it. I think the Lord would like to be a companion in our business life as well as in our home and church life."

"And do you think he would really bless a man who took him into partnership with him?" I asked. Because I wanted to be sure of my ground before I took any step in the matter.

"Yes," said he; "I think that the man who followed the teachings of that sermon would be blessed in the long run."

That made up my mind. I went to my room in the hotel, and then and there decided that I would give the message of that Sunday morning a try. Not that I have ever been a man to jump at conclusions. But the sermon of the morning had come to me just at a time when I was calculating in my mind whether or not to go into a certain Wall Street speckilation.

As I have wrote somewheres in these papers, when I went in with Gould and Fisk in the movement to lock up greenbacks, I saw that they were working for a decline in prices. I fell out with them. But they had gone on with their plan. And I had been wondering whether it wouldn't be a good plan, since they were working on the short side of the market, for me also to put out a line of shorts. By being independent, I might clean up even more money than if I had stood in with them; because then I'd have had to divide my profits by three, whilst now I could pocket all my profits. I was turning the thing over in my mind one way and the other, without being able to come to a decision. And now, suddenly, that sermon had come into my life. It seemed providential. I took it to be a leading of the spirit.

So that night in my room in the hotel, I got right down on my marrow-bones — it's knee work that brings the blessing, every time — and told the Lord that I was going to try the thing, and see if he really wanted to be taken into partnership in my business. I prayed good and long — in fact, I prayed right out loud, so earnest was I in the deal I was making then and there with the Lord. If he went in with me as a partner, and helped in the work, I saw, from all my experience in partnerships, that I'd have to divide up some of the profits with him. So I told him that if he'd prosper me in this stock-market move that I was now about to venture into, I'd pay up in cash the promises I had made toward the benevolences that my name had been attached to. Because, although I had told the trustees of Drew Theological Seminary, when they named the school after me, that I would give them a quarter of a million dollars as an endowment, I had kind of hated to pay over so big a sum of money. For the reason that that amount put up as margins in stock-market speckilations, promised to earn large profits. Even though I was now a rich man, I hated to take that amount of money out of my business. A full cup must be carried steadily. So, instead of paying over to them the money outright, I wrote my check each year for the interest on the endowment. Of course, that was just as good to the school, because all they wanted was the yearly income, anyhow.    But the Trustees were after me to pay over the full amount, in order, as they said, to make the thing sure.    And they kept reminding me, also, that I had said I was going to swell the endowment to half a million.    So, there on my bended knees in that room, I made a covenant with the Lord.    I would take him into partnership with me in this business dicker that I was about to go into; and, if he prospered me, I vowed that I'd pay over in full — and without going back on it this time — all the gifts I had thus far made in the form of agreements to pay.

When the Sunday was over, I came back to the city with a glad heart.    I went down to Wall Street the next morning feeling a young man once more. Without waiting for anything or anybody, I went onto the market and began my operations.    I had learned in my associations with Gould and Fisk that Erie was the stock they were planning to centre their Bear operations on.    Besides, I knew of a large issue of Erie stock — 23 millions — which they had secretly put through about three months before. So I gave orders to my brokers to sell that stock heavily short.

I didn't find any difficulty in getting my offers taken.    In fact, these offers of mine were snatched up so quick on the floor of the Exchange that if I'd been a little more cautious I might have suspected something. Because, and I found it out later, it was no other than Gould and Fisk themselves who had turned tail and instead of Bears had suddenly become Bulls. They had changed their tactics without giving me notice.

Our lock-up of greenbacks, with purpose to tighten the money market and produce a fall in securities, had been so successful that great pressure had been brought to bear on the Secretary of the Treasury at Washington to put back into circulation some of the currency that had been called in by him in preparation for our country's resumption of specie payments. First along Secretary McCulloch hadn't listened to these appeals. He thought they were cries of some stock-market speckilators who had got themselves in a tight hole. But when the leading business men of the country began to urge it, he finally yielded and had reissued some four millions of money. Fisk and Gould, seeing that the authorties in Washington had begun to turn against them and were now siding in with the business interests of the country, had taken it as a warning. They suddenly turned from their Bear campaign, and now were Bulls.

Unluckily, I didn't know of this. I was an outsider now. To speckilate as an outsider, is like trying to drive black pigs in the dark. So I kept on selling Erie short just when Gould and Fisk had turned and were buying Erie for a rise. I learned later that they had made this sudden turn in their tactics partly in order to squeeze me. Because they had been all-fired mad when I deserted them in the campaign of locking up greenbacks. Jimmy at the time had called me "'Fraid Cat," "Danny Cold-Feet," "Turn-Tail," and such-like. But I hadn't cared. I was determined to look out for number one, no matter what names he called me.

The long and the short of it is, by and by my contracts to deliver seventy thousand shares of Erie matured; and I wasn't able. Gould and Fisk had bought up the entire floating supply of Erie, and now I couldn't buy it for love or money. Erie shot up suddenly from 35 to 47, a rise of 12 per cent. almost in an hour.

This was on a Saturday. A week from that time a steamer would be in from England bringing a large consignment of Erie stock which English investors were shipping over. But that would be too late — my contracts would mature by the following Wednesday. I was in a bad fix. The other boys who had been caught along with me in this corner held a meeting. I was there. It was voted to go to the courts and get an injunction restraining the cornerers from demanding the stock.

I was glad I had been present at this meeting. It put information into my hands which I might be able to make use of. So the next morning, although it was on a Sunday, I went to Fisk at his office in the

Grand Opera House building. It was a beautiful building. If I'd had time, most like I'd have stopped to admire all the costly fixings that Jimmy had put into it. After he'd bought this Opera House, he rented some of its space to the Erie Railroad for its offices. He had his own office there also. Opposite the main entrance was an anteroom for his visitors to wait in. Behind the door opening from there was a screen of red curtain. There, behind that screen, Jimmy sat at a big black walnut desk. The doors of the offices were of black walnut, and over each was a silver-plate sign to tell the department. Even the ceilings were painted with all kinds of fancy pictures. Fisk had springs all round his desk, for sending signals to every part of the building. Under the same roof he gave his French operas; and he was manager of this also. By pushing one spring, French ballet dancers would be ushered into his private office. Another signal would bring a messenger boy. Another would bring the heads of the Erie Railroad. Another would bring the managers of his steamboat lines. He also had a room where he could give banquets. Jimmy there was a kind of Solomon in all his glory. For under that roof he had power and money, and all that money could buy. He called himself "Prince Erie."

But I wasn't in any mood to stop and think of those things then. I was in too much grief of mind.

So I walked into his office and went straight to the gist of the matter. I told Fisk I was in a fix. Those deliveries of Erie stock that I had contracted to make — unluckily I was unable to meet them. I asked him to help me out by not pressing me for the stock just on the tick of the minute, but to give me a few more days.

He replied in what I thought was a very unfeeling manner. He said that he wasn't running a benevolent institution; this Wall Street business, as he understood it, wasn't a distribution of Christmas candy or a Charitable Relief Society. If I was squeezed I must make the best of it.

"Look happy, Uncle," he added; "look happy. Of course, we shall be under the necessity of taking nearly all of your earthly possessions. But there are other things in life besides money. Grin and bear it. In fact, I understand you have been 'Bearing' it!" And he roared with laughter at his joke. He leaned his big, blonde bulk back in his chair — Fisk was by this time as fat as a butcher's dog — and seemed to enjoy the thing immensely.

But I wouldn't give up. A rich person is like a man up a tree, liable to come down so much faster than he went up. I was afraid of becoming a poor man once more. So now I pressed my case home to Fisk every way I knew. I said that to let me off didn't mean that he'd have to let the rest of the Bears off who were also caught in this corner. In fact, he would make so much out of them that he could afford to be easy on me. My case, I tried to show him, was different from the others. He and I had been friends together a long time. Surely it wouldn't do to let any unpleasantness come between us now. He had all the money he wanted, anyhow; and it would be Christianity in him to let me off. I reminded him how the Bible says that we ought to be tenderly affectioned one to another. But he didn't soften.

"Call Gould in," said I. "I know Jay will have some heart, even if you haven't." First along Jimmy wouldn't do it. By and by he consented. He went into another room while Jay came in. I told him pretty much the same thing that I had told Jimmy. I didn't get any satisfaction.

Finally they said they were tired of discussing the thing at that time; if I wanted to, I could come around again that night at ten o'clock. So I left. I was there at ten o'clock that night, good and prompt. But I didn't get in to see them as soon as I had expected. They seemed to have a press of business on hand. Though they had told me to come at ten, it was eleven o'clock before I finally was admitted from the anteroom into the office where they were. I started right in.

"See here, boys," said I. "I'm not asking you to lose any money yourselves. All I want is for you to give that printing press another turn. Print a few more convertible bonds. They won't cost you any money; the Erie Railroad can easily afford it. You have the power to issue more bonds if you want to. If you are caught at it, I will buy the bonds from you in cash. Or, I'll buy the bonds of you with the understanding that I am not to pay for them unless they catch you at it."

But Jimmy all of a sudden seemed to become full of prickles in his conscience.

"Why, Uncle," he replied, and he pretended to be very serious and solemn, "as a high officer of the Erie Railroad Corporation I am sworn to honour, guard and defend her interests. Far be it from me, even at the sacred call of friendship, to prove recreant to my solemn obligation. They who pass to the harming and despoiling of the Erie Railroad," and he placed his fat hand over his heart, "must pass first over my dead body."

Jay grinned while Jimmy was going through all that stuff. But I didn't. I didn't see any joke in it. I told them that I would pay as high as 3 per cent. for the loan of thirty or forty thousand shares for fifteen days. I said: "You can call on me, and I'll write my check for a plump hundred thousand dollars. If that isn't a reasonable profit for you, what is?" But they refused to listen.

Then I changed my tactics. I said how I hadn't come there merely as a beggar; that I had it in my power to do a favour to them as well as to ask one.

"What's that?" they asked.

"Well," said I, "I was at a meeting of our Bear crowd yesterday. They are going to do something which it would be mightily to the interest of you two fellows to know. I'm willing to turn state's evidence, so to speak, against them, and let you into the secret, if you'll agree to let me personally out of the corner.

They said they wouldn't agree to anything. But it might soften their attitude towards me considerable, they said, if I showed that I remembered old times by doing them the favour, and tell the plans of my partners in the Bear party.

I tried to get them first to promise to let me off if I told them. They wouldn't. I finally decided to tell, and trust to their honour as gentlemen to do me the favour in return. So I said:

"All right, I'll show my friendliness of spirit. I'll let you in on the secret. Bright and early to-morrow morning those associates of mine are going to the courts and get out an injunction restraining you from demanding the deliveries of these Erie stocks."

They made believe to "pooh-pooh" the information; said it wasn't worth shucks to them; that they didn't care what injunctions were gotten out; they were going ahead and demand those deliveries, even if all the judges in creation got in their way.

But I could see, just the same, that it was a valuable piece of news I had given them. "And now," said I, "I have done my part. Are you going to do yours?"

"Couldn't think of it," said Jay. "Drew, we've got you just where we want you. You'll have to pony up."

"Boys," said I, "don't you drive me too far, or I'll fight back. I know a whole lot about you. You know during the whole of our other fights I objected to ever giving my affidavit. But I swear I will do you all the harm I can, if you don't help me in this time of my great need. So help me Heaven! if you don't let me out of this corner I'll go before the courts and make an affidavit telling all about our old deals, and show you up."

"It's a hard winter," said Fisk, "when one wolf eats another. And you would have to give away on yourself, too. You were with us, hand and glove. In fact, you were in it before we commenced."

"It don't make any difference," said I. "I'm willing to make a clean breast of the whole thing. I will hew to the line, let the chips fall where they will. For I am desperate. If you put that Erie stock up, I am a ruined man."

"Dan Drew," said Jimmy, "you are the last man in the world to whine over any position in which you may find yourself in Erie."

I didn't answer back. I didn't see any use of dragging out the talk. It was already one o'clock.

In fact, they themselves were plainly showing me
that they wanted the interview brought to an end.
I rose to my feet. I took my hat. I said just this:
"Gentlemen, I will bid you good night."

Jay grinned so wide it was almost a laugh —
about as near a laugh, I guess, as that graveyard
face of his could get. As to Jimmy, he bust out in
a roar. I didn't take any notice. I left them and
passed out.

It's a sorry colt that will kick its own dam. I
felt all the more sore at the unfeeling way in which
Gould and Fisk were treating me in this matter,
because I had been their foster parent, so to speak.
When they came into Wall Street as yearlings, I
had taken them up — had showed them how to make
money. And now, for them to turn on me in my
old age and strip me in this way, was an unthankful
thing to do. It was like a mare of mine once, that
got a stone in her foot. It was hurting her, and was
like to lame her for life. So I got off, and started
to help her. As I was bending over the hoof and
trying to dig the stone out, she reached down and bit
me in the seat. I remember it made me very sore
towards her — this ungrateful act of hers. So in the
present case. I felt I had never seen a more ungrateful pair of men than Jim Fisk and Jay Gould.

But it was no time to nurse feelings. Things had
to be done, and very quick, too. The Sabbath Day
was already at an end. (I was very sorry that I had

been forced to desecrate the day. As I was going home that night from Fisk's office, I felt myself a guilty and hell-deserving sinner, and have asked since to be forgiven for breaking that Lord's day.)

After a short sleep, I got up the next morning and set to work. I was in really a tighter fix than I had been the day before. Because, since I had given away on my partners in the Bear crowd, they were down on me. And it hadn't helped me any with Fisk and Gould, either. I was now between two fires, so to speak. I was sorry I had told those two men anything at all of our plans. They had pretended that they didn't care beans for the information. Just the same they used it. Before we could get out our injunction, they up and went to Judge Barnard before he was out of bed and got an injunction against us. In war it's always an advantage to attack first. In the case of lawsuits, to get out an injunction first is particularly helpful; it puts the party that comes out next with an injunction, in the light of mere quibblers and obstructionists; and they don't have a standing with either court or jury.

Now it was a case of fight it out to a finish. We tried to get Fisk and Gould ousted from their office, and the Erie Railroad placed into the hands of a receiver. I went before the court, as I had told them I would, and tried to hurt them by making a clean breast of some of our doings. This was my affidavit:

"Gould and Fisk have recently been engaged in locking up money; they told me so; they wanted me to join them in locking up money, and I did to the extent of $1,000,000, and refused to lock up any more; I had originally agreed to lock up $4,000,00, but when money became very tight, I deemed it prudent to decline to go any further, and unlocked my million; the object of locking up is to make money scarce — to make stocks fall, because people couldn't get the money to carry them.

DANIEL DREW."

The next few days were about as hard as I ever went through. I was like a snake under a harrow — couldn't wriggle out, no matter which way I turned. When my fellow Bears learned that I had employed Sunday to go to the Erie crowd, they thought of me as a Jack-on-both-sides. They called me an informer. They soured on me. Then, when the Street saw my affidavit, they turned against me also. Because it was the first news they'd had that I had broken with my old Erie partners. Fisk and Gould were powerful on the market at this time. It was seen that I was no longer in with the ruling clique as I once was; so a good many of the operators were not willing to follow me any longer. I was mortal lonesome.

As the time to make my deliveries drew nigh, I had

to do something. I went onto the market and tried to buy Erie. I offered any price. It was an awful fix. All the other Bears were likewise trying to buy. The price went up like sixty. Between Monday and Wednesday the price jumped from 47 to 57. And I couldn't get it even at that figure. If that steamer from England would only come! But she couldn't possibly arrive until the thing would be over. By Thursday afternoon our buying had forced the stock up to 62. This was at two o'clock. At a quarter to three the stock would have to be delivered. I thought I was a goner.

Just then a strange thing happened. Queer figures were seen coming into Broad Street — tailors from uptown, boot-makers, small cigar dealers, and the like. Each of them had one or more ten-share certificates of Erie in his inside pocket, which he now offered for sale. The thing was soon explained. Some time before, an issue of Erie stock had been put out in ten-share certificates. Nothing but stock printed in ten-share certificates is sent across the ocean to London. It had been calculated by Fisk and Gould, therefore, that this particular issue had been bought by English investors, and was safe across the water. They had taken account of all the rest of the supply on the market, except this ten-share issue. Now we learned, and it was a joyful surprise, that a good number of these ten-share certificates had been quietly bought up at the time by small buyers on this side — clerks, barbers, shoe dealers, and so forth; and now were being dragged out of their hoarding places by the high prices we were offering.

This help appeared none too soon. I grabbed at every ten-share certificate that was offered. Jimmy and his black-faced partner saw my move. They tried to head me off by themselves snatching up these new offers so I couldn't get them. It was an exciting time on the floor of the Exchange. They did succeed in absorbing much of what was offered. I worked like a house afire. Five minutes before closing time I got my shorts covered. But it had been at an awful cost. This squeeze in Erie cost me well-nigh a million dollars in good, hard money.

But the loss did me some good. It taught me once for all not to take up with new and strange doctrines. Some time later I met the man who had been with me in that church service up in the country. I said to him:

"Do you remember that new-fangled notion that was brought out in the sermon we heard some weeks ago, about taking God into partnership with you in your business?"

He said, yes, he remembered it very clear.

"Well," said I, "there's nothing to it."

## XXXVII

I WAS sorry at the time it happened that I had broken with Fisk and Gould. When you are in with an inside clique of operators, you have the pick of the basket, so to speak. Those on the outside take what's left. But I now see that even to have stayed in with my old crowd wouldn't have helped for very long. Because something was soon to happen which would have smashed up our ring, anyhow.

It came on a Saturday in January. I remember it, because the next day was Sunday. And I thought how awful it must be for Jimmy to be hurled into Eternity on that day, with no time to say his prayers and mind his soul. We had finished breakfast that morning in my house in Union Square; I was just about getting through with morning devotions. A coach drove up to the door with great style. There was a darkey coachman, togged out like a militiaman at General Training; the horses were all shiny with harness of brass and steel. You'd have thought it was some king paying a royal visit. In fact, it was "Prince Erie." Jimmy now came up the steps lively as a cricket, and into the house.

"Hello, Colonel," I said.  He liked to be called colonel.  By his offering jobs in the Erie Railroad to the officers of a militia regiment, he had got himself elected their colonel.

He said: "Good morning, Uncle," and I took him into the front room, where we could be alone.  We didn't refer to the late unpleasantness that had come between us in the matter of the Erie corner.  Business men don't carry grudges.  Every day is a new beginning.  If you can use a man to-day, it never pays to remember what he may have done to you, or you to him, yesterday.

He sat down in the plush chair in front of the fireplace.  I burned cannel coal in that fireplace.  How well I remember those little details now!  At the time, I hadn't any idea it would be the last I should ever see Jimmy alive — in fact, that it was to be his last day upon earth.

"I came," said he, as soon as he got seated, "to talk with you about those shares of yours in the Bristol Line of steamboats.  How would you like to get them off your hands and have the money?  Ready cash, you know, is a handy article, and often better than capital tied up, particularly in boats."

I told him I was always open to an offer.  I said that just now in particular I was in a position where ready cash would come in almighty good.  He made me an offer for the stock.  We dickered for a spell.  Finally I told him I couldn't give any answer then.

I'd turn the thing over in my mind, and would let him know later.

"So long," said he. "Think it over quick." And he started to leave.

"Going so soon?" said I. "Stay and visit a spell."

"No," said he; "I've got a busy day ahead of me. That Ned Stokes is putting me to an everlasting lot of trouble. But I'll trounce him, yet, you see if I don't."

I tried to shame him out of making such a big fuss over so little a thing as a love scrap.

"But, Uncle," said he, "it isn't a little thing. That rat has come between me and my Josie. Before he came along I had things my own way over at her house. I was the one who set her up in that house. Before she knew me she didn't have a decent gown to her back — yes, owed money for her rent! There's no end to the cash I've spent on that woman. And for her to turn me down for that young popinjay is more than I can stand. If he was even of some account on the Street, I wouldn't blame her so much. But for her to take up with a little two-by-four like him — put me out of her house to give him room — no self-respecting man could put up with it. And I'll smash him for it if I have to keep at it from now till the cows come home. If Tweed was only back in popular favour as he was a little while ago, I could get a couple of men from his gang of 'Dead Rabbits' to help me with the job." He went on to say how he had been getting even with his Josephine by buying her servants out of her employ as fast as she could hire them; and he said he had other aces up his sleeve which he hadn't played yet.   "I'll show them a thing or two, before I get through with this thing."

"Have a care, Jimmy," said I; "those light-heeled women are bad people to deal with.   They're devil's daughters, every last one of them."

"I guess I'm finding it out," he replied.   "There isn't any faithfulness in a car-load of them.   What do you think? She's suing me now for libel. Just at this minute I've got to get over to the York-ville Court and fight it out.   But, Uncle, there's as good fish in the sea as ever was caught.   Your Jim Jubilee, Jr., isn't down and out just yet.   I'm as bucksome as ever.   Why, as soon as I get rid of that pair of rascals at the Yorkville Court to-day, I've got an appointment with a woman and her daughter down at a hotel on Broadway.   Mothers do well not to hang onto their daughters too long. Dead fish and daughters are bad things to keep. Glasses and lasses are brittle wear, Uncle," he called out, as he was going through the door; "and the finer they are, the more brittle.   By-by."   That was the last time I ever saw Jimmy alive.   Who'd have thought that a man as gay as that was going to his death?   After he'd got through with the ses-sion of the Yorkville Police Court, Jimmy went down to the Grand Central Hotel on Broadway.   He was going in at the north entrance to meet the woman and her daughter that he had spoken about. Just as he got inside the door and was going up the short stairs to the parlour floor, Stokes at the top met him and shot him with a revolver. It hit him in the belly. Stokes threw the revolver under a lounge in one of the parlours leading off from the hall, and tried to get away. But he was caught, and taken to jail. Fisk sank where he stood, and hardly spoke after that. He was taken into one of the parlours of the hotel. He died the next morning about ten o'clock.

It was a sad Sunday for all of us. The thing had come so sudden. Jimmy was the livest one in all our crowd. Although I'd had some differences with him a little while before, still I hadn't allowed that to sour me against him. He was one that you couldn't stay mad at for any length of time. He had a way of making up with you, that you just couldn't resist. And now that he was gone, it seemed as though the king pin had been knocked out of our Wall Street clique. In fact, Jimmy himself had seemed to know how important he was. He used to slap me on the back hard enough to make my teeth rattle, and say: "Uncle, you and Jay couldn't get along without Jim Fisk, and you know it!"

I guess the others in our old crowd seemed to feel the loss just the way I did. After Jimmy was dead Jay went down to the room in the hotel where he lay, and sat near to the body while it was lying in state. Bill Tweed also came in and stood a while in the little party at the head of the coffin.   But the people, as they filed through to see Jimmy in his coffin, looked at Tweed; and soon he got up and went away. I can't tell how lonesome it was to all of us when the body was finally taken — on a special train — up to his old home, Brattleboro, Vt., and there put away in the ground.   They placed a big monument over his grave.   It had figures representing "Commerce," "Navigation," "Drama," and "Railroads," on the four corners; they tried their best to brighten up the gloom.   But it didn't work.   Somehow, we felt that it wasn't going to be so well with any of us after that.   And it wasn't very long before our fears came true.   That same year Tweed was hounded by the papers until the Sheriff got him and locked him up in the County Prison on Blackwell's Island, and he never got out alive again—that is, to go free.   With Tweed gone, the other prop that had helped us so much in our Wall Street speckilations was taken away.   Jay felt this as much as I.   He has gone on making lots of money.   But since Tweed was locked up and Fisk shot, Gould has become lonely and troubled.   He says he is going to give some of his Erie Railroad money to the New York Presbytery, to be used for Home and Foreign Missions.   Even Ned Stokes, who did the shooting, doesn't enjoy life, though he is out of jail at last.   He sees spooks in the night.

The papers, of course, had a whole lot to say when Fisk was killed and our crowd thus broken up. The *New York Times*, the morning after his death, came out in an editorial like this:

We shall probably be thought very eccentric if we suggest a reflection which must have occurred to many minds yesterday — namely, that the old-fashioned theory (as some people call it) about guilt bringing with it its own punishment, receives a startling illustration in the events of the past year. There are not a few persons in the world who think that we are too much advanced in knowledge to believe that there is any person in the universe greater than that which we create ourselves, or which is tangible enough to be touched; and that all human circumstances are the result of accident or chance. Yet the events of the past year might well disturb the conclusions of these philosophers. The men of whom Fisk was one seemed to be so strong that nothing could shake them. They had wealth and power unlimited; they altered laws to suit themselves; leaders of society bowed down before them. The world had nothing more to offer them. But to the astonishment of all men, and as it were in a moment, the whirlwind descends upon them, and they are swept away. Their wealth is gone; their names are become a by-word; some of them are vagabonds on the face of the earth; others perish, in the bitter language of Swift, like poisoned rats in a hole. We say again that it is an amazing spectacle, and though some may continue to assert, "It is all chance," and to cry out, "There is no God," there are others who will be inclined to take a different view of it, and to go back to the simpler faith of earlier years — that somehow or other, explain it how we will, the sin of every man finds him out, and the divine laws are just in execution, whether we choose to acknowledge their existence or not.

That editor bothered his head more than there was any use of, to prove that there's a God. I could have told him, without his trying to find it out in such roundabout fashion. In my own life, I've experienced the guidings of Providence in a way too clear to be mistaken — that is, up to the time when bad luck set in for me. And even now, when it isn't so well with me as it used to be, I try to trust even where I can't see:

> "From every stormy wind that blows,
> From every swelling tide of woes,
> There is a calm, a sure retreat,
> 'Tis found beneath the mercy seat."

Even in these later days of my life, I have been snatched out of ruin sometimes by such close shaves that I have had to fall down onto my marrow-bones in thankfulness. Why, I have come home at night sometimes so tuckered and down in the mouth, I've said, the first thing on getting into the house: "We're ruined, Danck, we're ruined! It's sure pop this time!" and I have gone to bed with my boots on and without stopping to undress, I have been that down-hearted.   But in the morning, on getting up, I'd say:

"Go out, Danck, and get the paper.   We'll look our fate in the face."

And when he had brought it in, and I had looked over the stock quotations, I'd have to exclaim:

"We're saved, Danck, we're saved after all!   That fall of two points does it!"

The way to keep your religion is not to be all the time arguing about God, but just believe him.   I don't see why, just because Ned Stokes put that bullet into Fisk's belly, that it proves anything one way or the other about religion.   And yet, the papers made it a big card against us.   They came out like this:

In every bad man's life there comes a moment when the machinery of wrong he has so laboriously contrived seems to be going wrong; when one after another of his elaborate combinations fails; when the building of dishonesty or cunning, with all its apparent completeness and splendour, seems breaking to pieces over his head.   He sees that it is not man that is defeating him.   It is some mysterious and higher Power.

These conspirators are now rounded up.   The vast wealth they had accumulated melted away like the snow of spring.   Even their very names became a proverb for rascality.   Surely the young men who have been dazzled and debauched by careers of flaunting vice and open and gigantic fraud, will gather some serious impressions from their tragic histories. They must see that there is a mysterious and gigantic Power ruling the issues of human life, and inexorably punishing the infractions of his laws, and not for a moment forgetting the smallest wrong: that Power we call God.

Which shows that the more educated you are, the harder it sometimes is to have religious faith.

The *London Times* was also in high spirits when our Erie crowd was broken up by Jimmy's death and by Bill Tweed's imprisonment. It was so bitter in its hatred of me and my whole clique that it said our bust-up now was a cause for rejoicing on both sides the water, and that we had been a bad thing for the country:

For a long time the British shareholders of the Erie Railroad have been making efforts to obtain that justice which we are accustomed to think would not be refused by the most turbulent Spanish Republic or the most effete Oriental despotism. In the Empire State and its splendid capital they laboured in vain. They were told by friendly advisers that their agents might as well go home again.

The revolution has come, and the Erie ring has been broken up. This incident has almost a national importance, for there can be no doubt that the audacious practices of the Erie Directors injured the credit of all American securities. It is difficult for foreigners clearly to distinguish between what is sound and unsound in a country so new and changing as the United States, and cautious people might well argue that if other companies were not so profligate as the Erie Company, there was nothing in the nature of American institutions to prevent them from becoming so.  Indeed, the pictures drawn by New Yorkers of their Legislature, their Judiciary, and the mercantile doctrines and practices of their citizens, were enough to sober the most sanguine speculator.  Whatever the truth of these assertions, they could hardly be contradicted so long as one of the chief enterprises of the country, involving millions of money, was notoriously under the management of a set of swindlers, befriended by a suspected legislature and a more than suspected judiciary.

That British sheet seemed to have the idea that I and my crowd should have served in Wall Street for the good of the country!  That would be a pretty way to get along in a stock-market deal!  If a fellow in a stock-market dicker stopped to think first how it was going to affect the country at large, he would have his hands so tied he wouldn't be able to move. The trouble with editors is, they see only the down-town side of a man's life.  They don't see the home and religious side of him.  It would be a great deal better if newspapers would pay attention to that part of a man's life that is open and above the surface.  Straight trees can have crooked roots.

# XXXVIII

THOUGH far beyond the Scripture limits by this time, and lonesome because of Jimmy's death, I was still able to find my way around in Wall Street smart and handy— as Jay Gould himself had to allow. For it was about this time that I gave him and Hen Smith that squeeze in Erie which they won't forget for some time.

I saw, by my reading of the tape and from the reports that came to me around the Street, that Jay and Henry were selling Erie for future delivery. I calculated that they were overdoing the thing. Because at this time, out of the seven hundred and eighty thousand shares of the capital stock of the road, fully seven hundred thousand shares were held abroad. So, with the help of a German banker, I got control of the floating supply of the stock here in the New York market. Then I waited.

Soon the time to make their deliveries came around. The short operators, Smith and Gould among the rest, were unable to get the stock. Then I set about. I had a good holt on them. I loaned them the stock. But it was at a rate which milked them fine as anything.

"I've known those two boys," said I to my broker, "a good long time. I guess we won't charge them 3 per cent. a day. We will just make it one and a half. They will give down freer then, and, more than that, they will feel better."

It wasn't pity in me so much as good business policy, to set the rate at one and a half instead of three. Because those two men, Jay and Hen, were so powerful, that if I'd squeezed them too tight, they might have gone into litigation and made it hard for me to collect anything. Even as it was, a cent and a half a day means a rate of 600 per cent. a year; and that's a decent enough profit for anybody. And they had to pay it. I had those fellows by the scrooch of the neck. The way they squiggled to get loose made me chuckle all over. (I always did have a knack, anyhow, of seeing the fun of the thing.) And just now they were squirmy enough. But I held on tight. In fact, I made them squiggle still more; for I wasn't through with this deal yet. After I'd got the stock all loaned out, I waited until the moment was ripe. Then, going down to the Street one morning, I issued orders to my brokers: "Call in now all of that stock that has been loaned out."

I knew that so unlooked-for a move would make a big howl in the Street. And, in order not to be pestered by the yells and cries of the operators when they suddenly found themselves caught, I drove away up town, and stayed there all day.  So, when the traders on the Exchange came to my office that day to beg for an extension of their loans, I wasn't there.   "Mr. Drew's gone away for the day," was the only thing the clerks could say.

A hungry horse makes a clean manger.  I finished this deal up good and thorough.  Some of the traders were sold out by order of the Stock Exchange Board.  Prices caught as pretty a tumble as anyone could ask for.  And I took a slice out of the boys that day which I guess they remember yet.

This was 'long about the end of September, soon after I had come back from my summer's rest in the country.  About a month after, Gould came around to my office one day.  He chatted for a while, and then said he'd stump me to go in with him and singe the Street by a Bulling movement in Erie.  I ought to have been on my guard; because it was so soon after I had caught Gould in the corner I have just wrote about.  And to hold that fellow for any length of time, was like trying to ride a cat in a wheelbarrow, he was that squiggly.  But Jay had a persuasive way with him.  You never could tell from his face what he was thinking about inside.  And now he put on such a friendly tone of voice that it made me think he was kindly affectioned towards me.

"We'll rocket that Erie stock," said he, "higher than Gilderoy's kite.  Anyway, Dan, you and I ought to be together in our Wall Street doings.

Let's forget some of the late unpleasantnesses — we're about even, now, I reckon — and start over again."

I was sort of tickled at the idea of getting back into partnership with him. Gould had a way of making a success of the things he went into. I knew him for a good mouser, one that never misses. So I said I'd go in with him. We agreed to buy Erie stock and hold it for a rise.

The thing went along for a while, smooth as a pan of milk. The price of the stock got up to 56. That was high-water mark compared with what Erie had been selling for a little while before. With that level reached, a lot of shares came dumping onto the market. In order to keep the price up, I had to take them. I didn't know at the time that it was Gould who was unloading on me. I trusted the man. I took all the shares that were offered, and locked them up in my safe.

It was about this time that Gould came over to my office and paid me another visit. He said that the market in Erie, from what he had noticed in reading the tape, seemed to be softening most unexpectedly. (Jay had so innocent a way of saying it, that I now believed he was as much worried as I over the sag in Erie.)

"Tell you, Dan, what I suspect," said he. "Most like as not the Street has got onto our Erie move and has begun to fight us. We must throw them off the scent. What do you say to going in on a side play in 'Northwestern' for a while, as a kind of blind for our Erie movements?"

The idea sort of took hold of me. I knew that Jay was getting rich hand over fist, and so felt I could trust his judgment. Besides, he put up some good arguments. He showed how the price of Northwestern stock was 'way above what it ought to be.

"You remember, Dan," said he, "how not very long ago that farmer out in Wisconsin gave a thousand shares of 'Northwestern' stock for a shanghai rooster; and now it's selling clean up at 75. It's a ridiculous price. We can go in, sell the market short at that figure, and play for at least a ten-point drop in the next three weeks."

I said I guessed it was safe to go short of "Northwestern"; and that it might tickle the boys to speckilate for a spell in something new. So I sent word to my brokers and they put out a line of shorts in "Nor'west" to the extent of twenty thousand shares.

I ought then to have watched that "Nor'west" deal more closely than I did. Because, as I found out afterwards, at the very time that Gould was getting me to go short of it, he was engineering a pool to Bull that same identical stock. For a report was around that Vanderbilt was after the road in order to get a western connection through to Chicago, and Jay was giving out to that Bull clique of his that it was, therefore, a good time to operate for a rise. I didn't know these facts. I was so busy watching our campaign in Erie, and trying to support the market there, that I didn't pay hardly any attention to "Nor'west." Until one day — it was Friday, I might have known something was going to go wrong — as I was watching the ticker, "Nor'west" jumped up from 83 to 95 in a single hour. Then it bounded up to par, dropped back to 90, and finally went to 105.

Even then I didn't realize how tight the corner was. I ought to have covered my shorts without a moment's delay — cut short your losses and let your profits run, is the rule. But I stood to lose so much at the 105 figure, that I decided to wait and hope for lower levels. So I kept up a good show of spirits. That Saturday afternoon some one said to me, in a teasing way: "Uncle, Northwestern is rising."

"Rising?" I replied. "Why, it's riz!"

But though I made believe I wasn't scared, I was as uneasy as a toad on a hot shovel.

Hen Smith was also a Bear with me in this Northwestern movement. He was short even more shares than I. He knew of some doings in the Erie Railroad Company in the last few months that would look bad for Gould if they came out. So he went to the president of the Erie Railroad and got him to obtain a warrant for Gould's arrest. We calculated that if Gould could be put behind the bars, it would take from the Street the man who was supporting the "Northwestern" market, and so cause it to drop.

We got Gould into the hands of the Sheriff.    But he secured bail; and was madder than ever when he got back into the Street.

Well, to cut it off short, we were cornered.    The price was ballooned to 230.    The rest of our Bear party were let off at from 150 to 160.    Hen Smith and I were the only ones who couldn't arrange a compromise.    I went over to Gould's office several times to get him to let me off.    He was very polite.    We got along fine so long as our talk was about former days and the pleasant times we had used to have together.    But the moment I switched the talk around, sort of gradual like, to those Northwestern shares that I'd agreed to deliver, he got as cold as charity.

"No use, Drew," he said finally — this was Saturday — "I was caught once, and I paid up man-fashion.    Now you've got to pay up.    I've learned some lessons from you in financiering, and have taken them well to heart.    The entire difference between the stock at its present level and the level at which you made your contracts, must be paid in cash, and good solid cash at that.    Don't come again unless you bring the money with you."

I thought of two or three ways to get out of the hole. One was to get out an injunction.    But the Stock Exchange had made a ruling that any one interfering with an officer of the Exchange in the discharge of his duty, such as enforcing deliveries when they fell due, and such like, would be put out. Then I thought of repudiating the contracts my brokers had made in my name. I figured that my brokers were more able to carry these losses than I was in my present condition. But the trouble here was, I myself was financially interested in the very firm of brokers that had done the work. For when I came back into the Street, after my war with Vanderbilt and my few months of retirement, I had become a special partner in the brokerage house of Kenyon, Cox & Co., by paying three hundred thousand dollars into the business. So, if I fell down on them now, I would really be falling down on myself.

The Saturday came to an end without any result. The next day, Sunday, was a hard one. At the price at which the stock then stood, I would lose over two million dollars; and I could see no way out. It was a long, dark day. When the Exchange opened Monday morning, I tried Gould again, but without any success. I made up my mind I'd have to stand a loss, and set about to make it as small as possible. I borrowed a part of the twenty thousand shares I was short. I also got hold of some convertible bonds which could be turned into stock. In this way I made a settlement. It was at about 125. The difference between $83 and $125, was the amount of my loss on every share! And there were twenty thousand of those shares! My loss was over three-quarters of a million dollars. The price of the stock then sank to 75. But this didn't do me any good. I had been chiselled out of my good money. It didn't make any difference to me then if the stock sank to nothing.

You don't get much sympathy in Wall Street when you stub your toe. All I could hear was snickers, wherever I went. About this time, also, the newspapers let loose on me again. One of them came out like this:

We cannot affect to have any sympathy with these men, and least of all with Drew. He has been one of the curses of the market for years past. If he has now received such a blow as will result in his being driven from the Street altogether, no one will be sorry for him.

Daniel Drew does not care a fig what people think about him, or what the newspapers say. He holds the honest people of the world to be a pack of fools, and you might as well try to scratch the back of a rhinoceros with a pin as to scratch his mind — if he has one — by preaching about morals. When he has been unusually lucky in his trade of fleecing other men, he settles accounts with his conscience by subscribing towards a new chapel or attending a prayer meeting — as a sharper he is undeniably a success.

The mud-thrower who wrote that said one true thing, that I'm not fidgety as to what people think of

me.  It was the loss of the money that hurt.  Gould
was the person I felt sore against.  When he was
getting me to go into that "Northwestern" dicker, he
was nice as anything.  That's the way with a
treacherous man — to come up to me holding a
knife behind his back, smile in my face till he got
close up, and then dig me in the guts!

Gould and his crowd tried to give out that Vanderbilt was in with them in the "Northwestern"
deal.  But the Commodore came out with a plump
" 'Taint so":

The recent corner in Northwestern has caused
some considerable excitement in Wall Street, and
has called forth much comment from the press.  My
name has been associated with others, in connection with the speculations, and gross injustice has
been done me thereby.  I beg leave, therefore, to say,
once for all, that I have not had, either directly
or indirectly, the slightest connection with or interest in the matter.  I have had but one business
transaction with Mr. Gould in my life.  In July,
1868, I sold him a lot of stock, for which he paid me,
and the privilege of a call for a further lot, which
he also settled.  Since then I have had nothing to
do with him in any way whatever; nor do I mean
ever to have, except it be to defend myself.  I have,
besides, always advised all my friends to have nothing to do with him in any business transaction.  I
came to this conclusion after taking particular notice
of his countenance.

C. VANDERBILT.

So many people got to tittering at me because of this "Northwestern" affair, that by and by it made me sore.    Rub a scalded horse on the gall, and he'll wince, no matter how tough a set of nerves he's got.    My cronies in the Street poked fun at me over this squeeze! — they laughed as though they'd split.    I didn't see anything so all-fired amusing in it. To be sliced out of the earnings of half a lifetime, and by so beneathen a trick that I've hated to put it down in these papers — let such a trick have been played on them, and I guess they'd have winced, too.

But I got back at them.    One day, soon after, I walked hastily into the Union Club, on Fifth Avenue.    Most of the people there knew me.    I had hurried, and now was considerable het up.    So, when I got inside the door where they all were, I pulled out my handkerchief and mopped my face and neck.    In doing so, I flicked a paper out of my pocket, making believe that it was by accident. It fluttered to the floor.    I passed on without seeming to notice it.    After looking around a minute or two, as though trying to find somebody, I went back into the Street.    Of course, after I got out the people in there picked up the paper, and there they saw what looked to be an order from me to my broker:

"Buy all of the Oshkosh you can, at any price you can get.                    D. DREW."

They gathered at once that a Bull movement in "Oshkosh" stock was under way. As always happens in such cases, they told their friends. A buying movement started in. When they started to buy I started to sell. I unloaded on them at a good figure a lot of "Oshkosh" that I was holding at that time, and that I had feared I wouldn't be able to get rid of. They didn't laugh at me after that. They saw now how it feels to be parted from good money.

# XXXIX

A REPORTER came to me one afternoon in
my office, which was now in Whitely and
Neilson's, at Exchange Place. He said
the Erie Railroad was going to sue me for the seven
million dollars I carried with me when I scooted
from Vanderbilt to "Fort" Taylor in Jersey City.
The news scared me.

"Sue me?" I said. "What can the Company
sue me for? Why, I haven't been in that concern
for four years! I finished up there as treasurer,
and squared up all the accounts before I left. I
don't see why they want to sue me."

"Mr. Drew, they are about to sue you for one
hundred thousand shares of stock which you issued,
they claim, illegitimately."

"Well, now!" I answered. "I don't see what they
want to do it for. I credited the Company with
the proceeds of the sales, and unless it had the
money at the time it would have bust; for the fact is,
the road was just dead broke. It's queer that they
should pitch upon me."

I made believe that I wasn't bothered by the news.
Just the same, it worried me considerable. Law-

suits are expensive things, no matter which way they turn out; and then, too, even after the cost of the suit, I might lose in the end.

This suit by the Erie Company alone would not have been so bad. But my own flesh and blood now began to get at me. When my son-in-law died, he had made me one of the trustees of the property which he left to his children. I had contrived after a spell to become the sole trustee of this property. But now my grandchildren were getting into a complaining state of mind. They said I hadn't invested the money, as the terms of the deed of trust required. They didn't stop to think that by using the money in my Wall Street speckilations, I stood the chance of making a lot more than just the scrawny 6 per cent. you get when you put money away in a permanent investment. I tried to explain this to them, but they wouldn't listen. They began lawsuits against me in the open courts. By and by the Supreme Court dismissed me from my position as trustee of my own grandchildren's property, and put another person in my place. This got noised abroad in the Street, and hurt me a good deal in my Wall Street dickerings. People said: "His flesh and blood don't run any risk with Uncle Dan'l."

On the top of my other troubles came the Panic of '73. Stocks slumped right and left. Dividends fell off on all my investments. Now it was hard for me sometimes to get money for my living expenses. It began to look pretty scary for me. I was being threatened with lawsuits on every side. Flies come thick when a horse has a galled back. I didn't know but what every time my door bell rang at night, it was a process-server; or maybe the Sheriff, coming to sell me out.

By and by, as the summer passed and autumn came, the worst of the panic seemed to be over. The big men in the business world had got under the market and were supporting it from further slump. People began to breathe easier. Then I saw that the time had come to get out of the fix I had been in. During the last few months I had been like a man running away from a bull; the bull was pressing me so close that I hadn't had time for anything else but to run. Now was a little let-up. This gave me time to look about for a permanent escape. I took advantage of it. I set about to get my property out of my own name. Then if a crash came, I would have property to fall back on, and which my creditors couldn't get.

Unfortunately, this move of mine leaked out. My creditors learned what I was trying to do. They started in at once to foreclose on the firm of Kenyon, Cox & Co., Brokers, in which I was tied up. That was the firm through which I had worked most of my stock-market deals of late. Its name was signed to the obligations I had incurred. My enemies now charged that I was planning to fall down on that firm and leave it to its fate; and that therefore they were not going to be caught napping. So they brought foreclosure proceedings against it, and the firm went to the wall. The brokerage house of Kenyon, Cox & Co. was tied up with other big houses in Wall Street. So when this firm fell, it sent other houses tumbling headlong. Thus the panic started in once more, and this time in good earnest. The country was just then like a patient trying to recover from a hard fever, and now had suffered a relapse. Doctors say that a relapse is worse than the first sickness, because the constitution doesn't have the strength that it had at first. Anyhow, that seemed to be the case with the country. The men of means who had got under the market before and had been supporting it, got discouraged when this second crash came, and gave up trying. House after house tumbled. Each tumble left the houses next to it weaker. Soon a panic set in which spread all over the country.

As the panic increased, I felt as though I had kicked over a bee-hive. The way curses came buzzing around my ears now was a caution. They laid the whole thing at my door — said that thousands of merchants and farmers and people generally who were being ruined in this Panic of '73, and the poor people who suffered so in the winter that followed, would lay their woes to me for all time to come. Because I, at a critical time in the country's first recovery, had given that recovery a set-back and so started the fever raging worse than before.

But they said those things through ignorance. They didn't realize the position I had been in, that's all. When my neighbour's house is a-burning, I haven't time to help him — I'm looking to my own roof. When I started in on that scheme to get my property out of my own name, and so brought about the failure of Kenyon, Cox & Co., and those other failures that followed, I was in a tight fix. A broken ship has to get to land somehow. People said: "Dan Drew is willing to burn a house down, in order to roast a few eggs." They didn't stop to think that when a man is starving, he'll do most anything for food.

After the downfall of the brokerage house in which I had been general partner, I had to scratch around good and lively to keep from going under. I had put my house on Union Square out of my own name. Now I got it back and placed a mortgage on it. A mortgage on his house is a bad thing for a Wall Street operator, because the news leaks out and hurts his credit in the Street like Old Sambo. But I had to do it. Also, I told the trustees of Drew Theological Seminary that I couldn't pay any longer that $17,500 a year interest on the endowment I'd promised. (I wished then that I had handed over the full quarter-million when I had had it.)

By and by I saw I'd have to do something in

order to get cash.  My creditors were nagging me on every side.  When a tree is fallen, every man goes at it with his hatchet.  So, after the Panic of '73 was finally over, I set to work.  The market by this time had got settled.   Money was coming into the Street once more, so that there seemed a chance to get some of it.  I planned a dicker which, if successful, would bring me in a fine penny.  I gathered around me a few men.  I went in to sell stocks for a fall.  I put out a large number of "Calls" in "Wabash."  Of late years I had been doing quite a business, anyhow, in "Puts" and "Calls," because you can turn over your capital more quickly in that way than by buying and selling stocks outright.

I figured now that if I could put out a big enough line of shorts, I would know how to bring about a slump in prices at the right time.  This was my plan: I would sell stocks for a decline.  Then I'd corner the gold market and thus bring to pass the very decline in values that I was hoping for — seeing that when money is high, stocks go low. I remembered Fisk and Gould, and "Black Friday." There was Belden, for instance.  Billy Belden had made some money in that former gold speckilation by issuing those orders to Fisk which allowed Fisk to go ahead and make big contracts in the gold market in Belden's name and so escape any legal liability against himself when settling-up time should come.   I calculated now that with the more

or less tight condition of affairs that was upon the
country as a result of the panic, I also stood a chance
to turn a good penny by operating in stocks and in
gold at the same time.

In some way or other my plans didn't just carry
out as I had calculated.  I wasn't any longer an
insider, as I'd been back in former days.  So I had
to go into my speckilations unsight, unseen.  In
wading where you can't see bottom, you are very
like to step off into a deep hole.  And that is
what I did.  I found that I had issued my "Calls"
in the face of a rising market.  Do the best I could,
I wasn't able to head off the upward movement.
Gold was going down, prices were going up; and it
was whip-sawing me in both directions.  As the best
thing to do under the circumstances, I started in to
sell my holdings of gold before the rest of my crowd
— they were in the same fix that I was in — could
begin to do it.  This helped me a little, because
it got me out of the box I'd have found myself in if
I had kept saddled down with gold at a time when
our lock-up of gold was proving a failure.  But
this relief wasn't so helpful as it might seem.  Because,
when I began to release the gold which I had been
locking up, it made money more plentiful and so
made stocks rise still faster.  Thus it got me out
of the one hole, only to get me deeper into the other.

By and by the holders of my "Calls" began to
pester me for deliveries.  I saw that I wasn't going to

be able to meet them.   When the day at last arrived
I didn't feel that I wanted to go down to Wall Street
and look that mob of angry brokers in the eye, and
have them shake their fists in my face.   So I stayed
home, and sent word down that I was sick.   But
this didn't help matters so very much, because my
creditors in the Street complained that if I was
really in earnest to take care of my contracts, I would
have appointed some broker to represent me, while
I was away sick.

"Lumbago" is a good disease to tell people you've
got, when you don't want to go down to the market.
Because it's a disease that is serious enough to keep
you home, and yet will let you be up and around the
house if there is anything you want to attend to.
About noon that day, I sent a telegram down to
Dickinson & Co., from my home, telling how I was
too weak to come down to the Street, and asking
them to notify Robinson, Chance & Co., my regular
brokers, to take care of my "Calls."   This telegram didn't help as much as I had hoped.   In fact,
it got me in still deeper.   My brokers refused to
take the responsibility of taking care of my "Calls"
without a written and signed order from me, in my
own handwriting.   And the Street said I had
employed this roundabout way of notifying my
brokers, in order to lay down on those brokers and
repudiate my contracts when the time should
arrive.   Furthermore, the Street now got notice

that my clique to corner gold and depress values had been broken. So the price of gold now came tumbling headlong.

The next day, before the opening of business, I had to go down to Broad Street and meet my contracts. The break of the gold ring brought a good deal of happiness to merchants, whose business had suffered by the tightness of money which my manipulations in the "Gold Room" had made. But it hadn't brought any happiness to me. In fact, the whole affair, instead of helping me as I had hoped it would, hurt me considerable. I tried to give out that I hadn't been mixed up in it. But some of the papers came out the next day and charged me with it point-blank, in spite of anything I could say. For instance, one of them came out like this:

It appears that Daniel Drew is at the bottom of the present attempt to force up the price of gold. We should have thought that Daniel Drew might, at his age, have devoted what remains of his mind to some better purpose. Two or three weeks ago the rumour that he was engaged in this mischievous work was widely circulated and we sent a reporter to him to make inquiries on the subject. What he said on that occasion was as follows:

"My boy, I've really no interest in this thing. Some folks say I'm the leader of the pool, but I haven't anything to do with it. I almost never have any gold, and at the present time don't own a dollar

of it.   It's all folly; why won't they let me alone?
I'm trying to run along pleasantly with everybody
in the Street; but I can't.   First the Bulls charge
me with being a Bear, and then the Bears say I'm
a Bull.   They shouldn't.   I'm only trying to make
a few dollars in a quiet, easy way, and would like to
do it without being bothered.   Here's my brokers.
They'll tell you I haven't anything to do with the
thing — ask 'em — I won't keep them from telling
the truth.   They know all about me."

There are two things which this ancient person ought to know without our telling him.   One
is that it is very wrong to tell lies; the other, that it
is a very scandalous piece of work to deliberately
try to paralyze the trade of the country.   It appears
from our money article this morning that the people
who have been "in" with Daniel Drew in this
scheme are likely to burn their fingers.   We hope
they will.   At such a time as this, when the spring
trade is opening under favourable circumstances,
an effort to create a gold panic is about as vile an
act as it would be to set fire to a house.   The vener-
able Daniel will come to a very bad end if he goes on
in this way much longer.

But I was glad to see that I had been able to get
at least one of the papers to put some credit in that
report of sickness which I'd sent down from my
house.   Because, after I got back to the Street, the
*New York Sun* came out with this editorial:

Uncle Daniel Drew went down into Wall Street
yesterday morning in a coach.   His face was worn

with illness, but the traces of grief at the damage unintentionally done "the boys" by his sickness were deeper set and much more conspicuous than any left by a brief period of bodily suffering. Still, Uncle Dan'l's eyes sparkled with their wonted brilliancy, and the moment he cast them upon the stock-list tape his brokers knew that he was all himself again. His known goodness and liberality gave rise to a rumour that he contemplated a scheme of making good the losses consequent upon the rumour of his illness; indeed, Uncle Dan'l looked so benevolent and smiled so sweetly that this rumour did not seem so absurd as it would have been if coupled with the name of any other man; still, those of the victims who waited for the restitution were disappointed. Uncle Dan'l would rather found a college any day than restore a cent.

But the great bulk of the people said that my sickness was only an attempt to lay down on my brokers, and this hurt me with the very men whom I needed most to stand in with. It left me lonesome. Brokers would still take my orders, provided I paid my margins in advance. But they'd now get the shivers over the slightest bit of rumour about me, and sell me out quick — said they couldn't take any chances. I couldn't find men any longer to go in with me into deals. My "Wabash" dicker was going against me, because I was now all alone. I could have fought the thing to a finish, and have brought about a war that would have smashed railroad stocks as fine as anything; only I couldn't get enough men of means to go in partnership with me. People shut their doors against a setting sun. With the breaking up now of my gold clique I was brought pretty low.

I tried to keep my financial conditions secret. Because, when once a heifer is sick and laying down, the hounds will get after her and make her all the sicker. As long as you hold your head up, your rivals are scared of you, and let you alone. The moment they see you sickening, they pounce on you like crows around a dead cow. I tried to keep it dark that my property was melting away. But the reporters got wind of it. (It's well-nigh impossible to keep anything from those boys nowadays.) When the gossip which is going on about you in the Street gets into the public sheets, you're in a bad case. That very paper which had put some credit in the report of my sickness, was very unfeeling when the gold speckilation finally busted up. It said:

Yesterday Mr. Daniel Drew, ætat. 82, kindly took his patriarchal hand from the throat of trade, gold declined in price, and general business resumed the indications of activity which it has recently given. Deacon Daniel must often have heard wicked works of this kind denounced on Sunday; perhaps he has even lifted up his voice against them himself. We hope he will now try to practice what he preaches. He at least kept his business engagements yesterday, which was more than many people expected.  Let him now try to turn in an honest penny without striking a blow at the trade of the whole country.

And one of the other papers said:

We shall hope that there is no truth in the report that the recent "railroad war" is likely to break out again.  It caused quite enough damage while it lasted, and it is doubtful whether even the stock gamblers could have gained anything by it.  The trade of the country is not in a condition just at present to warrant any deliberate attempt to disturb it.  The gold clique in this city has for the present been broken up, and it is whispered about that the pious old Daniel Drew has been brought to almost complete ruin.  Thus, one by one, the "Kings of the Street" tumble down.  Whose turn will it be next?

It was not as yet true that this "King of the Street" had tumbled.  For I still kept on my legs.  But I was getting more shaky all the time.  The "Wabash" deal turned out an almighty loss, costing me a plump half-million.  The Street plucked me feather by feather.  Pretty soon Daniel Drew was declared a bankrupt.

# XL

MY BANKRUPTCY really came about because of the prosperity of the country. During the days of the Civil War, when things looked dark, I could turn a fine penny. Three days after Fort Sumter was fired on, stocks fell twenty per cent. And in McClellan's campaign, when those right and left wings of his were about to surround Richmond, all to once a fine slump in values set in. What was the reason? Why, we financiers had got advance information that McClellan was going to fall back, and that Abe was about to call for 300,000 more men. I made money on it. I have always felt more at home in depressing values than in boosting them. I guess I am a Bear by nature, so to speak, having always been sort of conservative and cautious-like in my make-up. During those days of my prosperity, my office with Dr. Groesbeck & Co., at 15 William Street, was the Bear headquarters for the whole Street. In these four little rooms, snug and cozy, most of the Bear campaigns in Wall Street started. In the front room were half a dozen clerks behind a railing, writing checks to pay for stocks,

with two or three boys as messengers. A little
room at the side was a kind of conference room
where we consoled the customers, and such-like.
In the next room were most of the customers of the
house. And in the rear room you'd have found
me, seated on a sofa. This was the starting-place
for most of the bearing down movements in Wall
Street all through that period. "Grossy" (that's
the name I used to give to Groesbeck) had gradu-
ated from the office of Jake Little, and so was fitted
to be my helper in Bear operations. Why, even
out on the sidewalk in front of our place, the talk
used to be all for a fall in prices. There was a
Bearish atmosphere about the office which spread
through the district.

But after the Civil War, stocks seemed possessed
to advance. I tried to check this movement, in the
case of Erie stock, by telling how the prices were
rising so that the road could hardly pay expenses
any more. I pointed out how she now had to pay
$20,000 for an engine that she could have bought
before the war for $10,000. But I didn't succeed
very hefty. There were a great many people who
now had faith in the future of the Country. Somehow or other I have never been able to feel at home
in this new age. The Country isn't what it used
to be when I was in my prime, back in the fifties.
There's a change in the very religion, to-day. In
my church, where I have sat year after year, and

even in my Theological Seminary, there are notions being taught which are different from the old-time ·eachings. Preachers are now talking so ever-astingly about this earth. I have done my best ro get them to stick to the gospel and not allow worldliness to get into the teachings of the church. Still, these new and strange doctrines are spreading more and more. The good old preachers have gone to glory. I am still found in my pew on the Lord's day. But I'm free to say that I don't enjoy it any-wheres near so much as I used to.

When I went into bankruptcy, I let everything go — made a thorough job of it. I thought I might as well go the whole hog, so to speak. The schedule of bankruptcy which I made out showed this. The following is all the property which I had in my hands at the time:

| | |
|---|---:|
| Watch and Chain . . . . . . . | $150 |
| Sealskin Coat . . . . . . . . | 150 |
| Wearing Apparel . . . . . . . | 100 |
| Bible, Hymn books, etc. . . . . . . | 130 |

That sealskin coat was a costly thing, which I wouldn't have had if I'd had to buy it myself. But Robinson came down from Montreal one day with three fur coats, one for himself, one for me, and one for Jimmy Fisk. I remember we had a merry time in the office when he made the presentations. Because all three of us had been, in some way or other, in the circus business.  So we pretended, after we had got the fur coats on, that we were all Bears.  Jimmy went cavorting around the room on all fours, so comical you'd have hurt yourself laughing.  I have missed Jimmy a good deal since he was taken away. He was as lively as a louse.

Besides the sealskin coat, there wasn't anything in my bankruptcy schedule, as anybody can see, which showed much property left in my hands. The hymn book was valuable to me, but it wasn't to anybody else.  In fact, my creditors said the bankruptcy was so complete that they doubted its genuineness;  and they started to have me examined by Commissioners, in order to get their clutches onto some of the railroad stock and other property which I had put out of my own name.  This examination put me to a lot of inconvenience.  I had never kept books.  Drovers don't keep books, anyhow. The way we drovers used to do, when two or three of us would go into a partnership, was to put what money each of us had into one big wad, which one of the partners would hold.  Any money paid out would be taken from the wad.  Any money we made would be put into the wad.  Then, when the partnership was dissolved, all we would need to do would be to count the money in the wad and divide it up even.  So when the Commissioners in Bankruptcy got after me to show checkbooks, ledgers, and so on, I didn't have any to show.  I had kept my accounts in my head. They didn't like that. They said it was only an excuse — which it wasn't.

They pushed me so hard that by and by I had to do something to get rid of them. So I made out that I was sick. I took to my bed. Even at my bedside they kept pestering me with questions. One day I made out that I was too feeble, and the doctor said to them that the examination would have to wait over for a day, while I recovered my strength. That gave me the chance I was looking for. After they were out of the house I up and dressed, and took the train, without letting anybody know where I was going. But this didn't help for very long. The Commissioners found I had gone up to Putnam County. They followed me there, to Brewsters', and said that the examination must go on. I had to consent. They put me under the drag, and harrowed me both ways. But I tired them out. By and by they left, without having got hold of anything.

I had had so much trouble in getting out of New York and back to my native county, that, now I was there, I decided to stay. After so many years in the city, the hills round about Brewsters' and Carmel looked good to me. So I settled down to live the rest of my life in the country.

But after a few months, Putnam County wasn't so attractive. There were a number of farmers up there whom I'd dealt with back in my drover days.

And now they kept dunning me to pay for critters
I had bought from them nigh onto forty years before.
Small creditors are worse than body lice. Why,
one day, right on the fair grounds at Carmel, old
Ebenezer Gay came up to me and bellowed out
before all the people:

"Mister Drew, isn't it about time you paid me
for that there calf?"

I told him I didn't know about any calf. He
said I'd bought one from him back in my drover
days and had never paid him. He went on to make
such a fuss about it, saying debtors have short memories, and such-like, that, to get rid of him, I up and
paid the money. But I saw that if I was going to
have any property left to live on, I'd have to get
away from there. A man could be nibbled to
death by ducks, if there were enough of them.

Besides, I began to feel a hankering for Wall
Street once more. After a few months, it got
almighty dull out in Putnam County. You can't tell
out there how the market is going, until the day
after; then it's too late. I found that I was tied
to the Street like a cat to the saucer. I felt that if
I could get back into the financial district, I'd be
able to make some money. I remembered how much
I used to make there. I was like a heifer lowing
for the green pastures. I couldn't be at ease.

Pretty soon I moved back to New York. I put
up at the Hoffman House. My wife had died before

we left the mansion at Union Square. That mansion had now been sold at auction. So I went to the Hoffman House, where I could be close to the Stock and Gold Tickers. I was talking there with a Mr. Knight, one evening soon after I got back.

"You mean to say that you have come back to go into active operations once more?" he asked.

"Yes," I answered; "the boys think I'm played out. But I'll give them many a twist and turn yet."

I spoke big then. But I have found it harder to get back into active affairs than I looked for. Who cares for old cattle? Brokers now are shy of me. Whenever the market begins to turn against me, I'm up and sold out. Besides, I don't seem to get over a loss as easy as I used to. One day I was so down in the mouth at a bad turn in the market, that I took more than I guess I ought to. Because, some time after, I found myself in a room in the Sturtevant House, in bed. A couple of my old friends called on me there. They had a bottle or two brought up into the room, and offered to treat me. But I didn't want them to see me taking anything. So I shook my head, No. They coaxed. Then they looked at each other as much as to say, "It's time we were going." By and by they went away. But they left the bottle behind. I felt that this was very good of them. Because I felt the need just then of something to cheer me up, and I wasn't feeling rich enough to buy it myself.

It was lonesome work, living at a hotel. So I have got my son to move down from Brewsters', and hire a house on East Forty-second Street, to make a home for me. I have had him put a stock ticker in the basement of the house. This saves me the trouble of going down to the financial district every day. Because there are times now when I feel so feeble that I can't go out of the house. And yet I don't just want to give up speckilating. You never can tell when you are going to make the lucky hit. Give up, and just then you might have been on the eve of a turn in your luck that would have brought you back all the money you had lost, and a lot more besides.

But the turn in my luck seems almighty slow in coming. To speckilate in Wall Street when you are no longer an insider, is like buying cows by candle-light. I don't know as I can keep the thing up much longer. The other night I had a bad spell — kind of an epileptic attack, the doctor called it. And he said, at my age it's likely to come on again at any time.

I manage to get to church still. I take part the best I can in the Lord's Day services. The preaching isn't like what it used to be. Still, I try to keep up heart.

From every stormy wind that blows,
From every ——

**THE END**